Social Work in the Age of Disconnection

This edited text brings together the stories of nine clinical social workers working during COVID-19, exploring the disconnections caused by a forced use of technology as well as the disconnections apparent in a time of social injustice.

Employing narrative strategies to capture this transformative moment of our history, these chapters explore the effects of technology and social media on psychotherapy, the delivery of services for the chronically mentally ill and elderly, as well as the consequences of recent cultural shifts on our conceptions of gender, sexuality, race, the immigrant experience, and political activism. While traditional research methodologies tend to address social problems as if they were divorced from the lives and experiences of human beings, these chapters employ phenomenological description of how the existing system functions, to identify theory-to-practice gaps and to recover the experiences of the person within the various institutional structures. Divided into three parts, each chapter begins with pre-reading and close reading questions and ends with writing prompts, allowing for practitioners and students to examine their own thoughts, and put what they have learnt into practice.

Suitable for students of clinical social work and practicing mental health professionals, this book is essential for those wanting to make sense of social work practice in our constantly evolving times.

Michael Jarrette-Kenny, DSW, LCSW, is a psychotherapist and adjunct faculty member at Bergen New Bridge Medical Center's Psychiatric Residency Program.

Miriam Jaffe is Associate Teaching Professor at Rutgers University, where she teaches writing. This is her fifth edited collection of case studies in Social Work.

Social Work in the Age of Disconnection

Narrative Case Studies

Edited by Michael Jarrette-Kenny and Miriam Jaffe

Routledge
Taylor & Francis Group

NEW YORK AND LONDON

First published 2022
by Routledge
605 Third Avenue, New York, NY 10158

and by Routledge
2 Park Square, Milton Park, Abingdon, Oxon, OX14 4RN

Routledge is an imprint of the Taylor & Francis Group, an informa business

Library of Congress Cataloging-in-Publication Data
Names: Jarrette-Kenny, Michael, editor. | Jaffe, Miriam, editor.
Title: Social work in the age of disconnection : narrative case studies / edited by Michael Jarrette-Kenny and Miriam Jaffe.
Description: New York, NY : Routledge, 2022. | Includes bibliographical references and index.
Identifiers: LCCN 2021055962 (print) | LCCN 2021055963 (ebook) | ISBN 9781032218304 (hardback) | ISBN 9781032218298 (paperback) | ISBN 9781003270225 (ebook)
Subjects: LCSH: Social service—Case studies. | Alienation (Social psychology)—Case studies. | Loneliness—Case studies.
Classification: LCC HV40.35 .S599 2022 (print) | LCC HV40.35 (ebook) |
DDC 361.301/9—dc23/eng/20211203
LC record available at https://lccn.loc.gov/2021055962
LC ebook record available at https://lccn.loc.gov/2021055963

ISBN: 978-1-032-21830-4 (hbk)
ISBN: 978-1-032-21829-8 (pbk)
ISBN: 978-1-003-27022-5 (ebk)

DOI: 10.4324/9781003270225

Typeset in Bembo
by Apex CoVantage, LLC

This book is dedicated to Jerry Floersch
and Jeffrey Longhofer

Contents

Introduction

Editors: Michael Jarrette-Kenny and Miriam Jaffe

Jerry Floersch, PhD, MSW, and Jeffrey Longhofer, PhD, MSW—to whom this volume is dedicated—together founded, in 2012, the Doctorate in Social Work (DSW) program that first connected our contributors. Their vision for a DSW program was radical because it featured an embedded writing program and interdisciplinary coursework. The mission was to de-silo social workers' knowledge: to expose social workers to ideas outside the traditional social work curriculum and to expose social workers' ideas beyond schools of professional caring. Together, we drew theories from the humanities, the social sciences, and the hard sciences to identify theory to practice gaps using narrative inquiry. Narrative inquiry brought street-level, practitioner scholars into an academic context. Programmatically, we developed a medium to convey our ideas outside of the established hierarchy, and this medium—this narrative approach, given to workshopping and revision and an open exchange of ideas—laid the groundwork for collaborations and emotional bonds that served to connect us to each other way beyond the classroom. Writing together brought us no small measure of comfort as social workers who needed deliberate writing spaces to process and to be able to teach.

This reflective communal process led to many publications, and as we started to plan *Social Work in the Age of (Dis)connection* in December 2019, desperate to process the social and political upheaval of the prior four years, we reached out to one another to discuss the fragmentation and brokenness in the world around us. We laid out a schedule to begin workshopping ideas about disembodiment in the age of technology and then, the pandemic. Our eerily prescient theme was made manifest in the worst global tragedy in modern history. Caught up as we were in adapting our practices to the quarantine landscape, writing this book became an important mechanism for us to connect and process our collective trauma and experiences. Our writing workshops took on the dual function of "producing" and "feeling"—a sort of meta-phenomenology. This study of our experiences documents the realities of social work during catastrophic crises.

In 2020, social workers stood out as essential, frontline workers. This book is made of their stories. These nine stories of practice, presented here as narrative case studies, are snapshots from across the field, each taken with a different lens. Our chapter authors explore disconnections caused by a forced use of technology as well as the disconnections apparent in a time of social injustice. We intend for this aggregate record of how experts in the field experienced various crises (on the micro, meso, and macro levels of social work) to serve as a space of reflection on how we might address human disconnection. As this world has shifted since the turn of the millennium, the conception of what makes us human has begun to shift along with it. Our identities have been shaped and have in turn shaped a world within our physical world. The consensual hallucination of the internet, once merely the speculations of cyberpunk mythology, now dictates our inner and outer landscapes, redefining our notions of the real and fake, often rendering them indistinguishable.

As much as practitioners want guides to help them navigate this new world that we have found ourselves in, we must first survey the landscape before we can speak with certainty about the terrain. The graduate of an MSW program is given a set of models by which to approach the challenges of real-world practice only to find that these models of practice have only limited utility in the real world. The editors and writers of this book all learned together in a Doctorate of Social Work program, in which our qualitative explorations of real-world problems helped us to see beyond forgone conclusions. The approach we have adopted in these chapters continues in the spirit of the program that shaped us as writers, the idea of practitioner scholars returning from the trenches to examine the complications and unaddressed needs of the clinicians and caseworkers in real-world practice. Our collective knowledge is what we hope to pass onto our MSW students at the various institutions in which we now teach.

★ ★ ★ ★ ★

In her book *Trauma and Recovery* (1992), psychiatrist Judith Herman discusses the notion of collective dissociation. It is a process by which we as a society, disavow uncomfortable truths, in the same way trauma survivors escape from the inescapable events that surround them. If we apply this notion to our treatment of the most vulnerable members of our society, we must acknowledge our lapse into this dissociative state. It is a cycle that has repeated itself again and again, returning the known suffering of the marginalized to a space of unknowing. In the spirit of tolerating the ambiguous spaces of unknowing, we present a textbook with no right answers or specific agendas. Instead, we hope to inspire reader engagement and connective thinking by presenting a series of explorations where writing is as much a method of inquiry as a statement about what is true. We begin with three accounts of "Connection During Times of Disconnection" in cases that show the ways that young and old have benefited from the technology. Then, in "Ambivalence and Connection through the Screen," we present cases that challenge hopeful views, worrying about the unique effects of 21st-century dissociation and disembodiment. Finally, in "Bridging the Gap: Disconnection and Reconnection During Times of Social Change," we explore the disconnection between humans in an age of racial conflict and inequality.

Employing narrative strategies to capture this transformative moment of our history, these chapters will explore the effects of technology and social media on psychotherapy, the delivery of services for the chronically mentally ill and elderly, as well as the consequences of recent cultural shifts on our conceptions of gender, sexuality, race, the immigrant experience, and political activism. Another important consideration is the use of multiple perspectives (psychotherapeutic, sociological, historical) acknowledging that diagnostic frameworks and institutions represent convergences of multiple epistemic cultures (legal, medical, scientific, etc.). We should recognize that no single discipline could attempt to capture the experience and complexity of open systems like human beings. While traditional research methodologies tend to address social problems as if they were divorced from the lives and experiences of human beings, these chapters employ phenomenological descriptions of how the existing system functions, in an effort to identify theory-to-practice gaps and to recover the experiences of the person within the various institutional structures.

Connection During Times of Disconnection

The profession of Social Work has as one of its core theoretical approaches the notion of the person-in-environment, that is, "the importance of understanding an individual and individual behavior in light of the environmental contexts in which that person lives and acts" (Kondrat, M. 2011). With this emphasis, one would assume that the profession has a mandate to explore the impact of our increasing technology and media-dominated world and its impact on the lives of those we serve. That being said, many in the field have been slow to see the benefits afforded by the rise of social media. While many practitioners have experienced a sense of disorientation during this period of rapidly accelerated change, the authors in this section have embraced this experience, focusing on the opportunities and possibilities for the development of identity that have emerged within this period of burgeoning technological advancement and physical disconnection. What does it mean to be human and how do we discover ourselves in the midst of the kaleidoscope of possibilities afforded by the constantly shifting landscape of the internet?

In the first Chapter *Are you "Following" Me?: Generation Z's Emotional Intelligence in Online Activism*, Biri, rather than accepting the prevailing narrative that adolescents are becoming socially impaired by technology, explores the ways in which digital natives have utilized and at times advanced beyond their forebears in terms of social intelligence, exploring the convergence of social, racial, gender, and political identity on the internet during the

COVID-19 pandemic. At the same time, she considers the experience of the psychotherapist wrestling with personal loss and attunement and repair within the therapeutic relationship.

Similarly, Lauren Busfield (*On the Online Self as an Extension of Personhood*) challenges the prevailing attitudes regarding technological change, arguing that the challenges of adaptation we are encountering are far from novel, but a recurrent theme throughout human history. Through the use of case narratives, she makes the case that

> Social workers must adapt along with the technology that both they and their clients are using and utilize it as a tool for exploration of identity formation, recognizing unique experiences in the online realm shape our perceptions of ourselves and the world around us.

Examining the lives of individuals who have grown up online, she explores the current challenge that all social workers face moving forward beyond the current historical shift, namely

> How do we ask our clients to limit time online when online is the primary-or only-option? Recognition of clients differing needs in regards to social media use can be a primary discussion point in social work, especially during a time of increased need to use the internet to connect with others and to preserve self-identity.

Shifting direction from those who have grown up with technology to the needs of the elderly, Lauren Snedeker, in "*Hi, I Can Hear You Now*," utilizes her experiences facilitating an Alzheimer's caregiver support group during the pandemic to explore the needs of this rapidly expanding population and those who care for them. Given the particular vulnerability of this population to the coronavirus. Snedeker notes the importance of this type of community for their caregivers, demonstrating that connection can be achieved in the most modest circumstances, in a space of relative anonymity: "Nothing complicated, and nothing that required a tutorial. We never saw each other, ran into each other at the grocery store, and could not describe each other's physical characteristics, but, together, we achieved a close-knit, therapeutic bond all through a free conference line." For some, however, this anonymity, or the shift to techno-relationships, is much more complicated.

Ambivalence and Connection Through the Screen

What is the relationship to the body to the practice of Social Work and how have practice and even the very notion of self been complicated and modified through the shift online? This section seeks, in contrast to the first, to explore the ambiguous ethical and philosophical implications of online practice as well as the complications of our recent abrupt shift into a world of disembodied interactions. In *Identity, Technology and The Shaping of Self*, Healy argues that beyond the age-old dialogue between nature and nurture, technology, both medical and information, has become a third factor regarding how we become who we are. Utilizing case material from his practice providing clinical case management for youth seeking gender reassignment, he argues that "[t]ransgender persons rely on all three realms in order to transition to how they know themselves to be." Understanding how these realms work will involve an investigation of how knowledge is acquired via information technology. Additionally, he posits that, for many youths, and certainly for transgender-identified youths, identity development is facilitated by the internet.

In the next chapter, *Connection and Separation Reconsidered*, Winograd further explores the role of the body, questioning whether attachments can be formed and maintained without physical presence and proximity. Drawing on theory from psychoanalysis, modern attachment theory, and communication and media studies, she explores therapeutic relationships increasingly impacted, interrupted, and mediated through technology, while focusing on themes of connection and isolation, attachment and separation, love, and loss. Extending the discussion regarding attachment and in particular the conditions stemming from complex trauma in the post-COVID-19 landscape, Jarrette-Kenny in *The Disembodied Self and the Future of Psychotherapy* observes that "Our experiences of self and others are increasingly mediated by the world of screens, a place which has promised a freedom from the constraints and inhibitions of the body. But does the experience of traumatic attachment and the attendant experiences of dissociation and disconnection affect changes in the emotional state of internet and smartphone users? Is therapy diminished by the digital world, that is, through video and text?" His chapter seeks to explore how the use of technology to address issues related to disembodiment may inadvertently reinforce the very problems that they attempt to redress.

Bridging the Gap: Disconnection and Reconnection During Times of Social Change

In this final section, the focus shifts to the arena of social justice. Given the current divisive political landscape, the need for social work to address the volatile political and social dimension of practice has never been more urgent. Despite this, as young practitioners venture forth into the field, there is a lack of awareness of how to integrate the National Association of Social Workers' (NASW's) directives to advocate for social justice and human rights in direct practice settings. In *The role of technology in community mental health: A strengths-based approach*, Zakia Clay reflects on the plight of a junior social worker as they attempt to provide services to the chronically mentally ill in the community during the pandemic. Her chapter uses the street-level bureaucracy framework to explore the existing systemic and practice dilemmas that were exacerbated by the pandemic, offering ways that technology can be used to engage clients both during a crisis and beyond. Her tenure in Community Based Outreach Programs and role in academia advising an overwhelmed newly licensed worker through the labyrinth of a collapsing system presents a unique opportunity to examine the toll that the public health emergency has taken on frontline workers and programs as they attempt to respond to client needs.

After identifying the limitations of our existing frameworks, it becomes essential to develop a plan of action. In this spirit, Edith Lori Slater (*Addressing Social Injustice in Social Work Practice: The Clinical Advocacy Model*) asks how the profession can be the beacon for change in society and instill trust in clients while simultaneously challenging and reinventing itself. Reimagining and strengthening clinical social work in her view depend on the profession's dedication to preparing social workers by focusing on scholarship that hones in on social justice. She proposes the use of CAM, a clinical advocacy framework, that can provide social workers with the knowledge and tools to ensure that clinical, advocacy, and social justice work are all central foci in practice. Utilizing a composite case study drawn from her own clinical practice, she illustrates the application of the model through the experiences of a 16-year-old girl, forced to migrate from her country of origin after being sexually assaulted by local gang members as payment for her uncle's debt.

In the last chapter, *Our Illusion of Separateness*, Anthony Nicotera presents a vision of reconnection through a recognition of our essential interdependence, sharing experiences, from 2001 to the present, as a teacher of social justice, lay chaplain, activist, social worker, and advisor to the Fellowship of Reconciliation, the nation's oldest, largest, multifaith peace and justice organization. These experiences have shaped the creation of the Circle of Insight framework, a tool for examining questions of connection and disconnection, and our illusion of separateness, in particular in a time of pandemic, and racial, political, and social unrest and division. These stories invite us to consider that if we hope to build a more socially just society, in the midst of a world divided and disconnected, desperately in need of healing and repair, we must see that our disconnection, our division, our devastation exist in the context of a deeper, more profound, more fundamental reality and truth, that of our need for one another, our common humanity, our unity, and interconnection.

We thank Jerry Floersch and Jeffrey Longhofer for making this humanity, unity, and interconnection our reality and for inspiring us to recognize the value of our role in contributing to the knowledge base of the social work profession and in healing through the act of writing.

Editors

Michael Jarrette-Kenny, LCSW, DSW, is a psychotherapist in Wyckoff, NJ, as well as an adjunct faculty member at Bergen New Bridge Medical Center's Psychiatry Residency Training Program. Upon completing his MSW, he began working on an acute inpatient psychiatric unit and as a screener for Care Plus NJ's Psychiatric Emergency Screening Program. He received advanced training in hypnosis at the New York Milton H. Erickson Society for Psychotherapy and Hypnosis (NYSEPH) and in EMDR prior to completing his Doctorate at Rutgers University. His areas of interest include the integration of hypnosis and mindfulness approaches in the treatment of complex trauma. His publications include "Attachment Patterns and Gay Male Identity" from *The Social Work and LGBTQ Sexual Trauma Casebook* and "Pulling Yourself Up By Your Bootstraps: Transcending the Stories of Ego" from *Spirituality in Mental Health Practice*, both from Routledge Press.

Miriam Jaffe, narrative activist, PhD (English, 2008), MSW (2018), was the director of a Doctorate in Social Work Writing Program for six years and now serves in the Rutgers University Writing Program as an associate teaching professor, mostly teaching graduate students across the disciplines. She is the lead editor of four mental health casebooks K-12 schools as therapeutic communities, sexual trauma, LGBTQ sexual trauma, and spirituality (Routledge 2016–2020) as well as a writer, including a chapter entitled "Queering Trauma Therapy: The Case of Ariel, a Gender Non-Binary Undocumented Immigrant in the US" and the article "Case and Frame: Teaching Case Study Composition," in *Clinical Social Work* (Spring 2017). She has developed the phenomenologically grounded pedagogy and case study format that comprises the chapters throughout these books using her two decades of teaching and training in scholarly composition. Jaffe is an associate editor of *Writing & Pedagogy* (Equinox) and since 2019 has served on the Editorial Board of the Trauma and Memory Book Series (Lexington). She recently published "The 'Practice' of Close Reading and Writing in Social Work Education" in *Writing and Pedagogy* and the article "Collaboration and 'Potential Space:' Creative Play in the Writing Alliance" is forthcoming in *Teaching in Higher Education*.

Contributors

Kristin Biri is a licensed clinical social worker in New Jersey. She completed her BSW degree at Marist College and her MSW degree at Adelphi University. Most recently, Dr. Biri completed her Doctorate in Clinical Social Work (DSW) at Rutgers University, where she focused on technology and social media's impact on adolescent and young adult identity development and interpersonal relationships. She completed a case study entitled "Identity Formation in the Age of Social Media: The Case Study of a Socially Anxious Adolescent" and also completed a small qualitative study using thematic analysis entitled "Disclosing the Self to Others Online: The Experiences of Socially Anxious College-Aged Females." Aside from these scholarly writings, Dr. Biri created a multimedia project, "Screen Smart Counseling," and developed an interactive website with tools for mental health professionals and parents to more effectively navigate online experiences with their clients and children. Dr. Biri has experience working with children, adolescents, and young adults in substance abuse, hospital, school, and private practice settings. Currently, Dr. Biri is employed as a social work consultant for a local school district where she collaborates with stakeholders in the school community to support the district's mental health initiatives by developing programs for both students and staff. In her own practice, Dr. Biri works primarily with adolescents and young adults with mood and behavioral disorders and conducts individual, family, and telemental health services.

Lauren Busfield, DSW, LCSW, received her Master's in Social Work from West Chester University of Pennsylvania and her Doctorate in Clinical Social Work from Rutgers University. She serves as the director of Field Education for Saint Elizabeth University, where she oversees the clinical portion of the BSW program. Lauren retains a clinical practice, working in both private practice and the nonprofit sector with adolescents, children, and families. Her research and publications have focused on ways technology impacts the culture of young people, mental health, family relationships, trauma, and development. She runs a resource and research site for parents and mental health professionals raising and working with children who are growing up in a digital world.

Zakia Clay is a licensed clinical social worker who earned her Masters and Doctorate degrees in Social Work from Rutgers University. In addition, she completed her undergraduate studies at Kean University, where she obtained a Dual Bachelor of Science in Psychology and Psychiatric Rehabilitation. She also holds a certificate in Clinical Supervision, Seminar in Field Instruction (SIFI), and Psychiatric Rehabilitation. For much of her career, Dr. Clay has worked in community mental health settings with adults living with mental illnesses. More recently, she engages in clinical work at a group practice and crisis intervention service. Her practice specialties include, but are not limited to, working with individuals diagnosed with anxiety, depression, schizophrenia, and bipolar disorder. She uses integrative therapeutic approaches that often include cognitive behavioral techniques and strengths-based models to help individuals move toward making positive changes in their lives. She also provides consultative services related to service delivery, policy, and policy implementation. In addition, she teaches both mental health providers and MSW students. Some of the topics include holistic approaches to improve well-being, social skills training, cognitive-behavioral techniques, and clinical social work practice. Dr. Clay has also contributed to several publications related to training, policy, and mental health.

Russell Healy, DSW, LCSW, is a clinical social worker who practices in Central New Jersey. He earned his MSW in 1987 and his DSW in 2016. Dr. Healy specializes in working with, and consulting on, issues regarding sexuality, gender, and ethics. He teaches in the Rutgers School of Social Work's continuing education program and has presented on working with transgender-identified youths and their families at NASW-NJ's annual conference. He has published case studies on forensic social work, the use of gay-affirmative therapy, and transgender-specific healthcare. Recently, Dr. Healy contributed a chapter, "Transgender-Specific Assessment, Counseling and Case Management," in the third version of Theory and Practice in Clinical Social Work. Dr. Healy is a member of NASW and certified as a gender specialist by the World Professional Association for Transgender Health.

Anthony Nicotera, JD, DSW, LSW, is an associate professor in Seton Hall's Social Work Program, Department of Sociology, Anthropology, and Social Work. He is a clinical social worker and directs NYU's Post-Master's Program in Spirituality and Social Work. He consults with the Fellowship of Reconciliation. He worked with Vietnamese Zen Master Thich Nhat Hanh, nominated for the Nobel Peace Prize by Dr. Martin Luther King, Jr., to help create the mixed-media films Planting Seeds of Mindfulness for Children, and The 5 Powers, which won best film at The People's Film Festival in Harlem, NY. He helped found Newark New Jersey's Cristo Rey High School. He served as a chaplain to the College of Law and School for New Learning via DePaul University's Center for Spirituality and Values in Practice, which he cofounded. He also helped found DePaul's peace and justice studies program. He has led numerous workshops, retreats, and healing circles and presented on panels pertaining to spirituality, social justice, and social work. He has been arrested or detained some 20 times for nonviolent civil disobedience. He spent six years as a member of the Society of Jesus, a religious order in the Roman Catholic tradition. As a Jesuit, he completed the Ignatian Spiritual Exercises, a 30-day silent retreat, and worked internationally and domestically in prisons, hospice facilities, inner-city parishes and schools, and legal and social service centers. He also lived in Latin America, working with community organizations and victims of war and violence, and he lived and worked in India with Mother Teresa.

Edith Lori Slater, DSW, LCSW, is a bilingual Spanish licensed clinical social worker in New Jersey and Hawaii. Presently, she is the director of a mental health agency in Bergen County, New Jersey, where her treatment approach is integrative of clinical advocacy, cultural responsiveness, and mind–body perspective. Her practitioner–scholar work focuses on the intersections of mental health and social justice. She advocates for social justice imperatives as an integral aspect of mental healthcare treatment. Her case study, Prioritizing the Dual Needs of Asylum-Seekers While Cultivating Therapeutic Alliances, and the qualitative study, Private Practice Social Workers' Commitment to Social Justice, are published in the Clinical Social Work Journal.

Lauren Snedeker, DSW, LSW, LMSW, is an assistant teaching professor and coordinator for the Aging and Health Certification Program at the School of Social Work. Her areas of practice and scholarly interests focus on the aging experience, mental health during older adulthood and caregiving. Educating and encouraging MSW students about the rich, clinical experiences that exist in gerontological social work is her passion. Dr. Snedeker's research goals focus on debunking dominant narratives of the aging experience through qualitative inquiry. Most recently, she conducted an explorative study with older women aging alone without readily available caregivers in New York City and the ways they channel their own resiliency. She hopes her research will contribute to better program and policy development for the aging population. She holds a master's degree in Social Work from the Silver School of Social Work at New York University and Doctorate in Social Work from Rutgers School of Social Work. Over the course of her career, Dr. Snedeker has worked in diverse settings serving the older adult population, such as hospitals, nursing homes, senior centers and privately by conducting home visits. She has experience working with individuals, families, and caregivers. Additionally, Dr. Snedeker has developed trainings, graduate-level curricula, content for continuing education events and professional conferences, and articles on age-related topics.

Wendy Winograd, DSW, LCSW, BCD-P, clinical social worker and certified psychoanalyst, provides psychotherapy to adults, couples, and children in private practice and in a school. She serves on the faculty of the New Jersey Institute for Training in Psychoanalysis and the Center for Psychotherapy and Psychoanalysis of New Jersey. She is on the Executive Board of the American Association of Psychoanalysis in Clinical Social Work, where she is the Recording Secretary, Book Review Editor, and Co-Chair of the Child and Adolescent Committee. She earned her DSW from the Rutgers University School of Social Work and her MSW from New York University. Her current research focuses on the psychoanalytic understanding of the relationship between play, identity, and relationship. She has published on female development, work with transgender adolescents, school-based psychotherapy with young children, and mother/daughter relationships, and she has presented her work nationally and internationally.

1 Are You "Following" Me?

Gen Z's Emotional Intelligence in Online Activism

Kristin Biri

Pre-reading Questions:

1. From early to late adolescence, individuals are exploring and experimenting with a sense of self. How do you think this process of development has shifted during the pandemic—not just for individuals, but for groups involving adolescents?
2. What are "intelligence quotients" (IQ) and how have they been used to determine success? What are some of the differentiators between IQ and "emotional quotients" (EQ) and how may these distinctions predict success?
3. Who is Generation Z and what are some distinguishing characteristics that set them apart from previous generations? How has Generation Z helped to redefine citizenship in the midst of the COVID-19 pandemic, BLM movement, and the political landscape of 2020?

We all snarl at tweens and teens who are "addicted" to their phones. We joke that their phones are an extension of their arms and permanently tied to their beings. We judge them, as we believe their texti young language and the way they communicate with one another is not proper English. We think they lack social skills because they exist online more so than they exist offline. And perhaps most importantly, we are eminently concerned that technology and social media are causing irreparable damage to teens' and tweens' mental health and well-being.

We as older generations, and we as parents, like to consider ourselves omniscient as our lived experiences have brought upon us knowledge, character, and wisdom. Yet, as I have come to learn, age does not always bring growth. Instead it may bring a strict set of values and outdated beliefs that leave us stagnant. I myself am an avid social media user, and when I look at my own social media feeds, I am inherently aware of the interactions that occur among my "friends" and exchanges that ensue among my online social groups. As of late, amidst the COVID-19 pandemic, 2020 presidential election, and Black Lives Matter (BLM) movement to name a few, many interactions come across as plain hostile. But these are not

DOI: 10.4324/9781003270225-1

tweens or teens, or even young adults. These are grown adults, Millennials, but even more so, Gen X-ers and Baby Boomers, who have taken to social media to bash, ridicule, and spew hate among their own turf. They are talking at one another, not with one another. No one is listening (or reading) for understanding of the other's perspective. The only noise they are listening to is that of their keyboards rampantly typing their follow-up response. Maybe we older generations fear the younger generations pose a risk to our established way of life, our homeostasis. Maybe we feel a sense of incompetence as we struggle to keep up with the new. Whatever it may be, the more we see technology and social media as the problem, or as the enemy, and the more we encapsulate ourselves in an all-knowing ideology, the more we create a profound rift between ourselves and the generations of the future.

I have been captivated by technology and social media's impact on child and adolescent identity development and the means in which this new generation, Generation Z, uses technology for their own connection, coping, and emotion regulation, long before COVID-19 came into the picture. *But, COVID-19 came, with a fury.* And my ideology that we must work with, rather than against, technology became more relevant than ever before. I teach continuing education courses through our state university's school of social work program on Screen Smart Counseling. I work to instill the belief that the more we become culturally competent about Generation Z, and the more we learn about technology and social media, the stronger the connections and the better rapport we can build with our children and our clients. Parents and clinicians alike often find themselves floundering when it comes to understanding this generation's adept use of media as a mechanism of personal development. In a session, clinicians may ask young clients to put their phones away or leave them outside the room. At home, parents may set strict limits and boundaries on how often and when they can use technology, while also restricting what apps and accounts they allow their children to create. Rightly so, they all have the best intentions—we hear technology and social media can exacerbate anxiety and depression, there are privacy and safety concerns, children may be catfished, worse yet, they may be kidnapped by an online predator, cyberbullying is rampant, children lack the ability to make well-thought-out choices—the list of fears and concerns is endless.

But by doing these things, parents and clinicians also are preventing themselves from seeing the bigger picture: technology and social media provide opportunities for self and other exploration and experimentation, the core psychosocial developmental task of adolescence. And, if you pull back the lens even further, I believe you will find that Generation Z is not just acting within their developmental schemas, they are also exemplifying how we can better integrate important social–emotional traits into our own online existence. Furthermore, through this integration, Generation Z is also highlighting how to more effectively engage in intellectual conflict online, a skill that will most certainly promote social justice, as well as better position us as a country to learn skills to better advocate for social change.

Psychosocial Theory

Erik Erikson is a pioneer of psychosocial theory and adolescent identity development. Erikson's psychosocial theory is based on four concepts: developmental stages, developmental tasks, psychosocial crisis, and process of coping (Erikson, 1994). There are eight stages of development that correspond to Freud's theory of psychosocial development (Erikson, 1994). These eight stages of development propose that we are all confronted with unique stage of life problems and that we must integrate our own needs and skillsets with the social demands of our culture (Newman & Newman, 1976). The shift from adolescence to adulthood is thought to be the most critical time period in identity development, as there is an increased focus on the self (Waterman, 1982; Valkenburg, Peter, & Schouten, 2006). Erikson's stage of adolescent development, between the ages of 12 and 18, is categorized as Identity versus Role Confusion (Erikson, 1994). The goal of this stage is to establish an ego identity, the sense of self that one develops through social interactions (Erikson, 1994; Bosma & Kunnen, 2001). Waterman (1982) defined identity as the combination of multiple facets: the definition of the term self, commitments to goals and personal values, goal-directed activity involvement, recognition of alternative identity options, self-acceptance, appreciation of personal uniqueness, and confidence in a successful future. Adolescents form their identities based on their exploration of the world and how they relate to society (Bosma & Kunnen, 2001).

Newman and Newman (1976) created a subsection of Erikson's identity development in early adolescence and labeled it Group Identity versus Alienation. They believed one of the four tasks of early adolescence was to attain membership in a peer group and establish close friends (Newman & Newman, 1976). Social connections are a central feature of normative adolescent development into adulthood (Allen, Ryan, Gray, McInerney, & Waters, 2014). Adolescents have an innate psychological drive to belong to groups and take part in meaningful social interactions (Allen et al., 2014). This need to belong is derived from three basic needs: inclusion, affection, and control (Gangadharbatla, 2008).

The friendship networks adolescents form online are much larger than offline networks (Manago, 2014). These online communities help adolescents build social capital (Ahn, 2011). Social capital is the resources accumulated by forming and maintaining friendships (Steinfield, et al., 2008). Ahn (2011) referred to social capital as "bridging and bonding," meaning communities of people with a higher level of trust have higher social capital, therefore, are more likely to help one another (p. 1440). Higher levels of social capital are related to higher levels of psychological well-being, such as self-esteem and satisfaction with life (Steinfield et al., 2008).

Emotional Intelligence

Intellectual ability is a globally understood concept that encompasses one's ability to use logic, plan, problem-solve, think abstractly, use language, and learn, and is of course, related to success in many different sectors (Drigas & Papoutsi, 2018). However, in the last three decades, researchers began to consider if this sole set of skills was enough on its own to contribute to individuals' life successes (Drigas & Papoutsi, 2018). The term "emotional intelligence" entered the mainstream with Daniel Goleman's 1995 release of *Emotional Intelligence: Why It Can Matter More Than IQ*, where he ascertained that a set of five specific traits was more integral to success than one's overall cognitive functioning and mental abilities. These traits include self-awareness, self-regulation, motivation, empathy, and social skills (Goleman, 1995). Before considering the concept of emotional intelligence, it may be helpful to first break down the concept of an "emotion." Drigas and Papoutsi (2018), drawing on a Darwinian framework, define emotion as "a complex feeling which results in physical and psychological changes affecting thought and behavior" (p. 3). Various theories, including the James-Lange Theory, the Cannon-Bard Theory, Schacter and Singer's two-factor theory, and cognitive appraisal, have all attempted to understand how and why individuals feel emotions from physiological and psychological perspectives (Drigas & Papoutsi, 2018).

Goleman (1995), referring to psychologists Solevey's and Mayer's definitions of "personal" or emotional intelligence, elaborates on how the ability to have insight and understanding into our emotions, handle feelings appropriately, delay gratification, attune themselves to others' social signals, and manage emotions in others through relationships, allows for individuals to excel in both the "practicalities of life" and to be "so highly valued in the workplace" (p. 42). In Di Fabio and Kenny's (2016) review of emotional intelligence literature, they noted a well-documented connection between emotional intelligence and positive outcomes in social, psychological, career, and academic domains along with strong associations to resilience, positive self-image, and social support. Drigas and Papoutsi (2018) note emotional intelligence leads to better social relationships for children, familial relationships, more positive perceptions from others, and overall improved well-being.

Scholars have questioned whether emotional intelligence traits are innate or can be taught to individuals (Zeidner, Matthews, Roberts, & MacCann, 2003). Biology, family dynamics, poverty, and culture act as exacerbating agents to complex social and emotional problems, and while the underlying basis for emotional intelligence traits is undoubtedly neural, due to the brain's plasticity, it is believed that emotional skills can be acquired at any age—but their acquisition takes much practice and commitment, particularly as age increases (Goleman, 1995, 2000). Goleman (1995) notes the frontal lobe, the part of the brain responsible for emotion regulation, matures through adolescence and discusses different "windows" for helping children acquire productive emotional habits as they enter into adulthood (p. 227). Additionally, developmental psychologists have mapped the growth of emotions, allowing them to consider what specific traits can be taught at which specific periods of child development, thus achieving the highest levels of mastery (p. 227). In Meena Srinivasan's (2014) release of *Teach, Breathe, Learn*, she looks at how mindfulness, a skill directly related to self-awareness and self-regulation can be built through constant practice, and refers to Hebb's rule: "neurons that fire together, wire together," discussing how the connections among neurons are "plastic" and can change over time (p. 109).

Ronald Kessler's research indicates that early intervention, not just information giving, but comprehensive trainings related to emotional and social competencies, has the ability to prevent more significant mental health diagnoses, even in children with a history of trauma and genetic predispositions (Goleman, 1995). Academic curriculum's integration of emotional intelligence skills across classroom settings indicates that in the sphere of K–12 education, there are believers that these skills may be manifested through instruction and practice (Ross & Tolan, 2018). Goleman (1995) notes that while emotional literacy classes may appear simplistic and dull, "the outcome-decent human beings-is more critical to our future than ever" (p. 263).

Unironically, the Collaborative for Academic, Social, and Emotional Learning (CASEL) coined the phrase Social–Emotional Learning (SEL) after Goleman's (1995) research positing emotional intelligence was attributed to higher school successes, inclusive of reduced conduct incidents, improved graduation rates, and more engaged citizenship (Ross & Tolan, 2018). CASEL, over the last two decades, has become a widely accepted holistic theoretical framework in schools across the country, with their five-factor SEL model emphasizing the skills of self-awareness, self-management, social awareness, relationship/communication skills, and responsible decision-making (Ross & Tolan, 2018; Elbertson, Brackett, & Weissberg, 2010). In addition to CASEL, in 2010, the National Governors Association Center for Best Practices finalized the Common Core Standards Initiative, shifting away from content guidelines in English Language Arts and Mathematics and instead focusing on expectations for student knowledge and skills in K–12 education (Porter et al., 2011). What this unprecedented, pedagogical shift required, was in essence, student acquisition of social emotional skills, with developmentally appropriate lessons designed for each grade level (Srinivasan, 2014). Prior to this model, traditional emphasis in schools was only on student acquisition of academic instruction; in other words, students were expected to learn a subject and regurgitate responses, with little room for critical thinking and academic debate (Elbertson et al., 2010). The new ideology emphasizes that learning takes place in the context of student relationships with others, such as their relationships with teachers, administrations, and peers; consequently, through these relationships, attachment, respect, and communication is enhanced, followed up with brain development (Elbertson et al., 2010).

New Age Thinking on Theoretical Concepts

In the decades since Erikson formulated his theories of identity development, much has evolved socially and culturally among the adolescent population, and as a result, other scholars have disseminated how the shifts in society have affected our views on identity development. Erikson (1994) suggested that an expanded social context introduces adolescents to new identifications, roles, rules, demands, and opportunities for growth and change. Bosma and Kunnen (2001) referred to this as the "person-context fit," but they have recognized how historical changes in social and cultural contexts have led to changes in how we should interpret Erikson's theory of identity formation (p. 46). While Erikson's (1994) work has been a cornerstone to understanding psychosocial development, some ideologies are not only antiquated but also invalidating to current adolescent experiences.

First, when disseminating beliefs on identity, Erikson referred to heterosexuality in regard to development of one's sexual identity. Heterosexuality is believed to be a derivative of our male-dominated, patriarchal social arrangements, allowing males economic, physical, and social access to women (Rich, 1993). When heterosexuality is socially constructed as a norm, however, it eliminates the option for healthy gender and sexual self-exploration by illegitimizing sexual exploration that falls outside of this purview (Konik & Stewart, 2004). Individuals may then commit to an identity, without experiencing an identity crisis, also referred to as identity foreclosure (Konik & Stewart, 2004). Marcia (1966) asserted that identity achievement could only happen once one is able to actively question his/her sexual identity to then deepen and enrich the commitment. Alessi and Martin (2017) highlighted the pivotal role of understanding minority stress when attempting to understand the comprehensive trauma among LGTB individuals. Even when LGTB individuals grow up in supportive familial environments, it does not minimize the structural societal forces in place that marginalize their gender and sexual identities (Alessi & Martin, 2017).

In 2020, the reach of societal forces has exponentially increased as adolescents are exposed to dual worlds every day: an online world and an offline world. Manago (2014) asserted that adolescents are growing up during a time of profound sociocultural shifts in technology. Today, average adolescents are spending far more hours interacting with their peers through the use of an Internet-connected device, rather than interacting in-person (Turkle, 2015). According to Wallace (2015), some 13-year-olds check their social media account upward of 100 times each day and spend an average of nine hours daily consuming media. Additionally, the social context of social media arguably introduces adolescents to roles and rules that differ greatly than in-person communication and interactions; consequently, adolescents must learn to navigate, integrate, and separate two distinct standards of living—online standards and offline standards—to form healthy identities. Without such navigation, integration, and separation of these two standards of living, the "wholeness" and "progressive continuity" that Erikson believed adolescents must achieve to form a healthy identity will be impossible (Waterman, 1982, p. 341).

Citizenship, one of the highest degrees of group identity encompassing its own set of rules, norms, and standards to adhere, has evolutionized to digital citizenship, a term suggesting safe, responsible, and respectful online choices (Jones & Mitchell, 2015). Jones and Mitchell (2015) discussed how digital citizenship education, aside from focusing on technical skills and cyberbullying prevention, focuses on respectful and tolerant behaviors to others and increase civic engagement opportunities. One of the goals of developing "good citizenship" involves moving away from one's own self-interest to being involved in the overall well-being of a larger group, where that individual may possess membership (Jones & Mitchell, 2015). In 2018, Drigas and Papoutsi put forth their emotional intelligence pyramid, a nine-layer model combining emotional, cognitive, and metacognitive skills, with the final level being emotional unity. They discuss how in a symbiotic world, what we do for ourselves, we do for others, and when we reach the potential to fully love ourselves and find internal harmony, we can then channel these feelings and energy into those around us (Drigas & Papoutsi, 2018).

Furthermore, Drigas and Papoutsi (2018) stressed that these skills can be learned and developed, citing Rivers, Brackett, Reyes, Elberston, and Salovey's (2013) research on improving the social and emotional climate of classrooms using the RULER approach to promote positive youth development from kindergarten through grade eight. A critical feature in SEL effectiveness is continuity and ongoing instruction of emotional literacy from preschool through the end of high school (Elbertson et al., 2010). The implementation of SEL in schools, and curriculum including lessons on digital literacy, is important to understand when considering digital citizenship because what it suggests is that only our youths, only Generation Z in K-12 education beginning in 1994 and later, have participated in empirically designed SEL activities. This would suggest that anyone over the age of 30 has most likely not been exposed to early education related to social–emotional traits; these older generations, therefore, may struggle to understand the importance of these traits in relation to life successes and may not as consciously recognize how these traits correlate to healthy, online civic engagements. Rivers et al. (2013) highlighted the need for professional development for school leaders, teachers, and staff to promote skill-building recognizing the need for universal application of these skills from the top down to enhance the learning environment.

As the COVID-19 pandemic imploded, we as humans transitioned to social (and academic) interactions that existed almost entirely online.

Physical distancing protocols and regulations made us forego our typical face-to-face communications and further engage in technologically driven forms of collaborating and connecting with our neighbors, our peers, our coworkers, and our families. And while controversial social media communications skyrocketed and political tensions escalated surrounding an international pandemic, CDC protocols, the 2020 election, and the BLM and antiracist movements, some members of Generation Z, already adept at technologically based communications, proved that the social–emotional skills that they had learned over the last one and a half decades could be used to proactively and productively incite change, rather than provoke conflict.

Through the use of case studies, the development, or lack thereof, of emotional intelligence traits both online and offline will be critically assessed as adolescents work toward meeting the developmental tasks of early and late adolescence, while navigating social media platforms as blossoming social activists and establishing digital citizenship.

Jesse

Jesse is a 21-year-old senior in college who uses they/them pronouns. While they were born biologically female and primarily date boys, they believe their gender identity and sexual orientation are fluid and they are open to all types of relationships. Upon having a conversation with Jesse about their sexual identity and preferences, it may seem as if they are confident and assured in themselves; however, after deeper discussion, it is evident this is a source of anxiety and depression for them growing up in a deeply religious, Black family. Institutionalized heterosexism and racism may be especially traumatic for LGTB minority youths, thus predisposing them to anxiety and depressive disorders (Alessi & Martin, 2017). Jesse never felt able to truly express themselves to their parents without being scolded or looked down upon, and as a result, as they began college, they slowly gravitated away from their parents as they were unable to discuss drinking, smoking, dating, or other controversial topic areas. By the end of their sophomore year, although they reveled in their newfound freedom from their parents, they were filled with anxiety about their new developing sense of their sexual self. Alessi and Martin (2017) discussed how LGTB individuals must chronically discern others' perceptions of them as they deviate from heterosexual and cisgender norms. More so, they may anticipate rejection as they assume a marginalized gender or sexual identity status (Alessi & Martin, 2017). After some sessions processing this source of anxiety during the summer, at the start of their sophomore year, they decided to join the LGTBQ Club on campus to find more connection and acceptance within their social environment. Within a few meetings, they became an active member and ran for a Board position as Secretary. With this position came a very specific duty: running the club's Twitter handle.

Jesse was already an active social media user and happily accepted this task. Twitter was already their favorite site to use. At the next session, I was blown away by how much research Jesse put into the Twitter page and the amount of knowledge they attained about the LGTBQ community. They had bought books and followed other similar Twitter pages, and during each session, they would share more and more information with me regarding their findings and their postings to the Twitter page. The conversation that was initiated via this Twitter page was astonishing, and Jesse was thrilled to be engaged in these back-and-forth exchanges within the community. It was as if running this page gave them a sense of not only purpose, but a sense of self. Too afraid and too concerned to engage in this discussion with close friends and family, they embraced the opportunity to be a part of this conversation online. Craig, Austin, and Alessi (2013) created a clinical adaptation of Cognitive Behavioral Therapy (CBT) for sexual minority youth, entitled Gay Affirmative CBT. They highlighted the need to distinguish between environmental problems versus dysfunctional thinking, validating clients' experiences of discrimination, emphasizing collaboration, and increasing personal strengths and supports (Craig et al., 2013).

Jesse and I were discussing the anonymity behind this Twitter page. I mentioned how they were able to post their perspectives on gender identity, sexuality, and acceptance without ever attaching their name to the perspectives they were taking. Jesse thought about this for a few moments and said, "Honestly, at first I felt as if I was hiding behind the Twitter page, but now I feel like the Twitter page has become an integral part of me." I added, "But people still do not know it is you, correct?" Jesse replied, "They[my followers] may not know my address or my social security number, but they know me. I am sharing with these people the deepest parts of me. I would say they know me better than some of my close friends and family know me at this point. And they accept me for all of it."

While using this Twitter handle, Jesse was cultivating a series of emotional intelligence traits, the first and arguably most important one being self-awareness. Research dating back to Socrates and Aristotle highlights the concept of "know thyself" and emphasizes knowing thyself as the origin of wisdom (Drigas & Papoutsi, 2018). Goleman (1995) stated that self-awareness must predate social awareness, emotion regulation, and relationship management. Self-awareness may be defined as the process of developing emotional consciousness and having an accurate self-assessment of one's own strengths and weaknesses (Goleman, 1995). Self-awareness is also referred to as knowing oneself as an individual entity (Drigas & Papoutsi, 2018). Gray (2009) indicated how LGTBQ youth may use social media to help legitimize their own sexual identities. By engaging with these individuals online, the person receives a sounding board for self-reflection, while also emboldening the pursuit of new experiences (Manago, 2014).

As Jesse further discovered their individual identity via their online interactions, it allowed them to more easily connect with peers and strengthen their sense of empathy toward others' experiences. The internet is full of individuals with various diverse backgrounds, but also allows for easier connection to individuals with similar views and values, which is why youths from minority ethnic or sexual groups may more easily find peers with sympathetic perspectives (Manago, 2014). Manago (2014) discussed how by easily accessing information outside of one's own social circle, it may strengthen the view that "everyone is connected" and feel a sense of closeness or belonging to a far-reaching community of others from diverse backgrounds (p. 515).

After years of struggling to accept their family's lack of acceptance of their sexual identity, after years of being dead-named by those they lived with on a daily basis, after years of multiple bouts of self-harm and hospitalizations, most recently even necessitating a withdrawal from their last semester, thus losing thousands of dollars in tuition, Jesse found a place, their own place, to settle themselves. And just as they were settling into their new idealized sense of self online, a place they were able to continue existing even through the COVID-19 shut down, on May 25 (or really May 26 and the days/weeks following) the world imploded, yet again. On May 25, George Floyd was arrested, and after about eight minutes of a white police officer kneeling on his neck, he lost consciousness, and soon later was pronounced dead. Jesse's rested mind about their sexual identity now found itself thrust into a world of civil unrest, encompassing their racial identity.

To little surprise, Jesse hastily enveloped themselves in the BLM movement via their social media platforms. They knew the power of social media to bolster one's voice among a sea of other like-minded voices, and they needed to feel validated and heard. Jesse was using what Manago (2014) referred to as "customized sociality" and was pursuing social resources such as social network support to meet one's social needs (Manago, 2014, p. 512). But unfortunately, Jesse did not find their needs being met as easily as they were when they used their social media platform for LGTBQ activism.

I recently participated in a Webinar, *COVID-19, Youth of Color, and Suicide Risk Indicators* with guest speaker Kimme Carlos, a motivational consultant and daughter of Dr. John W. Carlos, 1968 Olympian and civil rights activist. In discussing systemic racism, Carlos (2020) noted feeling as if "humanity has been stripped from you," "you are no longer of value," and "everything that is wrong with the world is embodied in you." The feelings of helpless and hopelessness become magnified as there is a real, intrinsic, and innate need to be seen and heard that is being overlooked in black youth (Carlos, 2020). While Jesse's sexual identity was being seen, heard, and validated, their racial identity was being undermined and invalidated by many other social media users.

LGTBQ rights are a radically accepted ideology in America: in 2004, a Pew Research Center poll indicates Americans opposed same-sex marriage 60–31%; however, in 2019, 15 years later, Pew Research Center polling indicates that Americans strongly favored same-sex marriage 61–31% (Pew

Research Center, 2019). Quantifying support for the BLM movement is not as simple with age, race, and partisanship having a strong determinant on stance; and most recently, as of September 2020, support has declined as confrontations between police and protestors have escalated along with Donald Trump's criticisms of the movement (Thomas & Mensace Horowitz, 2020). Pew Research Center also found that the partisanship divide between June 2020 and September 2020, which was already strikingly different in June, has grown even further (Thomas & Mensace Horowitz, 2020).

Kendi (2019) highlighted how it is no longer enough to simply not be racist, as a society we need to boldly analyze our own racist underpinnings and critically assess how we oppose racial inequity in ourselves and in our society. He referred to this as antiracism (Kendi, 2019). Case in point: #BlackoutTuesday. The premise for #BlackoutTuesday originated from two music producers to pause business on Tuesday, June 2, 2020, disrupt the current narrative, and allow individuals to pause, reflect, and find ways to move forward in solidarity to support the BLM movement (Coscarelli, 2020). Instagram became a never-ending feed of black squares with captions of #BlackoutTuesday and #BlackLivesMatter, thus rendering the ideology of #BlackoutTuesday powerless by hiding the critical information and resources that activists and organizers were trying to share with their online platforms (Coscarelli, 2020). Instead, when one searched the aforementioned hashtags, rather than stumbling upon a plethora of new knowledge and resources, they found black boxes, null of any relevance toward making proactive changes (Coscarelli, 2020). Social media users mistook the idea of "doing something" as posting a black square on their Instagram, instead of marching, mobilizing, and inciting community change (Coscarelli, 2020).

Social media users' motivations were questioned when they posted black squares. Were they doing so for "likes"? Were they doing so to jump on the bandwagon? Were they posting because they wanted to make a difference and cared deeply about the movement? Or were they ill-informed? Motivation falls under the purview of emotional intelligence traits. Jesse posted a black square on the morning of June 2, 2020. But by noon, their post was down and their repost looked very different: Jesse's motivation was to help themselves and others work toward understanding and personifying the concept of antiracism. Goleman (1995) suggested that motivating oneself is dependent on emotional self-control, delaying gratification, and stifling impulsiveness. Those posting black boxes for ill-intentioned reasons may be seeking instant gratification of "likes" and acting based on their uncomfortable emotions. Jesse was acting based on their own self-efficacy, their belief that they could have mastery over the events in their life and meet challenges as they arose (Goleman, 1995). Drigas and Papoutsi (2018) referred to the ideology of self-management in relation to motivation, where you possess the capability to control your impulses to more productively manage emotions and amend our behavior to initiate change.

Throughout June, Jesse was easily triggered by others' posts and found difficulty connecting with offline friends whose posts dissented from their personal beliefs about the BLM movement, particularly those who showed support for police officers. In a heated political landscape with the 2020 election just over the horizon, it was not surprising that posts were escalating. And while Jesse's friends were not supporting *the* police officers who Jesse deemed murdered one of their own, Jesse felt the way their friends were using their online voices to stand in solidarity with other police officers were ignorant, condescending, and racist. We worked, a lot, on online and offline social skills in the weeks to come. Developing the emotional intelligence trait of social skills suggests that one has "the skills needed to handle and influence other people's emotions effectively to manage interactions successfully" (Drigas & Papoutsi, 2018, p. 7). When one develops this skill, they will then have the ability to more effectively lead, communicate, manage conflict, collaborate, and build bonds (Drigas & Papoutsi, 2018). Goleman (1995) referred to social skills as "handling relationships" (p. 43).

Although Jesse typically found respite through their online networks, it was imperative that Jesse recognized how online banter was exacerbating their symptoms of anxiety and depression. The more they read and the more they posted, the more they struggled to regulate themselves. Social media is a wonderful tool to connect with others, receive validation, find resources, and gain support, but I often work with my clients on recognizing how part of being a mindful, productive social media user is also knowing when it is time to snooze the alerts and pause the posts.

Renee

I have been seeing Renee, a 16-year-old Caucasian female since she was in middle school, when she developed obsessive–compulsive thoughts and behaviors after the death of two family members in a short period of time. Renee stood out to me from our initial evaluation session together. I created a visual addendum to the biopsychosocial intake that I use with clients; I call it the biopsychosocial (media) assessment. I use this tool to gather information on how clients use, interact with, and are affected by technology and social media. I remember Renee, only 12 years old at the time, speaking so matter-of-factly about how she went on a "social media cleanse," a feature she had seen on Good Morning America, with tweens and teenage girls taking a break from social media in an attempt to improve their mental health. Her school was also promoting the concept to see if students could last two weeks without their smartphones.

I quickly learned in sessions that Renee was a pleaser and was not just willing, but eager to use skills we talked about together in sessions. As her obsessive–compulsive thoughts and behaviors waned through weekly psychotherapy sessions, we focused more on reducing her symptoms of generalized anxiety disorder in relation to her high school experiences on the swim team, with romantic relationships, and with peer conflict—very typical psychosocial stressors for her developmental period. Overall, I had minimal concerns with her general functioning and thought she was adjusting well to life stressors and implementing coping mechanisms, as necessary. In early 2020, we reduced our regularly scheduled weekly or bimonthly sessions to once per month, or only as needed.

But then COVID-19 came. As the world shut down and school came to an abrupt close, Renee demonstrated a sharp, precipitous increase with her symptoms of anxiety. At the very beginning of COVID-19 she was paralyzed by not only fear of contracting illness, but more so, fear of contracting and spreading it to family members. The fear of another family member dying became a prominent, ruminating thought, and she had difficulty detaching herself from the anticipated blame she would feel if she caused a loved one harm. Renee's parents were both frontline workers during the pandemic, her mother a healthcare worker in a local hospital, and her father a police officer in town. Their jobs, both requiring them to be physically present at work, made Renee further exclude herself at home, meaning the only in-person interactions she had were with her two older brothers, but even those were minimal, as she convinced herself they may be carriers of the virus. Since Renee and her siblings ate dinner with their parents in the evenings, Renee continued to struggle.

These new intrusive thoughts led to almost complete social isolation, in addition to new obsessive–compulsive thoughts and behaviors. Goleman (1995) stated,

> When fear triggers the emotional brain, part of the resulting anxiety fixates attention on the threat at hand, forcing the mind to obsess about how to handle it and ignore anything else for the time being. Worry is, in a sense, a rehearsal of what might go wrong and how to deal with it; the task of worrying is to come up with positive solutions for life's perils by anticipating dangers before they arise. The difficulty is with chronic, repetitive worries, the kind that recycle on and on and never get any nearer a positive solution.
>
> (p. 65)

Renee and I would label these types of thoughts as "spiraling." Early on in sessions, when Renee spiraled, it was quite difficult for her to exhibit any type of mental flexibility or employ any coping skills, feeling trapped in her flight of thoughts and paralyzed by her pervasive worries. The first step, when Renee was engulfed in this cycle, was working on reducing her physiological symptoms through relaxation and mindfulness techniques. However, as we practiced the skill of self-awareness, being aware of her early physiological symptoms of anxiety and labeling her emotions, she was better able to identify situations that triggered her concern and catch her worries earlier before they spiraled (Goleman, 1995). After a client is able to name or label his/her emotion, he/she may then begin to better manage the emotion that exists, the trait known as emotion regulation (Goleman, 1995). In a 2018 study on promoting wellness and reducing burnout in US physicians, the utility of emotional intelligence training was discussed as a means to promote effective coping strategies and stress management and to build resiliency (Shahid, Stirling, & Adams, 2018). Later, I also discuss how therapists' own use of self-awareness may serve as a tool to combat negative countertransference.

After we worked on validating her feelings of fear and implementing self-soothing strategies to reduce the emotional burden she was experiencing daily, we focused our attention onto her locus of control. With COVID-19, for many clients, so many verbalized feeling a profound sense of imbalance, as there were too many things that fell outside their locus of control and not enough things within. Knowing that social media was often a catalyst for anxiety with news reports bombarding users with (mis)information, we discussed in sessions ways to limit her exposure to this news by hiding or blocking some accounts and individuals, instead of completely avoiding all use of her accounts. This allowed her to have autonomy to decide who and what was peaking her pervasive worry, delete, or block them to foster a sense of control over her feeds, while also allowing her to find a sense of connection with others who she wanted to remain in contact. Self-awareness is more than knowing what annoys, frustrates, or bothers you, it is also about knowing what satisfies you (Shahid et al., 2018). I have seen many update the verbiage of social distancing to physical distancing, as although we need to be six feet apart physically, this does not need to translate into emotional or social distancing. We have means of connections through technology and social media that we can use advantageously and productively with some adjustments.

It was near impossible to hide all COVID-19 news from her feed, or simply to avoid exposure to any COVID-19-related information. In sessions, we began looking at her cognitive distortions, particularly that of emotional reasoning, and naming how she was allowing her feelings to determine whether or not things must be true. We recognized the difficulty in filtering through fact and fiction online, as information was constantly being challenged and changing. It was not necessarily true that we were always being fed lies and misinformation purposely, but that as the weeks and months progressed, we, as a country, were just progressing in our understanding of the virus. I often employed Renee's mother as a semi-expert to help facilitate this discussion with her ability to share first-hand accounts of what she was experiencing in the hospitals, combined with her background knowledge of viruses and medicine from her nursing education. Through this ongoing dialogue, it allowed Renee to engage in more meaningful, rational decision-making in lieu of her making more emotionally based decisions, thus slowly increasing her level of comfortability interacting physically with the world.

In one session, Renee discussed how she had seen a few groups of people create different GoFundMe accounts to raise money for frontline workers. Recognizing the toll that COVID-19 was taking on her parents, it brought her joy knowing that others were banding together to provide support and relief in the best capacity they knew how: by providing food, water, and PPE. When we look at Maslow's Hierarchy of Needs, we know that one cannot climb the ladder toward self-actualization without meeting his/her basic needs. However, so often, in the midst of stressful situations, particularly a global pandemic, basic needs are often the first to go as we fight to help ourselves and others. We forget to rest our bodies. We forget to drink water. We forget to pause and eat throughout the day. Renee knew quite well her parents seemed to be foregoing those needs and was touched by others' recognition and gestures.

Renee, riddled with her own anxiety about leaving the house, knew the difficulty her parents, too, faced. Goleman (1995) stated, "Empathy underlies many facets of moral judgement and action" (p. 105). He uses the example of how when a bystander feels for a victim, they are more likely to intervene and take action (Goleman, 1995). By the next session, Renee, too, had joined in to support frontline workers. It was apparent by her demeanor and affect as she spoke about her own GoFundMe account that by fostering a sense of control through organizing this support for frontline workers, by connecting with others' who had shared values, and by finding the eternal good in people who she found so often wrapped in social media squabbles about political discourse, eventually, she found a sense of peace and a sense of purpose.

But, again, just as Renee was settling into her new norms and routines, the world imploded yet again on 5 May. I checked in with Renee during subsequent sessions about the impact of social media and the BLM movement on her overall well-being, particularly knowing how social media is a trigger for her anxiety, but also knowing this one may have hit even closer to home—her father was a police officer. When Renee is struggling with symptoms of anxiety and depression and embodying a negative sense of self, seeing online content that goes against her own beliefs often exacerbates her negative feelings, and although she is not being personally attacked, it often feels as if she is. During COVID-19, healthcare workers were often praised as heroes, but throughout the BLM movement, police officers were often verbally attacked with strong rhetoric regarding defunding the police. Again, we engaged in education and open discussion, this time surrounding what "defunding" the police meant along with dialogue regarding the concept of "antiracism" and "systemic racism."

Session after session, Renee impressed me as although many of her friends' were voicing views that differed greatly from hers' and her family's, she shared that she was simply listening, not sharing, and trying her best to learn and not react. I realized, however, that although Renee's lack of online participation about the BLM movement may have been due to her trying to listen and learn, that it may have stemmed more from fear of going against the narrative and being shunned both online and offline. Here enters another concept I recently learned: cancel culture.

The notion of "cancel culture" also complicates the quantification of online support for BLM and the antiracist movement. When an individual acts in ways that are deemed racist, against equality, or morally unjust, other social media users may "call them out" on their political and social injustices to show their allegiance to vulnerable populations (Bouvier, 2020). There has been debate surrounding individual's motivations and their own morality when they "call out" others; for instance, perhaps they are calling out others' behaviors in a way to highlight their own righteousness for the wrong reasons or perhaps their "call out" is out of proportion to the primary unjust offense and they, in turn, are verbally attacking others (Bouvier, 2020). What happens, however, is an adult game of telephone where messages become miscrossed or morphed as it is repetitively shared online. When an individual is "called out" online, others who do not know the person may join in the "calling out" either by also verbally attacking them or by sharing the offensive posts in a way that goes viral online, thus allowing many others to also attack them. These individuals, who have been pegged as doing something heinous, may then become victims of online bullying or shunning. This can happen on a small scale throughout a school building or on a much larger scale across the nation. Renee, knowing many of her peers were Biden supporters, felt as if by showing her family's allegiance to Trump and the police, that she, too, would be shunned.

Ott (2017) believes that Twitter, in particular, trains us to devalue others and cultivates malicious discourse. Bouvier (2020) asserts how although social media users share news and resources, Twitter feeds are often "not so much characterized by rational coherent discussion, but more by floods of emotion and affect" (p. 2). There is an ephemeral nature to Twitter, whereas when individuals Tweet, it is not always well thought out or planned (Bouvier, 2020). Social media is also incredibly fast moving, meaning users may not always take the extra time to assess or gain a better understanding of others' posts and therefore respond on a shallower level (Ott, 2017; Bouvier, 2020). However, adolescents posting ill-thought-out content may actually be acting within their typical psychosocial developmental schemas. We know that until our mid-20s, our brains are not fully developed. Newman and Newman (1976) posited that between the ages of 14 and 17 years, one of the four developmental tasks was the development of formal operations, and between the ages of 18 and 22 years, one of the four developmental tasks was establishing internalized morality. Formal operations, derived from Piaget's Theory of Cognitive Development, includes hypothetical thinking and potential consequences of actions to anticipate future events and to understand logical implications of events (Newman & Newman, 1976). Internalized morality, a derivative of Kohlberg's Theory of Moral Development, is the ability to have empathy and an anticipated sense of guilt when making decisions regarding our own behaviors (Erikson, 1994). When posting, many adolescents are not fully considering the potential ramifications of their words, nor are they feeling poorly about its potential effect on others' well-being.

Renee became aware, through observing her online "friends" posts, that some of them certainly fit this description and responded in a shallow and/or crude manner online when posting about their political views or affiliations. When individuals post online, they do not always consider how their interactions will impact others, and sometimes post or respond to online content in a way they may not typically respond offline (Ott, 2017). Goleman (1995) asserts that empathy builds upon self-awareness, as the more we understand our own emotions, the better equipped we are to read others' feelings. People rarely come outright with how they feel. Instead, they express feelings through cues: tone of voice, gestures, facial expressions, and posture to name a few (Goleman, 1995). Thus, online empathy can be complicated because we lack the ability to read many of these cues from behind a screen.

To better facilitate meaningful discussion, whenever possible, I encouraged offline conversation (or via FaceTime, an online, but face-to-face platform) to allow Renee to share how she felt about her friends' posts and to allow her friends to read nonverbal cues from her if she struggled in explicitly stating her feelings. Incredibly apprehensive, and at times even resistive to having these conversations with her friends for fear of going against the crowd and being belittled and harshly judged, when Renee had her first conversation with her closest friend of whom had a differing political affiliation, she found that her friend was positively responsive, supportive, and even apologetic that she had offended her with her posts attacking the police.

Discussion

We clinicians like to think of ourselves as culturally competent, ethically sound, and morally social just beings after our years (or decades) of social work education and mental health training. But we are not posthuman robots. We have faults of our own and feelings that we must continuously work through behind the scenes of the work we do with our clients. As a mental health clinician, particularly as a mental health clinician through the BLM movement and COVID-19 pandemic, I have often found myself examining my own fault lines as an evolving white, heterosexual psychotherapist in a suburban upper-middle-class town, coupled with my own anxieties surrounding the safety and well-being of my family.

Connecting With Trans Youth

Jesse was not always Jesse. Eight years ago, when we first started our therapeutic relationship, they were Stephanie, and Stephanie was referred to as a she.

It was not until six years into therapy that Jesse shared they no longer wanted to be referred to as Stephanie. I empathized with Jesse's parents, who after 19 years of raising a daughter, their eldest child, were unable to shift from she to they and from Stephanie to Jesse after the reading of a letter left for them clarifying their gender identity as "trans." They birthed a firstborn daughter and agonized over what "her" name would be and referred to them by this name for the last 7,000 days of their lives. I believe I am a strong advocate for trans youth to be able to identify, and be identified, as the gender of their choice when choosing what bathroom to use, on their educational records, and regarding what sports teams they can participate on. But I am also a healthcare provider in—network with insurance, that of whom uses the name on the birth certificate and social security card to bill for services, and therefore, on my clinical records, Stephanie was imprinted.

Jesse and I were going back-and-forth via email to reschedule a session. The heading of the email, which came directly from the billing service I use, was Jesse's birth name: Stephanie. Haphazardly, in the midst of a chaotic work day, I replied back, "Sounds good, Stephanie! See you on Tuesday!" Two minutes later, in a moment of panic, I abruptly stopped what I was doing and logged back into my email, clicking on the sent messages. I dead-named them. Scrambling to write a follow-up email apologizing for what I had just done and correcting myself, I saw a response. It simply read, "Jesse:)." I paused for a few moments, something I had probably not done enough of that week, or month. This moment of disconnection, both disconnection from what I was doing trying to be in multiple places online at once, and disconnection from the individual of whom I had just spent months processing their gender and sexual identity with, rattled me. Aside from my uber-apologetic follow-up email response, Jesse and I spent the first 15 minutes of the next session discussing what it felt like for me to dead-name them and how to move forward from there. I was taken aback by Jesse's seeming disregard of the email. When I noticed, it appeared as if I needed to process the event more than they did, I immediately redirected the focus of the session to Jesse's needs.

Connecting With Parents and Children

Reflecting back on this series of interactions, as a clinician, my focus was on the willingness to repair the fault that had been made and reconnect as a clinician and client. My own feelings, for the most part, were put aside to prioritize the clinical needs of Jesse. But with family members of trans youth, living through the experience of their own children transitioning with their own cultural frameworks and belief systems, and with their own feelings embedded into the current reality, the willingness to repair, or willingness to reconnect, gets lost. Not lost as in absence from the ideology, but lost as in whose feelings and whose beliefs get to be prioritized more.

The parent–child relationships and interactions are integral pieces to the clinical work I do. Many parents exist from this framework of "I'm the parent and I birthed you and I know what's best for you," in addition to that of, "I love you so much and just want to keep you safe so will not let you do the things I deem as scary or dangerous or ill-suited for your age." Either of these frameworks, or the combination of them both, causes a disconnection between the parent and child, particularly between the parent and adolescent who is growing into their sense of self and experimenting with who they want to be. We know the adage of "to be old and wise," but sometimes the ego of the old (the parent) interferes with the adolescent development of self so significantly where the adolescent's new idealized sense of self believes themselves to be so distinct and separate from the parent that it leads to a profound rift in the relationship. Fariselli, Ghini, and Freedman (2008), using the Six Seconds' Emotional Intelligence Assessment, found that emotional intelligence only increases the most slightly across the lifespan and that there are many younger people with very high emotional intelligence and many older adults with lower emotional intelligence. Age only accounts for 1.6% of the emotional intelligence variance (Fariselli et al., 2008). By sharing this information with both the client and the parent, it allows me to even the playing field between parent and child, while subtly partnering with the status of the parent.

Much of the work I do in family sessions with youth surrounds the opposite ideology of "child should listen to parent," and instead flips the session where I request the parents take the time to listen to their child. We discuss the notion of really hearing not just the context but also the feelings. And often, I ask that the parents do not even respond and instead take those words home with them to reflect first. I may even give the parents homework to read an article or research the words their children are using, too. Generation Z is exposed to the ideas of transexualism both online among their social networks, and in also their public education depending on age and grade level, and it is therefore normalized through these online and offline forums. Older generations typically lack this online and offline exposure and, consequently, have a completely different frame of reference. Creating a shared language creates opportunities for reconnection.

Connecting During COVID-19

In March 2020, many mental health clinicians transitioned to virtual and telehealth services across the United States as the pandemic imploded. As recommended by my OBGYN, at 32-week-pregnant with my second child, compounded by an underlying diagnosis of hyperthyroidism, I transitioned all of my sessions to telehealth for the foreseeable future. I trained my two-year-old to know when the bedroom door was closed, that meant mommy was with clients and he would get to spend special time downstairs with daddy. The first few weeks were rough as I struggled to compartmentalize my work life from home life. I had to practice abruptly switching my gears from mom to a tantruming toddler to a composed therapist while also navigating what were and were not work hours at home. My work life rarely fell within the nine to five framework, but it did typically fall into days of the week I was versus was not in the office, as per terms of my sublease. As I met with clients virtually, all days somehow became fair game for booking appointments.

After taking a few weeks off in May after the birth of my healthy baby boy, I jumped right back into virtual sessions and continued throughout the summer. Virtual sessions worked well with a toddler and a newborn as I could craft my schedule based on what worked best for our now family of four, and clients tended to be home without in-school classes and without many social plans, so their schedules were also fairly flexible. More so, virtual sessions seemed to work really well with the primarily adolescent and young adult population I work with. They already existed and communicated with others regularly on their phones via FaceTime or other apps that the transition to telehealth sessions posed little to no concern for them at all. I found the offline therapeutic connections we had formed were easily maintained virtually. But then in September, as schools were finalizing their reopening plans, someone asked me if I, too, would be returning to the office for in-person sessions. My immediate reaction was a firm, "no," but then I thought, "I don't know . . . Am I?" And that thought paralyzed me with fear.

As I was finalizing my first draft of this chapter, Renee reached out requesting to schedule an appointment as soon as possible as her nightmare, the moment she had been dreading for eight months, had come true. Her brother tested positive for COVID-19. We scheduled a session that afternoon, and for the first 45 minutes, she struggled to string together full sentences describing her current state of being. While listening to her, despite how present and engaged I attempted to be in the conversation, my mind reverted back to my own first "scare" with COVID-19 the week prior. Clinicians are not immune to loss, nor do they possess all the coping skills necessary to emotionally regulate 100% of the time. Three days prior to the birth of my son, I lost my grandfather. Thirty-eight-week pregnant with a toddler at home during the pandemic, there was no opportunity to grieve in the normal, prepandemic ways of grieving, and there was no extended support system I could be around as I needed to physically protect myself and my family. This loss, coupled with the birth of my son, who I so vehemently wanted to keep safe from all potential illness, directed me to make choices that most certainly aired more on the side of caution.

Sigmund Freud introduced the idea of countertransference referring to therapists unconsciously displacing their own feelings onto the therapeutic exchange, but more recently, it is also more simply known as the feelings evoked when treating a client (Breivik et al., 2020).

Clinicians are living parallel lives to their clients as we both are experiencing the COVID-19 pandemic concurrently. As therapists, being more acutely self-aware of our own emotional responses throughout this time is critical to avoid a rupture in the therapeutic relationship with our clients. This may be accomplished through clinical supervision, team meetings inclusive of self-care circles, regularly implementing our own self-care regiments, frequent introspection, and/or continued professional development focused particularly on treating clients during the COVID-19 pandemic.

Conclusion

I have indicated multiple times that our youth, Generation Z, may be better equipped with social–emotional skills due to comprehensive SEL education in schools. This would mean that Generation Z, with this educational background, is better positioned to cope with mental health triggers and stressors. But if this is true, it seems difficult to then account for the 56% increase in youth suicide over the last two decades (Curtin & Heron, 2019). Some experts have attributed this sharp increase to child and adolescent social media usage, as this has been the most apparent difference in how children spend their leisure time, while others do not see a clear association between technology use and rising depression rates, suggesting a correlation does not equal causation (Heid, 2019). Other researchers have examined the impact of the wildly popularized, "13 Reasons Why" Netflix series on suicide rates, with April 2017, the month following the show's release, logging the highest number of suicides in any single month over a five-year period (Bridge et al., 2019).

The Social Dilemma, a Netflix film released in 2020, daunts a chilling narrative of the online social sphere. In 2017, Ott highlighted how our individual social media feeds are distinctly tied to what sites we visit, what we "like" and comment on, and who we become friends. For instance, on the most basic level, if I "like" a picture of puppies, more puppies will start to pop into my newsfeed. *The Social Dilemma* depicts how essentially we are puppets of digital creators and being exploited for capital gains. Technology is smart, sometimes too smart. And if we are not learning how to be responsible, mindful, productive consumers of social media and emphasizing the need to cultivate emotional intelligence traits both offline and online through SEL and digital literacy, we will most certainly find ourselves riddled with technological addictions and other significant mental health impairments inclusive of rising suicide rates among more avid online users. Through the development of emotional intelligence skills, we learn to coexist better in this world creating harmony and cooperation; the better we are able to cope inwardly and regulate ourselves, the better we are able to interact with the outside world, thus benefiting society as a whole (Drigas & Papoutsi, 2018).

While the aforementioned increase in youth suicide is a startling statistic, what is even more alarming is the 73% increase in suicide attempts among youth of color (Lindsey, Sheftall, Xiao, & Joe, 2019). In her webinar, Kimme Carlos also discussed how systemic racism has traumatized communities of color and traumatized black youth, and how the lived experiences of black youth are risk factors, as they are far more often victims of persistent stress, acute trauma, family disruption, and acute loss or rejection than their non-minority peers. Integration of SEL and digital literacy/citizenship in schools has proven advantageous and elicited many positive outcomes as highlighted earlier in this chapter, but it may not be enough. Lindsey, Sheftall, Xiao, and Joe's (2019) study suggested that we could take things one step further by increasing access to in-school mental health providers, as black youth, in particular, are not well enough connected to treatment to combat deeply societally engrained mental health struggles.

Additionally, while the notion of trauma-informed training for schools had been steadily gaining traction over the last two decades, it has skyrocketed following the pandemic. Trauma-informed schools acknowledge that children face significant hardships and adversity and that it is imperative to universally establish kindness, compassion, and flexibility across classroom settings (Winninghoff, 2020). Another goal of trauma-informed schools is to build resilience among students through offering unifying messages of hope, aligning with social justice ideologies (Winninghoff, 2020). But it should go without saying that teachers, staff, and administration bring their own trauma into the school, and without acknowledging, addressing, and supporting this trauma, these individuals will most certainly feel socially and emotionally depleted and therefore unable to adequately provide the social-emotional guidance their students have grown to accustomed to receiving (Luthar & Mendes, 2020).

Yes, SEL, digital literacy, targeted counseling programs, and trauma-informed approaches have been adopted by many schools across the country, and there are undoubtedly multifaceted benefits among our younger generations. And yes, it may feel almost impossible for schools and their staff to undertake more responsibility as we trudge through the COVID-19 pandemic with hybrid and virtual learning regiments in place. But with the appropriate allocation of resources and thoughtful consideration put toward our youths' role in shaping the political and social climate of our country in the decade to come, one can easily argue that we can never do enough to help shape both the cognitive and emotional minds of our future leaders. If you need a little more convincing, Georgia's voter turnout in the 2020 election paints a clear picture. Generation Z made up 21% of the total votes, the total number of eligible youth voters was nearly equivalent to the number of youths who voted in the election, and they supported Biden over Trump with the largest margin of any age group, 62–33%, giving Biden a significant bump in the race for the state's 16 electoral votes (Sternlicht, 2020). So even if we are not "following" Generation Z right now, we soon will be. They are the voices, they are the activists, and they are the future change agents of the world.

Close Reading Questions:

1. What does Biri update about psychosocial theory? How has psychosocial theory evolved from Erikson's original assertions over the course of the last few decades?
2. Manago coined the term "customized sociality." How can youth who identify as trans or BIPOC use this ideology to promote social emotional well-being while using technology and social media?
3. COVID-19, coupled with a polarized political landscape, induced high levels of fear in some of the population leading to social isolation and pervasive worry about well-being. How can we use Goleman's ideas about self-awareness to combat intrusive thoughts and encourage a shift in thinking when feelings of safety and security are deeply impaired?

Prompts for Writing:

1. Reflect upon your own early childhood educational experiences with social emotional learning. Consider the decade, political climate, and predominant theories guiding educational curriculums across the United States and how these factors may have impacted your SEL or lack thereof. Assess your own use of emotional intelligence traits in relation to how you use technology and social media.
2. Mental health professionals have had parallel lived experiences to their clients, concurrently experiencing the COVID-19 pandemic, BLM movement, and the polarized 2020 election at the same time as those they were working with. In what ways has countertransference impacted the helping profession? Do you believe emotional intelligence and self-care assumed a more critical role during this time?
3. Is it possible that generational differences between clinician and client could cause a potential rupture in the therapeutic relationship? In what ways can clinicians work toward developing cultural sensitivity with Generation Z to boost therapeutic rapport?

References

Ahn, J. (2011). The effect of social network sites on adolescents' social and academic development: Current theories and controversies. *Journal of the American Society for information Science and Technology, 62*(8), 1435–1445.

Alessi, E. J., & Martin, J. I. (2017). Intersection of trauma and identity. In *Trauma, resilience, and health promotion in LGBT patients* (pp. 3–14). Cham: Springer.

Allen, K. A., Ryan, T., Gray, D. L., McInerney, D. M., & Waters, L. (2014). Social media use and social connectedness in adolescents: The positives and the potential pitfalls. *The Australian Educational and Developmental Psychologist, 31*(1), 18–31. doi:10.1017/edp.2014.2

Bosma, H. A., & Kunnen, E. S. (2001). Determinants and mechanisms in ego identity development: A review and synthesis. *Developmental Review, 21*, 39–66. doi:10.1006/drev.2000.0514

Bouvier, G. (2020). Racist call-outs and cancel culture on Twitter: The limitations of the platform's ability to define issues of social justice. *Discourse, Context & Media, 38*, 100431.

Breivik, R., Wilberg, T., Evensen, J., Røssberg, J. I., Dahl, H. S. J., & Pedersen, G. (2020). Countertransference feelings and personality disorders: A psychometric evaluation of a brief version of the feeling word checklist (FWC-BV). *BMC Psychiatry, 20*, 1–12.

Bridge, J. A., Greenhouse, J. B., Ruch, D., Stevens, J., Ackerman, J., Sheftall, A. H., . . . Campo, J. V. (2019). Association between the release of Netflix's *13 reasons why* and suicide rates in the United States: An interrupted times series analysis. *Journal of the American Academy of Child and Adolescent Psychiatry, 59*.

Carlos, K. (2020, September 30). *COVID-19, youth of color, and suicide risk indicators* (Webinar), Mercer County Division of Mental Health. Retrieved from https://content.govdelivery.com/accounts/NJMERCER/bulletins/2a1d148

Coscarelli, J. (2020, June 4). #BlackoutTuesday: A music industry protest becomes a social media moment. *The New York Times*, Section C, p. 6.

Craig, S. L., Austin, A., & Alessi, E. (2013). Gay affirmative cognitive behavioral therapy for sexual minority youth: A clinical adaptation. *Clinical Social Work Journal, 41*(3), 258–266.

Curtin, S. C., & Heron, M. P. (2019). *Death rates due to suicide and homicide among persons aged 10–24: United States, 2000–2017.* NCHS Data Brief, No. 352. Hyattsville, MD: National Center for Health Statistics.

Di Fabio, A., & Kenny, M. E. (2016). Promoting well-being: The contribution of emotional intelligence. *Frontiers in Psychology, 7*, 1182.

Drigas, A. S., & Papoutsi, C. (2018). A new layered model on emotional intelligence. *Behavioral Sciences, 8*(5), 45.

Elbertson, N. A., Brackett, M. A., & Weissberg, R. P. (2010). School-based social and emotional learning (SEL) programming: Current perspectives. In *Second international handbook of educational change* (pp. 1017–1032). Dordrecht: Springer.

Erikson, E. H. (1994). *Identity and the life cycle.* London: W. W. Norton & Company.

Fariselli, L., Ghini, M., & Freedman, J. (2008). Age and emotional intelligence. *Six Seconds: The Emotional Intelligence Network*, 1–10.

Gangadharbatla, H. (2008). Facebook me: Collective self-esteem, need to belong, and internet self-efficacy as predictors of the iGeneration's attitudes toward social networking sites. *Journal of Interactive Advertising, 8*(2), 1–14. Retrieved from www.researchgate.net/publication/258846959

Goleman, D. (1995). *Emotional intelligence: Why it can matter more than IQ.* New York: Bantam Books.

Goleman, D. (2000). Leadership that gets results. *Harvard Business Review, 78*(2), 4–17.

Gray, M. L. (2009). *Out in the country: Youth, media, and queer visibility in rural America* (Vol. 2). New York: New York University Press.

Heid, M. (2019). Depression and suicide rates are rising sharply in young Americans, new report says: This may be one reason why. *Time Magazine*.

Jones, L. M., & Mitchell, K. J. (2016). Defining and measuring youth digital citizenship. *New Media & Society, 18*(9), 2063–2079.

Kendi, I. X. (2019). *How to be an antiracist.* One world.

Konik, J., & Stewart, A. (2004). Sexual identity development in the context of compulsory heterosexuality. *Journal of Personality, 72*(4), 815–844.

Lindsey, M. A., Sheftall, A. H., Xiao, Y., & Joe, S. (2019). Trends of suicidal behaviors among high school students in the United States: 1991–2017. *Pediatrics, 144*(5), e20191187. doi:10.1542/peds.2019-1187

Luthar, S. S., & Mendes, S. H. (2020). Trauma-informed schools: Supporting educators as they support the children. *International Journal of School & Educational Psychology, 8*(2), 147–157.

Manago, A. M. (2014). Identity development in the digital age: The case of social networking sites. *The Oxford Handbook of Identity Development.* doi:10.1093/oxfordhb/978019993654.013.031

Marcia, J. E. (1966). Development and validation of ego-identity status. *Journal of Personality and Social Psychology, 3,* 551–558.

Newman, P. R., & Newman, B. M. (1976). Early adolescence and its conflict: Group identity versus alienation. *Adolescence, 11*(42), 262–274. Retrieved from www.researchgate.net/publication/232519061

Ott, B. L. (2017). The age of Twitter: Donald J. Trump and the politics of debasement. *Critical Studies in Media Communication, 34*(1), 59–68.

Pew Research Center. (May 14, 2019). *Attitudes on same-sex marriage.* Washington, DC: Pew Research Center. Retrieved from www.pewforum.org/fact-sheet/changing-attitudes-on-gay-marriage/

Porter, A., McMaken, J., Hwang, J., & Yang, R. (2011). Common core standards: The new US intended curriculum. *Educational Researcher, 40*(3), 103–116.

Rich, A. (1993). Compulsory heterosexuality and lesbian existence. In B. C. Gelpi & A. Gelpi (Eds.), *Adrienne Rich's poetry and prose* (pp. 203–224). New York: W.W. Norton.

Rivers, S. E., Brackett, M. A., Reyes, M. R., Elbertson, N. A., & Salovey, P. (2013). Improving the social and emotional climate of classrooms: A clustered randomized controlled trial testing the RULER approach. *Prevention Science, 14*(1), 77–87.

Ross, K. M., & Tolan, P. (2018). Social and emotional learning in adolescence: Testing the CASEL model in a normative sample. *The Journal of Early Adolescence, 38*(8), 1170–1199.

Shahid, R., Stirling, J., & Adams, W. (2018). Promoting wellness and stress management in residents through emotional intelligence training. *Advances in Medical Education and Practice, 9,* 681.

Srinivasan, M. (2014). *Teach, breathe, learn.* Berkeley, CA: Parallax Press.

Steinfield, C., Ellison, N. B., & Lampe, C. (2008). Social capital, self-esteem, and use of online social network sites: A longitudinal analysis. *Journal of applied developmental psychology, 29*(6), 434–445.

Sternlicht, A. (2020, November 4). High youth voter turnout in Georgia creates significant Biden contingent in deeply divided state. *Forbes.*

Thomas, D., & Mensace Horowitz, J. (2020, September 16). *Support for Black lives matter has decreased since June but remains strong among Black Americans.* Washington, DC: Pew Research Center.

Turkle, S. (2015). *Reclaiming conversation: The power of talk in a digital age.* New York: Penguin Press.

Valkenburg, P. M., Peter, J., & Schouten, A. P. (2006). Friend networking sites and their relationship to adolescents' well-being and social self-esteem. *Cyberpsychology and Behavior, 9,* 584–590. doi:10.1089/cpb.2006.9.584

Wallace, K. (2015, November 3). Teens spend a "mind-boggling" 9 hours a day using media, report says. *CNN.* Retrieved from www.cnn.com/

Waterman, A. S. (1982). Identity development from adolescence to adulthood: An extension of theory and a review of research. *Developmental Psychology, 18*(3), 341–358. doi:10.1037/0012-1649.18.3.341

Winninghoff, A. (2020). Trauma by numbers: Warnings against the use of ACE scores in trauma-informed schools. *Occasional Paper Series, 43,* 4.

Zeidner, M., Matthews, G., Roberts, R. D., & MacCann, C. (2003). Development of emotional intelligence: Towards a multi-level investment model. *Human Development, 46*(2–3), 69–96.

2 On the Online Self as an Extension of Personhood

Lauren Busfield

Pre-reading Questions:

1. How has technology enhanced connection within your lifespan? Why might there be generational disconnections that interfere with the benefits of the online landscape?
2. In what ways has the current media landscape shaped our perceptions of generational differences in our experience of technology? How has the concept of "media" changed from your grandparents' generation to now?
3. What is the most dominant technological innovation in your generation? What about your parents and grandparents? How has your own identity been shaped by the dominant technology of your generation?

Throughout the course of history, humans have had a tumultuous relationship to technology. Our advancements both thrill and frighten us, open our eyes to possibilities both exciting and devastating, and push us to keep up or be left behind. As social workers, we need to be acutely aware not only of the impact of technology on our own lives and psyches but also of the impacts on society and our populations. Advancements change not only our everyday life but also the relationships that people have with each other, but also themselves. As we struggle to keep up in a rapidly changing world, we can start to question our place through those changes, our identities as persons existing both in "real life" and in a virtual world, and our ability to adapt to shifts in technological dynamics can become the most important indicator of our well-being in a digital world.

As social workers, understanding the environment in which a person exists is as important as understanding the person. In his 2011 book *Sapiens*, Yuval Noah Harari discusses our common myths that serve to unite us into large groups, a tool that we use to connect across societies and cultures. Our shared myths are more accessible in the technological age than ever before, resulting in widespread flow of ideas that help to shape individuals' senses of community and belonging, as well as their personal identities. Have we

DOI: 10.4324/9781003270225-2

also begun to develop a shared sense of what it means to exist in the world online? Social workers must adapt along with the technology that both they and their clients are using and utilize it as a tool for exploration of identity formation, recognizing unique experiences in the online realm shape our perceptions of ourselves and the world around us.

As we see a rapid shift to online life and explore what it means to have an identity while existing in a technological society, we can also examine whether this experience is a truly unique one to the current generations living through a turbulent relationship with technological advances, or whether this is a part of a predictable pattern of human advancement and development. As we examine the course of history and our relationships with all types of changes in how we utilize and relate to technology, we can start to see the possibility that this was always meant to happen. The speed at which global populations turned to the online world due to the COVID-19 pandemic, when they were perhaps underprepared to do so, has complicated our feelings about being digital and skewed the discussions of online life to focus on the struggles of lacking "normal" human interactions. Our new reality has certainly brought complications of online living to light, but has also showcased the adaptability and the ingenuity present in so many people, and how our society as a whole integrates new technologies as needed in order to continue advancing and surviving.

In order to make the connections from where we've been historically to our current relationships with technological advances, we need to examine previous responses in human history, in order to compare with current reactions. Are the fears and hesitations we have about our online world justified? Or are they part of a larger pattern that has occurred over and over again throughout our collective history, varying by degree of response but still just a normal part of our human development? When we look at our past, we gain insights into our present and future. To understand where we as a society are now, we turn to the people we work with. As social workers, we emphasize the importance of the person's environment in their lives and the impact on their overall well-being, and we recognize the range of lived experiences that our clients can have. The case study model allows us to get a glimpse into a client's lives, opinions, and reactions to current events, and we can see patterns begin to emerge societally from those insights. We pull from these experiences not universal truths, but concepts that may challenge our one-size-fits-all opinions on where we are headed as a society as we integrate technology more fully into our daily lives.

Everything Seems New, But We've Been Here Before

Each generation believes that its experiences as a collective are unique, new, and extraordinary. While this is true, the similarities and patterns that tie societies together are less unique to an individual generation than we may believe. Knowing that we, collectively, have lived through similar experiences throughout the development of humankind and have grown and adapted to our new worlds should help us on our path to understanding unique human experiences within the broader context of patterns of human behaviors, repetition, and survival.

In their book, *A Social History of the Media*, Asa Briggs and Peter Burke note that throughout history, the reactions to new technology have resulted in similar reactions in society, regardless of the form that it takes. Whether television or the internet, people tend to initially denounce all media that they view as new and unfamiliar (Briggs & Burke, 2009). As society adapts and gets used to the new media, they accept it, integrate it into their daily lives, and collectively forget the outcry that occurred at the onset of the invention. Later, a new form of media is developed and appears as new and uncomfortable as the last, and the cyclical nature of responses to technology is perpetuated. Our discomfort with new technology has long been part of the human tradition. As we look back at the history of machines and inventions that revolutionized the ways in which humans communicate and relate to each other, we can observe patterns of outrage and distrust emerging as early as the 1440s. William Berkeley is quoted by Elizabeth Eisenstein in her 2011 book, *Divine Art, Infernal Machine: The Reception of Printing in the West from First Impressions to the Sense of an Ending*, when he wrote of the printing press that "learning has brought disobedience and heresy and sects into the world, and print has divulged them . . . God keep us from both" (p. xi). In Tom Standage's book, *The Victorian Internet*, he makes the connection that our feelings related to the internet, of our "concerns about new forms of crime, adjustments in social mores, and redefinition of business practices-mirror the hopes, fears, and misunderstandings inspired by the telegraph . . . they are the direct consequences of human nature, rather than technology" (Standage, 2007, p. 212). In his later historical analysis of social media history, *Writing on the Wall: Social Media the First 2,000 Years*, Standage examines the human relationship to social media, which he stated has been much longer running than our modern-day society cares to believe. Standage claimed that our ties to social media run deep into the time of the Romans, where gossip and wide social networks became essential to everyday life (Standage, 2013). When we take the concept of social media and place it in the bubble of modern-day applications and websites, we disregard the vast and rich history of human relations, narrowing it down to clicks and "likes," without seeking the meaning-making that is occurring through those actions, we do a disservice to ourselves as well as our clients. Why things matter to people is a critical question in social work discourse (Sayer, 2011). Why is it that social media platforms have become such a time-consuming part of so many people's lives? Saying that we are addicted to our phones is a simplified judgment of societal responses to advancements in connection technology.

When we discuss the history of technological advances, what is most important is not what the technology is, but rather how we are responding to it. If we use Moore's Law to discuss advances, every 18–24 months previous technologies are outdated and capabilities have doubled (Thompson, 2011). In *User Friendly: How the Hidden Rules of Design Are Changing the Way We Live, Work & Play*, Cliff Kuang and Robert Fabricant highlighted this idea by saying that "technology should become simpler over time. Then it should become simpler still, so that it disappears from notice. This has already happened with stunning speed, and that transformation is one of the greatest cultural achievements of the last fifty years" (Kuang & Fabricant, 2019, p. 10). The speed of our advancements seems to be what current society has the most trouble adapting to. While we attempt to keep up with an ever-changing world, spending time on social media and technology, scholars worry most about terms like "addiction" and "overuse" (Savci & Aysan, 2017; Turel, Brevers, & Bechara, 2018; Hou, Xiong, Jiang, Song, & Wang, 2019; Balakrishnan & Griffiths, 2017; Walters, 2017; Worsley, McIntyre, Bentall, & Corcoran, 2018). Frequent, even "excessive" use of new technologies could be reframed as means of adaptation and learning. Standage discusses the use of technology as answers to problems—when successful and designed effectively, our devices assist us not only with small-scale problems that we experience in daily life but also with large-scale problems that face us as a society (Standage, 2013). As we create new technologies that keep us engaged with an ever-expanding social circle, with a globalized economy, and with the largest knowledge-based that we have ever experienced in human history, we may find that achieving a balance between needing to learn the constantly changing technology and needing time "unplugged" can be a struggle. We need time to learn, to adapt, and to adjust, which happens to be something that our society was short on when we made the switch to life online.

Dan Carlin, a historical commentator and popular podcaster, writes in his uncannily timed 2019 book *The End Is Always Near* of the disasters and following adjustments of societies as they adapted to the troubles of their times. In his section focused on pandemics, he writes about the pessimistic attitude that befell the survivors of the time after the worst of the plagues had passed. While our society has not witnessed nearly the same traumatic effects such as seeing nearly half of the population die of incurable and unexplained disease, the human psychological impacts of living through an upheaval in the way of life are as profound now as they were hundreds of years ago. Looking at the historical context and the potential for future public health crises, Carlin wrote of the "fear, uncertainty, and irrationality on the part of the public" (Carlin, 2019, p. 143). We can choose to view this as disheartening; we've learned little about how to effectively cope with disaster over the years. On the other hand, there is some comfort in the familiarity and relatability of the assessment; human behavior is extremely predictable, even over the span of centuries. We think we would respond differently to stressful situations than our ancestors did, but in reality, we are simply facing different stressors and fail to give enough credit to the previous generations who adapted and survived their own troubling times.

As we face our current crises ourselves and standing by our clients, exploring how they are living with their current challenges can help us see not only where they are struggling the most but also the adaptability that some of them show as they navigate the changes in their worlds. Taking a closer look at individual stories can shine light on the range of lived experiences arising from the shift to an online world and highlights the need for an individualized approach in assessing how each person sees themselves online and offline. While using phenomenological approaches to seeing an individual, we hold in perspective the environmental history of societies before us, living through disaster, upheaval, and change, to see patterns arise in behaviors that can lead us to the best analysis and support of our clients as they develop or continue lives in a digital world.

Client Perspectives in the Shift to Online Life

A dark-haired, blue-eyed teenager fiddles with her ripped jeans in the chair across from me, not meeting my eyes. Normally energetic and talkative, Natasha's made strides over the past year in managing her anxiety, focusing on the positive relationships she's built with close friends, and diving into hobbies as positive coping skills. The sullenness is new; she's been at home for months, and her contact with friends has dwindled. What contact she does have is over text, and this is something she's never liked; large group chats that focus on every topic in general, and yet nothing in particular. They overwhelm her, and she likes the one-on-one relationships she usually has with close girlfriends—sleepovers, late nights, and movie marathons are how she bonds. We'd talked before about making connections with friends outside of time spent together because sometimes life gets in the way of those in-person meetings, and she would suddenly feel isolated, but Natasha insisted that "hanging out" is the only way to socialize. When friends move away or switch schools, the friendship ends for her—she no longer sees how she can connect with someone she doesn't see. Encouragement from her parents and her therapist to maintain contact with faraway friends fall on deaf ears, as she is closed off to the idea. She needs to be with someone, read facial expressions, hear tone of voice, and have physical contact with someone in order to consider that friendship valid. Now, forced into a world of social distancing, her social life has collapsed, unable to adapt quickly enough in a changing situation to the new requirements of distanced friendships. She cannot keep up with texts in which she cannot read the intended tone; she quickly gets angry, snaps at friends she previously considered to be close, and "cuts out" anyone who she sees as starting drama. When in-person, these common friendship tiffs are resolved through talking it out in the hallways at school, through having to sit in close proximity on the bus rides home, or through friends noticing that something is wrong between them and stepping in to offer encouragement to repair the friendship. Without those external pressures, some of the friendships start to deteriorate; small arguments turn into long periods of not texting or calling, and without a need for physical contact, a rift expands that feels impossible to repair. Natasha describes her friend groups as close to one another, but as with most teen cliques, a member's social status changes rapidly within them, and without other regulatory forces, Natasha's struggles to maintain its members at all.

Adolescent Identity Online

Dana logs on as usual to her weekly D&D meeting, where her friends immediately greet her. She typically does not bring up where she knows her best friends from when talking to new people, afraid that she will be ridiculed for her involvement in online gaming. Her reality is that this has been a constant; through her mother's illness and death, and now her father's declining health this year, she's counted on her online friends as support, more than her own estranged family. She has had to move several times over the last few years to care for her sick parents, to go to school, to find a job, but during all of those times, losing friendships has never been a real concern for her. She shares all of her challenges, thoughts, and emotions with her friends over a typed chat or over the headsets while they play—her connections to her friends is as deep as if they were there with her. Dana has told her online friends things that she would never be able to share with others. Even if she ventures out to make new connections in a new place, she does not feel she can get as close to them as quickly and prefers to go back to her online group of friends, where she feels safer, and feels she does not need to be constantly offering explanations of her life story. The game is a connection—while she may not have much in common with other members at first glance, they at least know that they all enjoy the same game and that is enough for a basis of a relationship. She expresses that it is harder to meet people "in person," as you have to start from a point of not know-ing anything about a stranger and learning slowly if you have anything in common at all, whereas in the game, you know at least that you all enjoy one activity together and that creates an immediate bond. At times, though, she admits that she struggles. At the end of a really hard day with her father, she has no one to hug or a shoulder to cry on. She has focused on building these relationships online, but feels a lack of "real life" friends and struggles with where to start to build them. Her friends live across the country, and she knows that while they will provide words of comfort when needed, no one will be there to help her make arrangements for her father, to hold her hand at the funeral, or to help her go through boxes of memories piled in her parents' garage. When she starts to consider this, she questions her version of reality: does she have anyone she would consider a friend at all? What does friendship mean if you do not have someone you can count on to be there for you in the times you need them the most? Talking through this, she begins to question her perception of herself, as well. She has a firm identity online, a confident one, where she has friends, meaningful conversations, does well in a game, and can present the things she likes best about herself. Offline, she struggles with self-confidence, friends, and her actual career. Melding the two identities into one reality of herself leaves her feeling conflicted; which version of herself is more real, and which would she rather be?

Online Communities

Anxiety, as well as a list of physical health problems, is what prevents Erica from doing things she thinks she would like to do. She only thinks she would like them; but even in high school she held back, never fully participating in life, just in case something went wrong. Now in her mid-thirties, Erica can give a list of things that have gone wrong, and a longer one of what still might. She thinks about her diagnoses, the accompanying limitations of her physical conditions, and wonders if there is anyone else in the world who understands how overwhelmed she feels just managing her health. She tells me that she felt like her family and few close friends would never really "get it," that she would always be facing her body's betrayal on her own. She has tried and failed to make people understand her—her parents, her siblings, her ex-boyfriends—and feels that they all misunderstand her physical issues as manifestations of imagined issues. Erica has been told by many people in her life that she makes excuses for herself, and every time she tries to describe this happening, it brings her to tears. She cannot describe to them how much she wants to participate in her life but feels unable, or crippled, or so afraid of having an issue that even when she feels well she cannot venture to try. She is alone in suffering, which only increases her anxiety about meeting new people, as she thinks that no one new could understand any better than those currently in her life; she feels exhausted even thinking about trying to explain everything she experiences to another new person only to face rejection, again. Erica is resolved to distance herself from others, until she discovers that there are groups of others online. A group of people who have the same diagnosis; she joins and starts reading. She reads about symptoms that sound like hers, about pain that she knows all too well. She comments, and someone tells her how they have felt over the last few years, isolated with a diagnosis that does not always seem to make sense. Erica understands and tells her so. Soon, she has discovered other groups; more people, more stories, and more connections. Searching for other groups for another diagnosis adds more understanding to the conditions she struggles with. She adds online "friends" to her network and begins to talk to some regularly, sharing tips and tricks for dealing with issues that doctors deem subclinical or incurable. Through their conversation, she finds not only information that can be used to help her manage her symptoms, but even more importantly, she finds that the feeling of isolation has lifted. Discovering that she can have meaningful relationships online, she gets braver and sets up a dating profile on an app, figuring that friendship and love can both at least begin online and that her circle can be bigger now than the people on the block she has lived on for the last 20 years.

Nate jumps up from finishing his homework and runs to grab his headset. He has a standing date with Logan, a boy around his age who he has never met in "real life." Logging on, the two start laughing almost immediately about a game update, then discuss strategies about what they will build that day. Over time, they introduce each other to other online friends and talk about their families, their pets, their schools, and their interests. Nate's parents are a little hesitant to encourage the online relationships, reading horror stories about adults impersonating children and grooming them online. Nate's mom checks in with Logan's, and the parents decide to be lenient; no red flags are obvious, and online friendship seems to agree with the boys. Both have relationships with others who live close to them that have been either eliminated or lessened because their lives have switched to an online format. Friends from class seem far away, and distance no longer seems to be the deciding factor for either of them in forming friendships, as much as a common interest to start from. Logan sends Nate funny videos through email between their gaming sessions, and Nate emails about ideas for in-game advancement and articles about updates coming soon. They start to play other games together and soon they're playing several times a week, talking hours more than they would have if they had gone to the same school together. They casually bring up the possibility of meeting someday, but neither focuses on the need to take the relationship offline—for now, they are content to have found someone else who thinks that building a virtual factory on an alien planet sounds like a great afternoon.

(Virtual) Reality Shift

Our clients' lives are irreparably intertwined with the online world. While for years, many people have tried to limit the amount of time and energy that they put into their online lives, our changing landscape has forced many who had little interest in living lives online to grapple with their identity in a virtual world. The impact of COVID-19 in 2020 highlights the differences between people who enjoy online life and those who thrive in solely "real-life" situations and magnifies the challenges which people of all ages find when they are thrown into an increasingly virtual reality that they may not be comfortable in. This is certainly not the first time people have been placed in online situations they were not comfortable in; jobs have moved to a remote format before, and children have certainly had to learn how to function in a cyber school. This is, however, the first time that a move to online life has happened so quickly, so widely, and for so many people at one time, so much that we can view it as a shift in how our society as a whole function. The advancement of society from a production economy to an intellectual one has allowed more flexibility of what we consider to be productive work for people to do (Harari, 2015). Of course, not all work can be digital—we still need a significant number of people working in hands-on jobs in order for society to continue running as we know it, but more and more people are able to do work from a distance who were never able to before. We have opportunities for more members of society to be creative, to be productive, to share knowledge, and to be employed doing so: all without a need for a physical presence in a physical space. This change was inevitable with technological advancements; COVID-19 was a catalyst, but not a cause of the world going online.

What does it mean for an entire society to simultaneously move their social lives and identities online? This has been a question explored before, asking the question based on a smaller scale of how adolescents exist in the world and form a sense of self through their social media platforms as an increasing majority of them have access to iPhones and the internet. Adolescents who have already for years been forming their identities through an online world are participating in similar experiential activities that the generations before them have, but the means and mode of doing so have changed (Boyd, 2014). Compounded by the suddenness of a virtual shift and lacking options for exploration outside of an online world, the conversation about internet use can switch focus from how much time and information are people putting into the internet, to a concentration on meaning-making and the quality of online experiences. Each person may experience this differently; we can look for patterns in clinical work to better meet the needs of our clients to be able to.

The case vignettes given in this chapter are meant as examples, not of judgments of good and bad online experiences, but of the vast range of experiences, thought processes, and intentions that our clients have about their online lives. While we may be tempted to fall into the trap of labeling online time as "too much" or "too little," doing so ignores the nuances present in the use of the virtual world as a part of what makes a person who they are, as so many other aspects of their lives do as well. We accept that sports, hobbies, school, and work are things that help a people form their identities and express themselves as an individual, but we often fail to consider the vast variety of impacts that an online life can have on a person, either because it is a positive, integrated part of life, or because there is a lack, or a negative experience associated with online life.

Many adolescents and children who had robust online experiences before the switch to virtual means of maintaining relationships had an easier time with the transition. Those who have done the best with the transition seem to be those who have been developing an online presence, sense of self, and relationships that can exist regardless of in-person contact. This is not something that can be developed overnight, and a focus on online relationships may have been developing years before it became a necessity. Gretchen

McCulloch points out in her book *Because Internet: Understanding the New Rules of Language* that "the first people to socialize over computer networks were united by their dissatisfaction with the offline social options available to them" (McCulloch, 2020, p. 225). Those who struggled previously finding satisfactory social interaction opportunities in "real-life" may have previously been ostracized, but they now have the advantages that come with being well-prepared for a fully online social life. Standage observes of social media sites that "users of such sites do more than just passively consume information . . . they can also create it, comment on it, share it, discuss it, and even modify it. The result is a shared social environment and a sense of membership in a distributed community" (Standage, 2013, p. 7). As highlighted in the client perspectives, many individuals were thrust into isolation and loneliness, faced with either struggling to maintain relationships despite limited in-person interactions or quickly developing a group of acquaintances that related well through text messages and Zoom calls, those with well-developed social systems in place were able to continue a relatively normal level of interaction.

Others who focus on in-person relationships and avoid social media in general struggle to find connections when school and activities suddenly stop. Adolescents, some of whom have parents that had restricted their technology use, were thrown into an online world that requires a new set of social skills; some of those skills were underdeveloped or unpracticed as they shifted to texting, emailing, sharing on social media. Parents have been advised to restrict and monitor the internet use of their children, but consider how this plays out in a world that has gone mostly online, and what the consequences of lack of autonomy and privacy are for an adolescent at a critical identity-formation point. We understand the need for an adolescent to have some freedoms, as well as some leeway to explore their "selves" and their relationships as a part of growing up, but struggle with the balance when teens are online in a world we want to protect them from.

Adults are not immune to the struggles with online life, and in some ways, may find it harder to establish a new online identity. Dating especially may have become more complicated for adult clients who previously enjoyed meeting new people "through friends" or through shared interests and activities. The online presentation of the self through dating apps has become more important; if waiting months to meet someone might be a reality, then the first impressions gained from an online profile may make or break a potential new relationship. This was old news to some adults, who had been seeking love online for years, but for some, faced with the choice of an online meeting or loneliness, even a less-than-ideal first date online seemed preferable. Dinner over a video call or a long-distance chat while taking separate walks is not the "first date" our society has ever considered before, but new virtual rules bring about new opportunities, and new experiences to adaptable social beings.

Phenomenological Perspectives

Not every client will have a life full of online experiences; as with any other realm, the range where a person might fall is vast. The online relationships that someone has may be as in-depth as their "real-life" connections, they may be a shallow imitation, or they may be the most important attachments in that person's life. The issue lies when social work practitioners make judgments about what they deem to be healthy amounts of online time, or what is a healthy interaction, without considering the individual more fully, and how that person may be impacted by their online life. Our person-in-environment approach has not always allowed space for an environment based entirely or partially online, when the reality is that a client's life may take place mostly sitting in front of a screen. What does it mean when we observe the forces working in a person's life and move them to an online format? Does it change how we perceive those forces? Does it change how a person sees themselves?

Using phenomenology to better understand our clients, ourselves, and the world in the context of clinical social work is a well-established method (Longhofer & Floersch, 2012; Duckham & Schreiber, 2016; Newberry, 2012; Houston & Mullan-Jensen, 2012; Pascal, 2010). The concepts of exploring lived experiences on an individual basis are closely aligned with the ethical principle in social work practice of respecting the dignity and worth of each individual person (National Association of Social Workers, 2015). In their 2017 release of standards for technology use, National Association of Social Workers (NASW) discusses the importance of assessing a client's relationship with technology and focuses on access and abilities to use available technologies, rather than the relationships that clients may have *through* technology (National Association of Social Workers, 2017). This difference in phrasing may seem like a small change, but in order to more fully understand the lived experiences of people living digitally, we need to shift our perspective from viewing people as merely consumers of technology to active participants in online lives. This passive-to-active switch allows more space for a person to develop themselves in an online world; moving from simplistic analysis of person-as-consumer, or, even, person-as-victim-of-technology, and start a conversation about ways in which technology is working for someone (or not), relationships, and puts the person back into control of their online worlds.

The phenomenological perspective can give us insights into a person's life that may otherwise be missed using other theories; it can also help us to understand the human condition and the experiences unique to human beings growing up and living in a digital age. As with all preceding generations, our experiences are an experiment in humanity, and no one has ever lived out our scenarios before to tell us the answers. As we grasp for answers to questions we haven't entirely formed, we can gain an understanding of personhood as a lived experience through examination of individuals and implications for people on a large societal scale. If we bring Harari's concepts of shared myths being a uniting factor in societies into the conversation about identity in a technological age, we can broaden our perspective of what our shared conceptions of social media and technology mean for our identities as human beings.

A problem facing social workers currently is that we are presented with alarmist research the majority of the time, and this can limit our view of how social media presence might be impacting our clients in their current realities. While studies seem to focus on mental health concerns, screen time limitations both for children and for adults, we've reached a point of conflict—how do we ask our clients to limit time online when online is the primary—or only—option? Recognition of clients' differing needs in regard to social media use can be a primary discussion point in social work, especially during a time of increased need to use the internet to connect with others and to preserve self-identity. The impact of social media and well-being cannot be considered to have the same impact on everyone (Beyens, Pouwels, van Driel, Keijsers, & Valkenburg, 2020). Michael Harris is critical of our relationship with the internet in his book, *The End of Absence: Reclaiming What We've Lost in a World of Constant Connection*, and encourages readers to examine their relationship with the online world and to schedule in times away. He questions whether our experiences online and offline are often at odds with each other, and if they can coexist in our realities and all actions be considered authentic to our sense of ourselves. Harris writes that through this dilemma, "we are learning to embrace both worlds as real" (Harris, 2014, p. 102). He also recognizes that this is a unique dilemma for people living in the time "before" the internet and also in the "after"; within a generation, there will be no more "translators," as he terms them, but replaced by digital natives who accept the world online as the only reality (Harris, 2014).

We need to be able to adapt to the reality that our clients are living in, in order to understand them more fully as people with both an offline and online identities. If we are meeting with a client and they are discussing their online gaming, social media, or even dating habits, our initial instinct might be to turn to the familiar questions of length of time spent online and perhaps a lead-in to other, more "productive" hobbies that we could explore with them. We need to challenge ourselves to recognize these questions as biased, as questions of an age that is quickly passing by, and focus instead on questions that might help us better understand the value that a person might be gaining from an experience that they consider worthy of discussing as a part of their life.

Throughout the sudden changes brought about by a global pandemic and a shift to online life, we have been asked to make adjustments in time frames that seemed unreasonable, but we have. We have been asked to move things online that could not be done, but we did. We needed to change how we related to the world and to the people in our lives, and through our advances, we were able to. Not always smoothly, not seamlessly, not painlessly—but change never occurs without struggle. If we accept that this change was more rapid than anticipated, but was an inevitable point of human advancement, perhaps we can look past the discomfort we experience and see that our nature is, at its core, the same. We long for connection, and we find it wherever we can. We need stimulation, we seek knowledge, and we continually develop our identities as we grow and change online and offline. Near the end of his writing, Harris says that "it's in moments of translation that we learn what's indelible about us. We see what cannot pass forward into the new language, the new life, but we also see what things remain" Harris, 2014, p. 209). Perhaps this moment in our time is a time of great reflection, on what we need to carry with us into the future, and how we remake ourselves as people coexisting with our own inventions, and renewed confidence that we will get through both the pandemic and the digital age as adaptable members of the human species. Our perspective can alter from a position of fear and loss of control to one of formation and growth, if we allow space to develop our selves both in the physical world and the virtual; these identities may not look the same at first, but as we adapt we will learn to integrate the two into a more authentic self, living through a time of innovation and connectedness.

Close Reading Questions:

1. Busfield emphasizes the use of phenomenology in contrast to the methodologies which dominate the current research landscape. How might this approach address theory to practice gaps within your own field?
2. Busfield says that if we are able to adapt to the shifts in our virtual and offline lives, then "we will learn to integrate the two into a more authentic self." Do you agree with this sentiment? If not, what do you foresee as the obstacles to this process?
3. Busfield and Biri discuss similar ideas regarding the generational differences in the construction of online identity. In what ways do their conceptions differ from each other?

Prompts for Writing:

1. Busfield asks, "What does it mean for an entire society to simultaneously move their social lives and identities online?" Discuss the ways in which this question has impacted you personally and professionally.
2. Busfield notes the apocalyptic tenor of much writing about technological shifts in social scientific literature. What scares you most about technology? Does Busfield assuage any of your fears?
3. How have your attitudes toward technology shifted over the course of your lifespan? How has it impacted your understanding of diversity and your experience of your own cultural background?

References

Balakrishnan, J., & Griffiths, M. D. (2017). Social media addiction: What is the role of content in YouTube? *Journal of Behavioral Addictions, 6*(3), 364–377.

Beyens, I., Pouwels, J. L., van Driel, I. I., Keijsers, L., & Valkenburg, P. M. (2020). The effect of social media on well-being differs from adolescent to adolescent. *Scientific Reports, 10*(1), 1–11.

Boyd, D. (2014). *It's complicated: The social lives of networked teens.* New Haven: Yale University Press.

Briggs, A., & Burke, P. (2009). *A social history of the media: From Gutenberg to the Internet.* Malden, MA: Polity.

Carlin, D. (2019). *The end is always near: Apocalyptic moments from the Bronze Age collapse.* HarperCollins Publishers, 195 Broadway, New York NY 10007.

Duckham, B. C., & Schreiber, J. C. (2016). Bridging worldviews through phenomenology. *Social Work & Christianity, 43*(4).

Eisenstein, E. (2011). *Divine art, infernal machine: The reception of printing in the West from first impressions to the sense of an ending* (pp. IX–XIV). University of Pennsylvania Press.

Harari, Y. N. (2015). *Sapiens: A brief history of humankind.* HarperCollins Publishers, 195 Broadway, New York NY 10007.

Harris, M. (2014). *The end of absence: Reclaiming what we've lost in a world of constant connection.* New York: Penguin.

Hou, Y., Xiong, D., Jiang, T., Song, L., & Wang, Q. (2019). Social media addiction: Its impact, mediation, and intervention. *Cyberpsychology: Journal of Psychosocial Research on Cyberspace, 13*(1).

Houston, S., & Mullan-Jensen, C. (2012). Towards depth and width in qualitative social work: Aligning interpretative phenomenological analysis with the theory of social domains. *Qualitative Social Work, 11*(3), 266–281.

Kuang, C., & Fabricant, R. (2019). *User friendly: How the hidden rules of design are changing the way we live, work & play.* New York: Random House.

Longhofer, J., & Floersch, J. (2012). The coming crisis in social work: Some thoughts on social work and science. *Research on Social Work Practice, 22*(5), 499–519.

McCulloch, G. (2020). *Because Internet: Understanding the new rules of language.* New York: Riverhead Books.

National Association of Social Workers. (2015). *Code of ethics of the national association of social workers.* Retrieved from www.socialworkers.org/About/Ethics/Code-of-Ethics/Code-of-Ethics-English

National Association of Social Workers. (2017). *NASW, ASWB, CSWE, & CSWA standards for technology in social work practice.* Retrieved from www.socialworkers.org/LinkClick.aspx?fileticket=lcTcdsHUcng%3d&portalid=0

Newberry, A. M. (2012). Social work and hermeneutic phenomenology. *Journal of Applied Hermeneutics, 20*, 1–18.

Pascal, J. (2010). Phenomenology as a research method for social work contexts: Understanding the lived experience of cancer survival. *Currents: Scholarship in the Human Services, 9*(2).

Savci, M., & Aysan, F. (2017). Technological addictions and social connectedness: Predictor effect of internet addiction, social media addiction, digital game addiction and smartphone addiction on social connectedness. *Dusunen Adam: Journal of Psychiatry & Neurological Sciences, 30*(3).

Sayer, R. A. (2011). *Why things matter to people: Social science, values and ethical life*. New York: Cambridge University Press.

Standage, T. (2007). *The Victorian Internet: The remarkable story of the telegraph and the nineteenth century's on-line pioneers*. New York: Bloomsbury Publishing.

Standage, T. (2013). *Writing on the wall: Social media-the first 2,000 years*. New York: Bloomsbury Publishing.

Thompson, R. L. (2011). Radicalization and the use of social media. *Journal of Strategic Security*, *4*(4), 167.

Turel, O., Brevers, D., & Bechara, A. (2018). Time distortion when users at-risk for social media addiction engage in non-social media tasks. *Journal of Psychiatric Research*, *97*, 84–88.

Walters, A. S. (2017). Solution to social media overuse? Put the phones away! *The Brown University Child and Adolescent Behavior Letter*, *33*(12), 8.

Worsley, J. D., McIntyre, J. C., Bentall, R. P., & Corcoran, R. (2018). Childhood maltreatment and problematic social media use: The role of attachment and depression. *Psychiatry Research*, *267*, 88–93.

3 "Hi, I Can Hear You"

Facilitating Telephone-Based Caregiver Support Groups

Lauren Snedeker

Pre-reading Questions:

1. What is caregiving? What happens to support for caregivers in absence of shared physical space? Aside from the social distance, why are some reasons that support for caregivers might need to be remote?
2. In what ways is a phone call different from a zoom or face-time call? Which would you prefer and why?
3. Which rituals are lost without face-to-face connection?

It was 7 pm. I closed my computer, adjusted my headset, and dialed into a conference line. My pen was poised on my notepad, headset in position, and there I was, ready to start a caregiver support group.

"Hello!" That's how I announced that I had "entered the room." Immediately, I heard Dena breathing. I knew it was Dena before she even greeted me because I can tell each client by their breath. Hers was quick and harsh. And she never had any background noise.

Dena's group, consisting of four resilient women from around the country, had been meeting with me for about a year. I'd heard them laugh and cry as they described their adjustment to caregiving roles. I heard them share fears about their family members becoming more forgetful, more depressed, and more dependent on them. I heard them express shame, guilt, anger, and resentment about their new lives caused by dementia. I often thought that the members may have known things about each other in this group more so than their closest family and friends. And all of this was done over the telephone. Nothing complicated, and nothing that required a tutorial. We never saw each other or ran into each other at the grocery store, and we could not describe each other's physical characteristics, but together, we achieved a close-knit, therapeutic bond all through a free conference line.

At this point, because we had been meeting regularly for months, I was able to recognize who was on the line and who was speaking, but this wasn't always the case, especially early on in the group. Identifying tone, inflection, and to some extent, normal background noises are all things that I,

DOI: 10.4324/9781003270225-3

as the facilitator, worked hard to categorize for each group member. Dena breathed in a way that allowed you to hear how she was feeling in a given day. Usually, she inhaled and exhaled audibly during conversations with other members, symbolizing the weight of the conversation, and how she related to the member speaking. Joan, another long-standing group member, always had the television on a low volume for her mother, so we always heard just a hum of daytime talk shows coming from her background. Identifying and matching sounds to group members to this degree undoubtedly took time, attention and focus, and is not something that most learn about in social work school. Coping with impromptu disconnections, call waiting, and other interruptions and modeling appropriate responses to group members when they began talking over each other were and will continue to be part of a new set of foundational counseling skills for social workers to adopt and incorporate into their clinical practices. The COVID-19 pandemic has created no other option but to accept virtual platforms into social work, especially because of the positive outcomes it can create for individuals in need, like the four women in this caregiver support group who were in need of a community to help them cope, and, because of a variety of barriers, were unable to access support like this in other way.

By 2060, the number of Americans aged 65 and older will double from 46 million to 98 million (Population Reference Bureau [PRB], 2016). The aging process inevitably includes the onset of physical, and for many, cognitive health changes that have an unyielding power to diminish independence for the person and often those around that person. Specifically, ten million new cases of dementia are diagnosed globally every year (World Health Organization [WHO], 2021). The impacts of dementia can cause an individual to become more dependent upon another, often a family member, for assistance with a myriad of tasks, ranging from helping someone find a word they've been trying to say to helping someone with their own personal, hygienic care (Hornillos & Crespo, 2012). In the United States, it is estimated that 16 million adult family members provide care to someone living with a dementia-related illness (Alzheimer's Association, 2020). Family or informal caregivers are usually relatives, partners, friends and neighbors in some cases, that are unaffiliated with an agency and are not being paid for the support they provide to the care recipient, as opposed to a formal or paid caregiver (Family Caregiver Alliance, 2016; Schulz & Martire, 2004).

Research has long since confirmed how informal caregiving, in other words caring for a relative or friend, can cause adverse physical and psychological outcomes for caregivers themselves (Papastavrou et al., 2011; Schulz & Sherwood, 2008). Family caregivers supporting someone living with dementia are at high risk for stress, depression, isolation (Papastavrou et al., 2011; Winter & Gitlin, 2007) and mortality (Schulz & Beach, 1999). It is important to consider the impact caregiving for someone living with dementia alongside other life experiences, like poverty, food insecurity, job insecurity unstable housing, natural disasters and most recently, a global pandemic like COVID-19. In addition to addressing and responding to the needs of their family member or friend, caregivers are presently responsible for infection control again the COVID-19 virus. This can mean forgoing vital support from someone, like a home-care worker, because of risks. This can also mean reversing the decision, which is not an easy one, to transition a family or friend into a long-term care facility back home even though the person's needs have gone above and beyond what can be addressed at home due to fear of the virus and its' outcomes. As we have and continue to witness, the COVID-19 virus is often deadly for older people and people living with chronic health conditions (CDC, 2020). Family caregivers are currently managing more with less. Along with COVID-19, individuals are still experiencing memory loss, still being diagnosed with dementia, and still experiencing the progression of symptoms to the point when someone needs to help them. The growth of the aging population, the incidence rates of dementia, and the impacts of caregiving are all reasons why providers and policy makers need to develop and sustain caregiver interventions that meet a board range of needs and reach caregivers from diverse backgrounds (Bank, Argüelles, Rubert, Eisdorfer & Czaja, 2006; Chi & Demiris, 2015).

Support groups are one such opportunity for caregivers to receive emotional relief, connection, and community. This type of support has been a long-standing intervention for family caregivers, providing opportunities to receive education, discuss and reflect upon concerns, and learn new ways of coping and strategies for care along with others who may share similar experiences (Hornillos & Crespo, 2012; Lee, 2015). Support groups can provide a space for validation and social connectedness that can positively impact ones' quality of life (Lee, 2015). In one group session, Joan described how hard it was to think about a time when her mother would no longer be there, and how it would be easier for her mother to peacefully pass away in her sleep as opposed to suffering. Dena agreed and shared how she also did not want her father to suffer. Another long-term member, Michelle, added how she knew that she was a caregiver to her husband, but that this was not what she wanted her entire life to be about. Discussions about death of their care recipient and dislike of the caregiver role can often be considered taboo and difficult for caregivers to reflect upon, especially when face to face with other members and professionals who may visually demonstrate their judgments or discomfort (Toseland & Larkin, 2010; Toseland, Naccarato & Wray, 2007). It is not easy to share with others how, as a caregiver, you may not be able to find joy in what you're doing each day, or, that you wish things were different. Because of we as a society often have this image of family caregivers and image of family for that matter, we hardly stop to recognize the possibility for different experiences and different narratives. Group members connecting over the phone have the opportunity to admit, share, and process difficult emotions and feelings safely over the phone without *seeing* people's judgment. Even though social workers are taught to have a neutral face during clinical sessions, we cannot expect group members to demonstrate the same control.

Unfortunately, caregivers experience difficulties with accessing support groups, some reasons being the amount of time, energy, and resources that someone living with dementia is in need of (Lee, 2015; Martindale-Adams, Nichols, Burns, & Malone, 2002). Attending a support group in-person often means that the caregiver, who may also be living with their own health limitations, must gather resources for transportation, arrange respite (or relief) care for their person, and locate a support group opportunity in their local area (Winter & Gitlin, 2007). For some caregivers, joining a group can even create more of a burden on their resources and schedule (Winter & Gitlin, 2007). Most of the women from the telephone-based caregiver support group I facilitated were unable to participate in local groups through senior centers and other settings because of the timing, distance, and lack of additional support to the person they were caring for while they went to a group. I want to also note how we in mental health fields must be mindful about how we introduce a support group to a caregiver, and the critical need for all providers in all settings to resist making assumptions or judgments about a caregivers' potential involvement in one. Caregivers of all kinds feel that particular type of judgment. That feeling in the pit of your stomach when you are trying to listen to your own needs, the needs of the person you're caring for and what society is telling you to do, especially the recent movement to age successfully and in place. The truth of the matter is that aging in place, or at home, is not a possibility for all people because of the inequities in healthcare and beyond. The resources needed to stay at home while living with a chronic health condition, such as dementia, are not always within reach. However, technology-based communication interventions, such as via telephone, email, or chat system, have been reported by dementia caregivers as satisfying, cost-effective, accessible alternatives to in-person support for an already overburdened and stressful schedule (Chi & Demiris, 2015; Dollinger, Chwalisz, & Zerth, 2007; Jackson, Roberts, Wu, Ford, & Doyle, 2016; Smith & Toseland, 2006; Tremont, Duncan Davis, Bishop, & Fortinsky, 2008; Winter & Gitlin, 2007). Technology-based interventions can be an opportunity to connect with vital support for a variety of populations that are impacted by chronic health issues (Chi & Demiris, 2015), disabilities (Smith & Toseland, 2006), financial limitations (Toseland et al., 2007), and those living in rural areas (Brown, Pain, Berwald, Hirschi, Delehanty, & Miller, 1999; Dollinger et al., 2007).

Integrating technology into mental health services is not a new concept. Prior to the COVID-19 pandemic, individuals have been accessing online support for over two decades (Toseland & Larkin, 2010). With the onset of the COVID-19 pandemic, many providers who may have been naysayers have also followed suit by adopting technology into their practices. Despite the presence technology has had in the social work field, the gains it can achieve for many unseen populations, and this "forced transition" (Békés &

Aafjes-van Doorn, 2020, p. 238), concerns remain about the effectiveness of online therapy (Békés & Aafjes-van Doorn, 2020; Mishna, Bogo, Root, Sawyer, & Khoury-Kassabri, 2012; Toseland et al., 2007; Wells, Mitchell, Finkelhor, & Becker-Blease, 2007). Specifically, how the absence of non-verbal cues can threaten (or impede) the therapeutic alliance and allow for misinterpretations and the loss of potentially meaningful expressions (Damianakis, Climans, & Marziali, 2008; Koufou & Markovic, 2017; Sucala, Schnur, Brackman, Constantino, & Montgomery, 2013). Some have feared that connective rituals, such as shaking a client's hand upon introduction, are also lost when not face to face, perhaps adversely impacting the working relationship (Koufou & Markovic, 2017). Although anonymity can be controversial in social work practice and group work as a result of these anticipated losses in connection, many clinicians who have actually facilitated technology-based support groups have noticed how anonymity encouraged more disclosure from their group members (Damianakis et al., 2008; Galinsky, Schopler, & Abell, 1997; Schopler, Galinsky, & Abell, 1998; Toseland & Larkin, 2010). Additionally, how in fact developing "virtual relationships" (p. 11) can alter the therapeutic alliance between client and clinician in a way that positively impacts the work and the therapeutic alliance (Roesler, 2017). As the COVID-19 pandemic continues, these rituals seem less critical because the feeling is that some support and connection are likely better than none at all, especially while in quarantine. A report conducted by the Rosalyn Carter Institute for Caregiving in October (2020) described how out of 400 caregivers, 83% reported to be experiencing an increase in stress related to their role as a caregiver since the beginning of the COVID-19 pandemic (Rosalyn Carter Institute for Caregiving, 2020). Now more than ever, caregivers are in need of support.

Family caregiving has been and continues to be a public health concern (National Alliance for Caregiving, 2018), and it is therefore imperative for interventions to be accessible, affordable, and evidence based, especially in a post pandemic world. Telephone-based caregiver support groups are one way for caregivers to access affordable, effective, and convenient support that also has the power to encourage more self-expression. This chapter will continue by reviewing prior research on the outcomes of telephone-based family dementia caregiver support groups in terms of their effectiveness, their accessibility and how this specific type of intervention can elicit more self-disclosure and help caregivers connect to others and themselves. Composite case material from various family dementia caregiver support groups that I have facilitated will be presented to highlight these effects as well as demonstrate the adapted engagement skills necessary for facilitating support groups through a technology-based medium. As that technology continues to proliferate and avail itself to social work practice, it is beneficial for social work practitioners of all professional levels to realize and adopt these skills and for these types of skills to be discussed in the classroom so that social work graduates avoid the pressure of adapting to telemental health while on the job.

Effectiveness of Telephone-Based Support Groups

Caregiving can impact an individuals' emotional, physical, economic and social health (Lee, 2015; Schulz & Martire, 2004). In an effort to meet the needs of the person they are caring for, family caregivers often neglect their own needs (Lee, 2015). Dementia caregiving has been specifically identified as a more stressful type of caregiving compared to those that, for example, support someone experiencing a physical disability (Schulz & Martire, 2004). If someone is living with dementia, they then experience a combination of changes with their memory, thinking, language, communication, and their abilities for completing simple, daily tasks of living (WHO, 2021). These symptoms can worsen overtime and create a heavier impact (or burden) for the person and their caregiver. Caregiver burden is an umbrella term used to describe an array of different impacts that may figuratively weigh heavily on a caregiver, such as an increase in the physical needs of a person living with a dementia-related illness, the pressure of role-change within the relationship between care receiver and caregiver, financial strains, and social isolation as a result of the role (Chi & Demiris, 2015; Schulz & Martire, 2004). Caregiver interventions like telephone-based support groups are often measured by their impact on caregiver burden through self-reporting scales such as the Zarit Burden Inventory (Zarit, Reever, & Bach-Peterson, 1980). Similar to in-person support groups, participation in telephone-based support groups have been found to lower burden scores for family dementia caregivers (Goelitz, 2003; Lee, 2015; Smith & Toseland, 2006).

While the impacts of both in-person and telephone-based support groups for family dementia caregivers have been studied separately, there is a small amount of research that compared these interventions side by side. Brown and colleagues (1999) examined the outcomes of a telephone-based support group with the outcomes of an in-person support group for caregivers assisting a family member living with a traumatic brain injury (TBI). TBIs cause significant chronic impacts for the individual and for their caregiver (Brown et al., 1999). Caregivers supporting a family member living with a TBI experience stressors that are similar to those experienced by dementia caregivers, including caregiver burden and burnout (Brown et al., 1999). Fifty-two participants in Brown et al.'s (1999) study received a telephone-based group intervention because they were impeded by location, having little available supports due to the great distance one would need to travel in order to access regular help. Thirty-nine caregivers participated in the in-person support group, as these caregivers lived within 25 miles from the rehabilitation hospital center where the group was held (Brown et al., 1999). Over two years, ten in-person caregiver support groups and ten telephone-based groups were conducted during evening hours for nine to ten weeks each (Brown et al., 1999). Group members selected the topics each week, and all groups were facilitated by a psychologist, neuropsychologist, or a social worker (Brown et al., 1999). Brown et al. (1999) found that these caregivers were significantly satisfied with both intervention styles and that the telephone-based group achieved similar results to the in-person support group in terms of reduced distress and lower caregiver burden based on self-report instrument scores. Subsequent to Brown et al.'s (1999) study, research continued to confirm the effectiveness of technology-based caregiver support groups for dementia family caregivers. Lee (2015) conducted a systematic review of five technology-based dementia caregiver support group intervention studies in order to examine their effect on caregiver burden. Out of a sample that ranged from 25 to 127 caregivers, all five studies showed that technology-based dementia caregiver support groups, including telephone-based groups, were effective in reducing burden (Lee, 2015).

Telephone-based family dementia caregiver support groups can also allow for more consistent and ongoing support. In-person support groups often meet monthly and are subject to reservation issues such as booking physical space for the groups, leaving caregivers increasingly vulnerable to access barriers. Telephone-based support groups have the ability to conveniently connect members more often, helping to create more cohesion among the group as well as a therapeutic alliance between members and the group facilitator, which help the group to become even more therapeutic (Goelitz, 2003). The group members from the telephone-based support group I facilitated hardly ever missed a session for the full year the group ran, and because the group met at 7 pm each Monday night, members could plan for this around their caregiving schedules and other responsibilities, like their jobs. Almost 50 conversations helped the women develop caring relationships with one another, to the point where they shared their personal contact information with one another willingly once the group closed.

Access to Caregiver Support Groups

Even though there are myriad benefits from participating in telephone-based support groups, access to support remains low for dementia caregivers (Brodaty, Thomson, Thompson, & Fine, 2005; Martindale-Adams et al., 2002). After interviewing 109 caregivers for people living with dementia or memory loss regarding their own help-seeking behaviors, Brodaty and colleagues (2005) identified that these dementia caregivers did not access general community services such as in-home care, transportation, or meal delivery services because they did not feel that these services were necessary. First, the feeling of not being in need of services can be related to denial many caregivers may internalize instead of acknowledging and accepting available help (Brodaty et al., 2005). Second, caregivers in the study reported that they felt reluctant to ask for help (Brodaty et al., 2005). Family dementia caregivers may feel a similar type of reluctance when exploring services like caregiver support groups. Reaching out for supportive services in general can be difficult, especially for caregivers who possibly may feel guilty or ashamed about no longer being able, or strong enough to cope with these life changes

(Brodaty et al., 2005). Caregivers from the telephone-based support group I facilitated had expressed frequently how they felt guilty for losing their patience with their family member and for not being able to manage their family members' needs at times. But, even when help is accepted, caregivers can still feel conflict. The guilt that Dena shared with the group consistently after she decided to transition her father to a care facility was surprising. It seemed as though once Dena made this decision and was able to transition her father to a setting that was supportive to his needs, she would feel weight lifted off her shoulders and begin to cope better with the way her father was changing. Now that he was being cared for, Dena could potentially have the opportunity to enjoy the time she did have with him while visiting, and enjoy time with herself doing things other than caregiving. Dena did express relief at times, but also described feeling guilty that she no longer helps her father the way the other members help their family members. It was difficult at the time for me to find a way to respond to Dena that would be supportive and not patronizing. After all, she was right. There was a difference between her and the other members now that Dena's father no longer lived at home with her. However, for some of the members, Dena's decision helped them to accept help into their caregiving scenarios and perhaps cope better with it. Michelle mentioned the benefit of her home health aide and the adult day program her partner attended. To Michelle, these were their lifelines. Allison also shared about family and friends visiting with her spouse in order for her to have a break. It was humbling to see the group members embrace Dena for the decision she made for her father's care and quality of life rather then turn away from her, or, even feel jealous of her. I worried for the group's longevity once Dena made the decision to move her father to a care setting because of knowing that this group was her support system. Dena, like most of the other women, had family but was solely responsible for her father's care. So, asking her to step back from the group did not seem like an option to me, and I decided to take the chance and allow the group members to navigate this change without my involvement. Roesler (2017) noted how "virtual relationships" (p. 11) created a way for clients to have more control, and I conjecture that this occurred in the group I facilitated. Truthfully, it was relieving to have more equal power between the members and myself as the facilitator. These members utilized our sessions as an opportunity to learn about ways to respond to changes in their family member, how to help, and resources such as statewide aging services and engage with them despite negative assumptions regarding available help, which is an additional proven benefit of participating in a caregiver support group (Bank et al., 2006; Brodaty et al., 2005; Damianakis et al., 2008; Lee, 2015). Because one group member, for example, had a positive experience with a local agency, other members felt more compelled to connect with their local organizations and believed in their ability to assist them in some way.

Reluctance and denial can result in higher or a more intense experience of felt caregiver burden and cause a hopeless outlook on the caregiving situation. These feelings may be especially experienced by adult children, like Dena, who tend to want to care for their parent in return for the care the parent provided to them while growing up. Smith and Toseland's (2006) study showed particular benefits for the adult children who were caring for an aging parent in their research on telephone-based support groups for caregivers with aging parents. Group members like Dena and Joan who cared for her mother in her mother's home connected to process the loss of the child role as they supported their parents, which many fail to address because it is an expected experience to occur across the lifespan. Similarly, Michelle and Allison reflected on the transition in their relationships with their partners as a result of the caregiving role. They too described a pressure that caused them to attempt to do it all, because of the vows they took with their partners and likely the lack of available options elsewhere.

Religion, culture, ethnicity, past experiences, and personality can also influence help-seeking behaviors among family dementia caregivers (Brodaty et al., 2005). Some members of this caregiving subpopulation may not feel permitted to grieve or feel stressed as a result of ingrained value systems or family dynamics that highlight caregiving as an expected part of one's life role whether they are a spouse, adult child, or other family member. Some may also feel embarrassed to ask for such support due to inherited perceptions about mental health services (Martindale-Adams et al., 2002).

The format of a telephone-based caregiver support group can provide a space and "lifeline" for dementia family caregivers impacted by a variety of factors that prevent them from accessing beneficial supportive services (Martindale-Adams et al., 2002, p. 181). Telephone-based caregiver support groups have the opportunity to increase family caregivers' support networks and provide a better quality of life for caregivers and thus those reliant on caregivers (Lee, 2015). Members of the group were able to connect with a supportive network despite geographical, physical, and financial limitations. Dena, in her late fifties, was receiving disability benefits at the time of our go up and did not drive. Dena resided in a Midwestern suburban area where, as she had stated in earlier group sessions, there is little public transportation and she mostly felt isolated especially since her father had recently been transitioned into a care facility and she lived alone in their family home. Given Dena's limitations both geographically and financially, the telephone-based support group was an opportunity for her to not only reflect on her evolving caregiver role but also discuss other roles and relationships in her life that she was able to reacquaint herself with due to her father permanently residing in a care facility. Like Dena, many caregivers feel stuck with this type of issue in their caregiving journey—unable to meet the needs of their person at home, but unable to commit to moving them to a facility because of the impact of these negative emotions. I find that caregivers especially are always living in a dual reality where there is the expectation of the role and the actual experience of the role. Deaux (1993) originally referred to this concept as individuals have a personal identity and a social identity.

Dementia caregivers are characterized by media and nonprofit organizations as being burdened by their role but nonetheless happy to, "give back to their family member," or, able to "find the joys in caregiving." This type of narrative is infuriating for someone who has spent time with caregivers processing both the good and the bad. Dena was able to change this narrative, reclaim her identity as a caregiver, and accept her strengths in her role by recognizing how asking for help was part of the role and symbolized a good caregiver.

Joan, caring for her mother at home, shared a passion for participating in her local synagogue and volunteered for a variety of community organizations in addition to supporting her mother's needs. Joan described how keeping active helps her cope with her mother's needs and changing capabilities as a result of dementia. Joan's sister is minimally involved in caring for their mother according to Joan, despite living nearby. In the group, Joan is validated by other members for feeling resentful of her sister for not helping more and appears to perhaps feel more comfortable expressing these feelings in the group as opposed to her faith-based community. Other members compared Joan's experience with her sister to their own experiences with their kids and other family who they also feel resentful toward for not helping more with their care recipient's needs. What's more is that Joan's mother was no longer able to have fluent conversations at the time of the group. This change at the time likely symbolized that the disease was progressing, causing more stress on Joan and her mother. In caregiving studies, many have reported that when their care recipients' needs grow, there is a likelihood for caregivers to feel more emotional distress (Goelitz, 2003; Lee, 2015). I often say that for family caregivers, they are coping not only with the practical needs of their family member change and increase, sometimes overnight, but also with the emotional turmoil that can exist when for the first time, your own parent does not recognize you. And, for some, are afraid of you or angry with you for something you never did. Family caregivers like Joan are mourning their parent, the loss of their safe space, and the loss of their child role all while performing medical-level interventions at home for their parents. It's one of those life experiences that you cannot imagine truly unless you have lived it.

Michelle, in her mid-sixties, was caring for her spouse living with dementia. Michelle lives in a metropolitan city and cares for her husband full time at their home. Their two children live across the country and checked in with Michelle monthly via telephone. Michelle began home-care services twice per week to provide her a chance to be more social and engage in more exercise classes which she enjoyed while she was a member of the telephone-based group. Because Michelle and her husband had to retire early due to her husband's diagnosis and they are on a fixed income. Michelle stated how she cannot pay for more than two days of home care for her husband at this time, and appreciated being able to connect with a free support group that helps her process the changes in her husband and their marriage.

Allison also was caring for her husband diagnosed with Alzheimer's disease at the time of this group. Both were in their mid-fifties and lived in an urban area. Allison worked part time while her husband attended an adult day program while she is at work, a service now not available for many like Allison because of the COVID-19 pandemic. Their adult children lived across the country as well and, according to Michelle, have their own schedules and families to care for. Allison also described struggles with the change in her marriage as a result of this disease, and due to coordinating both her and her husband's schedules, is unable to find energy to attend a support group after their long days and nights. Despite having different relationships to their care recipient, the members of the group share similarities in their feelings about the caregiving role and were committed to one another and the group as a whole.

A Brief Note on the Ways I Engaged Members over the Phone

When the members dialed in to the conference line, I invited the first person who joined the call to begin with a check-in of their week and how they were feeling since the last group discussion. It is especially important in telephone-based groups to ask each person to check-in through a "group go-round," so that no member feels pressure or confusion about when it is their time to speak (Toseland & Larkin, 2010, p. 28). Taking turns provides each member an opportunity to share what they would like, whether it is a reaction to another member's check in or in regard to how their own week has been. Interestingly, turn-taking can also be used to manage monopolizers of conversation within the group dynamic (Toseland et al., 2007). The group facilitator possesses more of an active role in telephone-based support groups in order to help members recognize one another and encourage more connections and cohesiveness (Goelitz, 2003; Toseland & Larkin, 2010; Toseland et al., 2007). Keeping track of who is speaking and what each caregiver is saying is crucial for cohesiveness and more challenging because the facilitator is relying only on a group member's voice in most cases (Toseland et al., 2007).

In the group discussion, Dena shared how her father continued to ask about when he was going home. She stated how frustrated she was by her father constantly asking about this as that the care facility would be his final home, and she has reminded him constantly. After a pause, which may feel a bit longer over the phone, I inquired whether anyone had a similar experience or perhaps a way of managing this to offer Dena. Joan identified herself to the group and offered different ways for Dena to answer her father, such as stating how it was the doctor's decision, and then encouraged her to try redirecting her father to another conversation. Dena expressed appreciation for Joan's suggestions, and Allison verbalized how she experienced a similar situation with her husband when he began attending the adult day program. I thanked Allison for her feedback in order to identify her to the rest of the group in the event that they were unsure who was speaking in that moment. Over time, the members have demonstrated familiarity with one another's tone of voice; however, it is important to not assume everyone recognizes each other initially. I then invited Joan and then Allison to check in with the group, providing a fluid transition in the dialogue.

Final Telephone-Based Support Groups for Caregivers

I facilitated this group years ago, prior to the COVID-19 pandemic and prior to the friendlier welcome for virtual, clinical social work. In fact, I recall seasoned clinicians telling me the work I did at the time was not clinical. After lessons learned and experience, I feel strongly that this is no longer the sentiment about telephone-based social work or virtual social work for that matter. I am happy to see so many professionals wanting to learn more about practical ways to have sessions over technological platforms and for students to embrace this way of working so readily. We need to continue exploring best options for the communities we serve. Finally, with the proliferation of technology in social work, we must also resist ranking technology. Specifically, we must offer support through the telephone, through video calls and through text and email. Each client and community will gravitate toward whatever mode feels comfortable to them. We may be surprised when an older adult wants to video chat or, when a Millennial wants to connect over the phone, but, we should commit to providing support through whichever medium works.

Close Reading Questions:

1. What do you notice about the sensory experience of Snedeker's remote techniques?
2. Look more closely at the literature review that Snedeker includes. How does Snedeker's research help make the case for her positive association with online caregiving? Pick one or two of Snedeker's references to read and relate more fully to Snedeker's case studies.
3. What do you consider to be Snedeker's most relevant adaptations of face-to-face group therapy gone online?

Prompts for Writing:

1. Imagine that you must design a therapy group that takes place by phone only. Which rituals would you borrow from Snedeker? What innovations could you bring to telehealth based on your life experience?
2. What generational differences impact telehealth?
3. Why have familial caregivers been less present in our age of technology?

References

Alzheimer's Association. (2020). *2020 Alzheimer's disease facts and figures*. Retrieved from https://alzimpact.org/media/serve/id/5ce4d2975314a

Bank, A. L., Argüelles, S., Rubert, M., Eisdorfer, C., & Czaja, S. J. (2006). The value of telephone support groups among ethnically diverse caregivers of persons with dementia. *The Gerontologist, 46*(1), 134–138.

Békés, V., & Aafjes-van Doorn, K. (2020). Psychotherapists' attitudes toward online therapy during the COVID-19 pandemic. *Journal of Psychotherapy Integration, 30*(2), 238.

Brodaty, H., Thomson, C., Thompson, C., & Fine, M. (2005). Why caregivers of people with dementia and memory loss don't use services. *International Journal of Geriatric Psychiatry, 20*(6), 537–546.

Brown, R., Pain, K., Berwald, C., Hirschi, P., Delehanty, R., & Miller, H. (1999). Distance education and caregiver support groups: Comparison of traditional and telephone groups. *The Journal of Head Trauma Rehabilitation, 14*(3), 257–268.

Centers for Disease Control. (2020). *Older adults at greater risk of requiring hospitalization or dying if diagnosed with COVID-19*. Retrieved from www.cdc.gov/coronavirus/2019-ncov/need-extra-precautions/older-adults.html

Chi, N. C., & Demiris, G. (2015). A systematic review of telehealth tools and interventions to support family caregivers. *Journal of Telemedicine and Telecare, 21*(1), 37–44.

Damianakis, T., Climans, R., & Marziali, E. (2008). Social workers' experiences of virtual psychotherapeutic caregivers groups for Alzheimer's, Parkinson's, stroke, frontotemporal dementia, and traumatic brain injury. *Social Work with Groups, 31*(2), 99–116.

Deaux, K. (1993). Reconstructing social identity. *Personality and Social Psychology Bulletin, 19*(1), 4–12.

Dollinger, S. C., Chwalisz, K., & Zerth, E. O. N. (2007). Tele-help line for caregivers (TLC): A comprehensive telehealth intervention for rural family caregivers. *Clinical Gerontologist, 30*(2), 51–64.

Family Caregiver Alliance. (2016). Caregiver statistics. *Demographics*. Retrieved from https://www.caregiver.org/resource/caregiver-statistics-demographics/

Galinsky, M. J., Schopler, J. H., & Abell, M. D. (1997). Connecting group members through telephone and computer groups. *Health & Social Work, 22*(3), 181–188.

Goelitz, A. (2003). When accessibility is an issue: Telephone support groups for caregivers. *Smith College Studies in Social Work, 73*(3), 385–394.

Hornillos, C., & Crespo, M. (2012). Support groups for caregivers of Alzheimer patients: A historical review. *Dementia, 11*(2), 155–169.

Jackson, D., Roberts, G., Wu, M. L., Ford, R., & Doyle, C. (2016). A systematic review of the effect of telephone, internet or combined support for carers of people living with Alzheimer's, vascular or mixed dementia in the community. *Archives of Gerontology and Geriatrics, 66*, 218–236.

Koufou, I., & Markovic, D. (2017). E-therapy: The psychotherapists' perspective-A phenomenological enquiry. *Journal of Psychotherapy and Counselling Psychology Reflections, 25*.

Lee, E. (2015). Do technology-based support groups reduce care burden among dementia caregivers? A review. *Journal of Evidence-Informed Social Work, 12*(5), 474–487.

Martindale-Adams, J., Nichols, L. O., Burns, R., & Malone, C. (2002). Telephone support groups: A lifeline for isolated Alzheimer's disease caregivers. *Alzheimer's Care Today, 3*(2), 181–189.

Mishna, F., Bogo, M., Root, J., Sawyer, J. L., & Khoury-Kassabri, M. (2012). It just crept in: The digital age and implications for social work practice. *Clinical Social Work Journal, 40*(3), 277–286.

National Alliance for Caregiving. (2018). *From insight to advocacy: Addressing family caregiving as a national public health issue.* Retrieved from www.caregiving.org/wp-content/uploads/2018/01/From-Insight-to-Advocacy_2017_FINAL.pdf

Papastavrou, E., Tsangari, H., Karayiannis, G., Papacostas, S., Efstathiou, G., & Sourtzi, P. (2011). Caring and coping: The dementia caregivers. *Aging & Mental Health, 15*(6), 702–711.

Population Reference Bureau. (2016). *2016 world population data sheet.* Retrieved from www.prb.org/2016-world-population-data-sheet/

Roesler, C. (2017). Tele-analysis: The use of media technology in psychotherapy and its impact on the therapeutic relationship. *Journal of Analytical Psychology, 62*, 372–394. Doi:10.1111/1468-5922.12317

Rosalynn Carter Institute for Caregiving. (2020). *Caregivers in crisis: Caregiving in the time of Covid 19.* Retrieved from https://www.rosalynncarter.org/wp-content/uploads/2020/10/Caregivers-in-Crisis-Report-October-2020-10-22-20.pdf

Schopler, J. H., Galinsky, M. J., & Abell, M. (1998). Creating community through telephone and computer groups: Theoretical and practice perspectives. *Social Work with Groups, 20*(4), 19–34.

Schulz, R., & Beach, S. R. (1999). Caregiving as a risk factor for mortality: The caregiver health effects study. *Jama, 282*(23), 2215–2219.

Schulz, R., & Martire, L. M. (2004). Family caregiving of persons with dementia: Prevalence, health effects, and support strategies. *The American Journal of Geriatric Psychiatry, 12*(3), 240–249.

Schulz, R., & Sherwood, P. R. (2008). Physical and mental health effects of family caregiving. *Journal of Social Work Education, 44*(sup3), 105–113.

Smith, T. L., & Toseland, R. W. (2006). The effectiveness of a telephone support program for caregivers of frail older adults. *The Gerontologist, 46*(5), 620–629.

Sucala, M., Schnur, J. B., Brackman, E. H., Constantino, M. J., & Montgomery, G. H. (2013). Clinicians' attitudes toward therapeutic alliance in e-therapy. *The Journal of General Psychology, 140*(4), 282–293.

Toseland, R. W., & Larkin, H. (2010). Developing and leading telephone groups. *Social Work with Groups, 34*(1), 21–34.

Toseland, R. W., Naccarato, T., & Wray, L. O. (2007). Telephone groups for older persons and family caregivers: Key implementation and process issues. *Clinical Gerontologist, 31*(1), 59–76.

Toseland, R. W., Rossiter, C. M., & Labrecque, M. S. (1989). The effectiveness of peer-led and professionally led groups to support family caregivers. *The Gerontologist, 29*(4), 465–471.

Tremont, G., Duncan Davis, J., Bishop, D. S., & Fortinsky, R. H. (2008). Telephone-delivered psychosocial intervention reduces burden in dementia caregivers. *Dementia, 7*(4), 503–520.

Wells, M., Mitchell, K. J., Finkelhor, D., & Becker-Blease, K. A. (2007). Online mental health treatment: Concerns and considerations. *CyberPsychology & Behavior, 10*(3), 453–459.

Winter, L., & Gitlin, L. N. (2007). Evaluation of a telephone-based support group intervention for female caregivers of community-dwelling individuals with dementia. *American Journal of Alzheimer's Disease & Other Dementias, 21*(6), 391–397.

World Health Organization (WHO). (2021). *Dementia fact sheet.* Retrieved from https://www.who.int/news-room/fact-sheets/detail/dementia

Zarit, S. H., Reever, K. E., & Bach-Peterson, J. (1980). Relatives of the impaired elderly: Correlates of feelings of burden. *The Gerontologist, 20*(6), 649–655.

4 Identity, Technology, and the Shaping of a Self

Russell Healy

Pre-reading Questions:

1. Read Healy's epigraph. What are your initial thoughts on how Meaney might figure into discussions about technology and sexuality? How might Meaney's quote relate to cancel culture or the cultural silencing of unpopular perspectives?
2. How might bioethics and technology collide or coincide with child-hood sexual development?
3. What are your assumptions about how children are "influenced" by medical technology? How do innovations in technology change the way we develop sexual identity?

What forces shape youth in the 21st century? In particular, what forces shape gender identity in youth at this moment in history? As modernism yielded to postmodernism in the mid-20th century, the debate regarding which primary dynamics make us *who we are* used to be binary, between the soft, social, and behavioral sciences and the hard sciences. Psychology, sociology, and anthropology emphasized the roles of learning, nurturance, socialization, and acculturation in our lives. How and where we were raised, and under what socioeconomic conditions were seen as the major forces in our development. Thus, we were shaped by socially constructed elements. Conversely, bio-genetic factors were seen by biologists and other sciences as being what constituted our life outcomes. Essential, natural elements granted to us through life's biological lottery were seen as what made us. Anatomy was destiny. If we strayed from, or deviated from what was seen as nature, we had pathology. This theory only works if we assume nature does not consist of diversity. Because the clinical cohort in the chapter will be transgender-identified youth, the chapter assumes nature produces diverse outcomes.

Once we entered the 21st century (having survived "Y2K"), it seemed to me that we became strongly influenced by technology specifically, information and medical technology. In the sciences, there has been a reconciliation of sorts between the nature versus nurture debate by acknowledging that

DOI: 10.4324/9781003270225-4

genes interact with the environment (Sherry, 2004). The idea of a synthesis between the nature and nurture dialectic was made possible the technology of the Human Genome Project. Some theorists write about the disunity created by the relatively new idea that genes and the environment interact, and caution us to be circumspect in our embracing of this new perspective. According to Michael Meaney:

> We have ample reason to celebrate the technical advances associated with the Human Genome Project. Yet, the same technology bears the risk of expanding the divide that lies between the biological and social sciences in the same way that access to computer technology expands the division between the developed and underdeveloped world: one group blindly infatuated with the explanations that might flow from gene technology, the other huddled in terror at the thought of a biological world of which they know nothing.
>
> (2001, p. 51)

Some researchers propose adding "Media Effects Theory" to the nature versus nurture debate, in an attempt at further integration of theories. Communication researcher John L. Sherry concludes, "There is no longer any question among most developmental psychologists, cognitive scientists, neuroscientists, and biologists that nature interacts with nurture to determine human behavior. Unlike other human sciences, communication has never seriously engaged the nature/nurture debate" (2004, p. 102).

In this chapter, I am proposing that technology, both medical and information, is a third factor regarding how we become who we are. Meaney implies that we may over-rely on the role of genetics by keeping the Human Genome Project in the essentialist realm, thus functionally keeping the pendulum swinging between essentialism and constructionism. He complicates the debate by advocating for questions that show the complexities involved in how we are shaped. Sherry approaches my notion that technology is itself a third variable by suggesting the role of communication theory be emphasized further in the debate, but communication theory is only one part of the larger technological realm.

In order to understand how we got to where we are in this 21st century moment, I will begin by discussing the role bio and medical ethics play in how medical technology became commoditized in the latter part of the 20th century, especially given that social work is a transdisciplinary profession. My sources will therefore be transdisciplinary. I will use a case vignette culled from an amalgam of the transgender youths I see for clinical case management because the lived experience of transgender youths is equal parts of nature, nurture, and technology. Transgender persons rely on all three realms in order to transition to how they know themselves to be. Understanding how these realms work will involve an investigation of how knowledge is acquired via information technology. Additionally, I will posit that, for many youths, and certainly for transgender-identified youths, identity development is facilitated by the internet. From there, I will also question the utility of the concept of identity.

Background: The Emergence of Ethics and the Uses and Misuses of Medical Technology in the Nature versus Nurture Debate

Most will agree that medical technology has become a commodity in the United States (Friedman, 1991). In order to understand how medical technology got to where it is today, it will be important to review the history of medicine since the end of World War II. Until the middle of the 20th century, medicine had always been privileged by paternalism. Revelations of the horrors of the Nazi regime, revealed during the Nuremburg trials and codified by the Nuremburg Code in 1947 (Corrigan, 2003, p. 771), created the context for a paradigm shift away from paternalism toward patient autonomy. One of the outcomes was the notion of informed consent, the idea that patients and research subjects are entitled to full knowledge regarding their treatments or participation in a research trial. However, according to ethicists Thomas L. Beauchamp and James F. Childress, informed consent "did not receive detailed examination until the early 1970's" (2013, p. 121). Most historians and bioethicists cite the Karen Ann Quinlan "right to die" case as instrumental to operationalizing various models of informed consent (Beauchamp, 2006, p. 644). Legally, informed consent can be described as follows:

> The doctrine of informed consent is based on the legal principle of battery, which holds that an offense to personal dignity occurs when one violates another's bodily integrity without full and valid consent. Generally, if a doctor obtains a patient's consent to medical treatment without informing that patient of the nature of the treatment or the extent of the harm that is necessarily involved, the patient's consent is held not to be an "informed consent." Legal informed consent requires the satisfaction of three criteria before a medical decision will be seen as legally informed. First, the decision must be informed. This requires the doctor to provide the patient with adequate information about the proposed treatment, including its alternatives. Second, the decision must be voluntary. This requires the doctor to abstain from coercing or otherwise improperly influencing the patient's decision. Third, the decision must be competent. This requires that the patient have an "appreciation" of the nature, extent, and probable consequence of the conduct consented to.
>
> (Ford, 2001, p. 474)

Informed consent ushered in the era of patient autonomy as a counter balance to physician paternalism. But, there are detractors who believe that

informed consent is problematic because it creates a context of moral abso-
lutes, which reduce the healthcare interaction to an "empty ethic" (Corrigan, 2003, p. 787) that ignores the complexity of healthcare encounters and
research trials. The traditional "standards of care model" has been displaced
by the imperative of informed consent. This will be explored in more depth
when I begin discussing transgender-specific healthcare.

To this day, debates continue regarding the utility of paternalism and
autonomy in healthcare (Chin, 2002). Paternalism can be benign, or it
can involve deception, manipulation, and coercion. Some see paternalism as being in the best interest of a patient. Bioethicists Beauchamp and
Childress define paternalism as "the intentional overriding of one person's
known preferences or actions by another, where the person who overrides
justifies the action by the goal of benefiting or avoiding harm to the person
whose preferences or actions are overridden" (2013, p. 215). In their definition, paternalism can be seen as a beneficent act, as the goal is to benefit
a person or keep a person from harm. The assumption made here is that
paternalistic healthcare providers will always act in a manner in which a
caring parent would act toward their children. Just as some parents do not
act in their child's best interest, the same can be said about some healthcare
providers.

My interest in bioethics grew out of a general interest in ethics and practice ethics, which I first encountered in undergraduate philosophy courses.
The idea that our behavior and choices can be grounded in secular values
that still reflect Judeo-Christian morality intrigued me. Enlightenment era
philosophers such as Immanuel Kant, David Hume, John Stuart Mill and
William James, offered me a way of understanding how a good and meaningful social life could be possible without the burdens of religious dogma.
When my licensing board required me to earn continuing education credits
in ethics during every cycle of licensure, I was eager. What I took from my
undergraduate courses in philosophy was the notion that ethical reasoning
can be about discovering what could be possible. I expected something similar in the new ethics licensure requirement. Instead, the continuing education seminars I took were focused on liability and defensive practice (Knapp,
Handelsman, Gottlieb, & VandeCreek, 2013, pp. 371–377).

Disappointed, I decided to create my own curriculum for the course I'd
want to take. To prepare, I began doctoral studies in the medical humanities, which allowed me to take two courses in bioethics. I was fascinated.
Although I work in mental health, I was able to generalize the foundations
of bioethics to the practice of mental and behavioral health treatment. My
perspective expanded, mostly due to the professor, Darrell Cole, PhD, who
was exceptionally skilled in his pedagogy. Much of what follows in the next
paragraphs is from notes I took during his seminars.

Bioethics involves four major principles: respect for autonomy, nonma-
leficence, as in the avoidance of causing harm, beneficence, as in providing the good or preventing the bad, and justice, as in a just distribution of

resources (Beauchamp & Childress, 2013, p. 13). These principles can be applied in a number of ways.

Deontology (Principlism: Immanuel Kant)—Involves assigning weights and measures to ethical principles in order to solve ethical conflicts. This approach is methodological. It is concerned with finding actions that preserve the integrity of the principles. Process, not outcome is what matters. Unwanted outcomes are countenanced if rules/statutes/principles were followed.

Consequentialism (Utilitarian: John Stuart Mills)—Requires us to find the best possible outcome for the most benefit. Ethical principles matter only with respect to the consequences they are likely to produce. Ends justify means. Act consequentialism states that a specific action must be taken on a certain occasion. Rule consequentialism states that the same action must be taken in all similar, relevant situations.

Virtue Ethics (Aristotle)—The character traits and motivations of the practitioner are what matters. This approach de-emphasizes analytical ethical reasoning and holds that ethical principles are too general and abstract for the complexities of the healthcare environment. Take, for example, the subject of justice. Resources do not have to be distributed equally to be considered just. In a healthcare context, justice is about proportion and necessity, concepts which are fraught in our current, complex healthcare situation. Virtue assumes that practitioners with a conscience, self-knowledge, and good intuitive abilities ("eminence") will behave ethically, especially if desirable traits are actively being cultivated and strengthened.

In social work, the virtuous, praiseworthy clinician reflects positive moral character. Most social work clinicians are virtuous in that we value self-knowledge and let our conscience guide our actions. This self-knowledge is distinct from attending continuing education seminars. We must do that to keep our licenses. Most social workers I encounter participate by choice in any number of activities designed to increase self-awareness, mindfulness, and compassion for others.

Deontology is the ethical decision-making model most of us are familiar with. It is an efficient methodology if one is concerned with issues of obligation (Reamer, 2018, pp. 78–79). Consequentialism, an applied form of utilitarianism, is how many experienced clinicians make ethical decisions. Most of us begin our careers as deontologists, but as we gain experience, confidence, and expertise, many of us become consequentialists out of a desire to do the most good to help our clients. For example, younger clinicians may interpret the prohibition against dual relationships rigidly. Over time, we learn that it is not pragmatic to adhere to rigid standards. In fact, it can dilute a therapeutic alliance if we don't acknowledge that we may encounter and interact with our clients in our various communities, especially if we specialize in working with a particular community. I will often see my transgender clients at various conferences, and I am comfortable with things like talking, or having a cup of coffee and a snack with them.

The feedback I get is that they feel respected, which is an important feature of a therapeutic alliance, especially for a population of clients vulnerable to stigma. In ethics, we must answer to ourselves as a matter of conscience. In morality, we must answer to authority.

Bioethics as a field of study, or perhaps a discipline, is relatively new. Its beginnings can be traced to the tumultuous decade of the 1960s (Jonsen, 2004, p. 31) and became more serious as issues such as the right to die emerged. As mentioned earlier, the right to die movement introduced the tenet of patient autonomy in the relationship between doctor and patient. This was met optimistically by some, such as Howard Brody, MD, who discussed paternalism in his book *The Healer's Power*, "I of course cannot accept it, since I wish my critique of the new medical ethics to be a step forward, not a cover up for reactionary retreat" (1992, p. 91). Brody's belief is patients and physicians can share power together and aim it at the problem, similar to the values we hold as social workers. His notion of a reactionary retreat means that we ought not hide behind a "legalistic model." Instead, he prefers a "conversational model" between healthcare providers and their clients or patients, an approach that respects relational and interpersonal dynamics (1992, p. 90).

Medical virtue ethicists agree that a therapeutic alliance is a relationship. In *The Virtues of Medical Practice*, physicians and ethicists Edmund D. Pelligrino and David C. Thomasma write, "respect for patient's self-determination, and thus the integrity of the person, is a moral requirement in all human relationships, especially in those like medicine, in which there is a *de facto* imbalance of power" (1993, p. 57). Although they are writing about physicians and their patients, we can assume that Pelligrino and Thomasma would agree that a way to bring balance to all clinical encounters is to acknowledge that clinical encounters are relational.

Other physician/ethicists, such as H. Tristram Engelhardt, Jr., believe that paternalistic healthcare, especially a paternalistic approach in which information is withheld, for example, is "vexatious" and can be "injurious" to patients because paternalism does not teach the patient to be responsible for their health (1996, p. 320). As a philosophical libertarian, Engelhardt believes that healthcare interactions should be private and based on agreement between doctor and patient. In an ideal universe, that would mean no third-party insurance, where ideally, costs could go down.

As the field of bioethics was solidifying in the 1980s and 1990s, other forces were at work that began changing how healthcare would be conceptualized and delivered in the 21st century. First was the rise of neoliberalism, which created a market-driven hegemony in the States, where education and healthcare have become commodified (Verhaeghe, 2014). Direct advertisements for specific medicines proliferate throughout most forms of media. Attorneys advertise for their malpractice litigation services freely, as well ("if you or someone you love was diagnosed with and took"). Patient autonomy has gone from a noble and empowering ideal to a kind of threat to practice.

Doctors have become passive providers of information, or "pill monkeys," as one of my clients says about his psychiatrist. Gradually, many doctors began to practice defensively. According to ethicist JJ Chin, many doctors have found themselves in a situation where

> in the name of honouring autonomy and freedom, physicians merely offer possible options without any professional input, then this informative model is unlikely to serve patient's interest. Under such a system, even non-coercive and non-manipulative attempts to discuss with patients the pros and cons of their decisions can be considered a violation of their freedom or rights when in fact, such efforts merely reflect appropriate care and concern for the patient's well-being.
>
> (2002, p. 153)

Our neoliberal hegemony is widely believed to have its roots in the 1980s, an era characterized by deregulation. Such deregulation gave pharmaceutical companies more freedom in how they compete to develop and market drugs. Deregulation allowed private industries within healthcare to shape a market-driven approach which favors a profit-driven motive. The cost of healthcare in America is so high, and training programs and licensing processes so arduous, precisely because healthcare is not subject to as much oversite as it is in other Western nations. This is not to suggest that what has become known as socialized healthcare would be ideal. Germany's healthcare system is fully privatized, but the government regulates costs, not the marketplace (www.ncbi.nlm.nih.gov/books/NBK298834/).

The act of diagnosis has changed as well; we have become a medicalized, and what I term, a "psychiatrized" society. The labels we are given through diagnosis become lifestyles. In Thomas Szasz' seminal essay, *The Myth of Mental Illness*, he offered his concern that psychiatry has the power to take autonomy from people by labeling, diagnosing, and medicating them or institutionalizing them, which functionally socializes people into the role of being mentally ill. Szasz, himself a psychiatrist, believed that much of what psychiatry addressed was not biologically based. Rather, psychiatry was addressing everyday "problems in living," albeit unwanted ones, and treated those problems as illnesses (1960).

I certainly see this in many of my younger clients. When I ask them how they feel, many will respond with statements like "I am feeling very OC," or "it's a bad ADD day," or they will tell me that because they are on the autism spectrum they don't possess the "spoons" necessary to function more robustly. Philosopher Ian Hacking calls this the "looping effect" (Hacking, 2002, p. 11, 2006, p. 1), wherein people tend to inhabit their labels and classifications. Their lived experience is informed by whatever diagnosis they believe they have. In fact, many of them diagnose themselves based on what they read online (more later in the chapter on the role of information technology in the lives of youth). Much of what they read has been subjected to "concept creep," a phenomenon observed by psychologist Nick Haslam. Taking his own discipline to task, Haslam argues that psychology has allowed for definitions of diagnostic categories and social phenomena to expand. Such expansions, or creep, dilutes the meaning of phenomenon such as mental disorders and abuse. He believes this functions to create a broader sensitivity to harm, which induces a sense of powerlessness and pathology in individuals. People embrace their labels, which impacts their self-perception and behavior (2016).

Anthropologist Paul Rabinow and sociologist Nikolas Rose are less sanguine about the power of biology in our lives today. Citing what they refer to as a "bioethical complex," a system "in which the power of medical agents to 'let die' at the end of life, the start of life or in reproduction, are simultaneously enhanced by medical technology and regulated by other authorities as never before" (2006, p. 203). They are cautious about what philosopher Michel Foucault termed "biopolitics," which I interpret as the danger that the State could enforce, coerce, or otherwise control us in the service of public health (Rabinow, 1997, pp. 73–79). Medical technology as an expression of Foucault's biopolitics has grown exponentially in the last two decades. For example, in 2014, Wake Forest Baptist Medical Center reported on their website they had successfully "grown" a vaginal prothesis using a 3D printer and the patient's stem cells. The condition being treated is known as Mayer-Rokitansky-Küster-Hauser (MRKH) syndrome. It is a rare genetic condition in which the vagina and/or uterus is absent or underdeveloped. Children with this condition typically underwent the kind of vaginoplasty performed in gender confirmation surgery, which requires extensive after-care and only creates a neo, or faux vagina (some transgender women I know characterize their neo-vaginas as a "wound"). The prosthesis, known as PACIENA, is printed from a biocompatible material known as PLA. Once printed, created, and grown, it is implanted and provides the recipient with a working vagina, one that self-lubricates and allows for pain-free sexual pleasure. According to a study published in Wake Forest Baptist Medical Center Women's Health, the procedure provides good functional and anatomical results without having to use skin grafts and has been used successfully on a number of young women with MRKH syndrome (https://newsroom.wakehealth.edu/News-Releases/2014/04/LaboratoryGrown-Vaginas-Implanted-in-Patients-Scientists-Report).

The Wake Forest researchers believed that the treatment can be used in cases of vaginal cancer, and it could also be used as a more effective gender confirmation surgery for transgender women. Several of my clients are looking into this option. This is but one example of how medical technology has begun to revolutionize what is possible in healthcare. For my transgender clients, medical interventions using synthetic hormones and surgeries actually make their bodies congruent with their lived experience of their known self and desired embodiment. Put simply, nature or nurture alone is insufficient. Information and medical technology are required to help them live as close as possible to an authentic lived experience.

While it may seem like I am less than enthusiastic about medical technology, the opposite is so. The issue, in my mind, is how medical technologies are used, and the context in which they are used. When I was a child in the 1960s, I saw a copy of Look magazine (my parents had a subscription). On the cover was one of the early "sex change operations." I recall thinking that it is amazing what medicine can do! I wanted to become a doctor myself, but got distracted by the humanities. I will finish this section with a discussion of how medicine has intervened in gender since the early 20th century, in order to establish how paradigms have shifted with respect to gender and identity in the 21st century, to be explored later in the chapter.

In the 21st century, consent and assent inform medical interventions for minors who present for gender-confirming treatments. Only parents can consent to medical interventions for their children who are under the age of 18. However, the capacity of a minor to assent or agree to a treatment is getting more attention. Some pediatric specialists believe that children as young as 7 can assent to medical treatments which have long-lasting effects (Katz et al., 2016).

In this next section, I will review two published case studies of medicine's involvement in gender from the 20th century. Jules Gill-Peterson is an associate professor of English and Gender, Sexuality, and Women's Studies at the University of Pittsburgh. Her book, *Histories of the Transgender Child*, challenges the contemporary idea that transgender children signify a new phenomenon. What is new is that young people are self-identifying as transgender, which was not the case throughout much of the 20th century. Urologists, psychologists, and social workers had a role in medical interventions involving minors with gender nonconforming behavior or intersex conditions, known now as disorders of sexual development. In the early 20th century, such interventions were informed by the now discredited, pseudoscience of eugenics. Later in the 20th century, gender itself was politicized (that will be the second case review). In many ways, the 20th century was a stage upon which the nature versus nurture debate played out, with youths at the center of the drama.

In her book, Peterson tells the story of the Brady Urological Institute of the Johns Hopkins Hospital (Johns Hopkins was a center for research and treatment on conditions of sex and gender throughout most of the 20th century). The Institute opened in 1915 and concerned itself with "producing a binary sex out of an intersex body" (p. 68). Intersex conditions, also known as disorders of sexual development, have been historically referred to as hermaphroditic conditions. Children whose genitals are ambiguous or whose reproductive organs are undeveloped are diagnosed as having disorders of sexual development. Such children were referred to the Institute. Most of the children seen at the institute were white and benefitted from white privilege. They were "promised alteration and normalization through medical intervention," whereas children from the poor, African-American families in Baltimore were regarded as being "difficult" and treated as "disposable" research subjects (p. 79). The Social Work Department at Hopkins would send social workers to the homes of resistant families to ensure they were complying with treatment plans recommended by the Institute doctors. Social and charity workers had a condescending attitude toward any resistance to medical treatment and characterized resistance to the medical model as irrational and unscientific. Peterson speculated that African-American families accepted their intersex children and were not concerned with whether or not their children's bodies reflected a binary gender. Thus, they were skeptical about whether medical interventions regarding gender were necessary (pp. 75–76).

The Institute was headed by a surgeon, Hugh Hampton Young. Synthetic hormones had not yet been created, so treatment often involved surgeries on the young patients. Assessments were intrusive, beginning with external and internal palpitations "to ascertain the existence and position of any gonads, glands and organs governing sex, including a phallus/clitoris, testes and/or ovaries, a prostate, uterus and fallopian tubes, and/or vagina" (pp. 68–69). This process would often be followed by exploratory laparotomies in an attempt to look inside the body for evidence of a "true sex," which was Young's project. Other attempts to look inside involved X-rays and the use of a cystoscope, inserted through the bladder, to look for evidence of a vagina. Young believed that the presence of ovaries or testes operationalized the person's true gender, "regardless of the rest of the body, or the patients sense of self." Based on the results of the exam, Young would usually recommend sexual reassignment surgery, which was in its nascent state early in the 20th century (p. 69).

If a child was assigned a gender that did not conform to their lived experience of their self, they might understandably show upset behavior during follow-up visits by tearing up. Staff referred such children to an ophthalmologist, who of course found no pathology. Peterson writes, "the doctors could not even imagine that constant crying might have been a traumatic effect of their aggressive medical protocol" (76). This is an example of how paternalism can be harmful. If doctors can't use empathy to connect to the emotions of their patients, maladaptive coping or suicide may result. It should be noted here that many children born with intersex conditions often face the same dilemma today. When ambiguous genitals are noted at birth, some doctors will recommend that parents' consent to surgical interventions to correct the gender of the child based on some of the same "true sex" criteria used by Young. One can only imagine how a person born with a disorder of sexual development feels when they reach adolescence and find out the doctor made the wrong choice. Those who advocate for intersex children advise that parents wait until their child is old enough to tell them what is their gender and let them choose a course of action.

Suicide is a theme that permeates the narrative of transgender youth. In the 21st century, suicidal ideation or attempts are often correlated with a lack of access to medical care and social support. In the 20th century, suicide phenomenon could be correlated with unwanted medical intervention. The Brady Institute, which is still in existence and highly regarded, operated for over 50 years before the emergence of bioethics and informed consent. Physician paternalism was the norm. So was the concept of "normalcy." One of the Institute's young patients was a 10-year-old child, assigned female at birth, but was raised as a boy in a farming family. The child experienced himself as male and presented as male. His parents were concerned that by age 10, his genitals had not yet descended, so they took him to Brady. After the typical, aggressive exam, the doctor informed the child's father that his son was in fact a girl. Sexual reassignment surgery was recommended, but the father refused, likely due to the expense. He was upset by the diagnosis, as he had five other children, all girls, and wanted a boy to take on more chores on the farm.

Twenty-one years later, the boy returned to Brady. He had lived his life as male and was about to get married. However, the Priest who was to perform the ceremony needed medical proof that he would be marrying a man and a woman. The young man's father had told the Priest about his son's hermaphroditic condition. Dr. Young did another exam, with the same conclusion the previous doctor at Brady reached. The young man and his fiancé were devastated. Three days later, the young man, Robert Stonestreet, ended his life by taking a lethal dose of mercury (72–75).

Despite the abuse of the Brady Institute, Johns Hopkins continued its research on gender and sex throughout the 20th century. In 1965, psychologist John Money cofounded the Johns Hopkins Gender Clinic. Whereas Young's approach was essentialist, the nature side of the dialectic, Money's theoretical approach was constructionist, as in the nurture side of the dialectic, and a reflection of the sociopolitical zeitgeist of the era. He conceptualized gender as a role, consistent with feminist ideas at the time (118–120). In 1967, Money was given a case that he hoped would be career defining. The case is now well known, but it eventually caused Money's downfall. The best telling of the case can be found in journalist John Colapinto's book, *As Nature Made Him, the Boy who was Raised as a Girl*.

Bruce and Brian Reimer were identical twins, born on August 22, 1965, to a working-class Mennonite family in Winnipeg, Canada. Approximately six months after they were born, they developed phimosis, a condition which caused their foreskins too tighten, making urination painful. The solution was a simple circumcision. Bruce went first, but his circumcision was far from simple. Due to an error, the procedure was botched. Bruce lost his penis as a result, and Brian did not get circumcised that day. The Reimers were devastated. In Colapinto's words, as Mennonites, they feared their child would have to "live apart" from others (2000, p. 17).

While watching a talk show on television in February 1967, they saw Dr. John Money, who was talking about sex reassignment operations to correct intersex conditions or damaged genitalia as the result of birth defects. The Reimers thought that Money might understand their situation and contacted him. They were naive regarding transsexuality (as it was referred to then), or intersex conditions, and certainly, unaware of the sociopolitical ethos surrounding such phenomenon in the late 1960s. Money replied quickly and urged them to come to Baltimore. He had an agenda, which he did not reveal to them.

To Money, the identical Reimer twins were a perfect research opportunity for a theory he wanted desperately to prove that, if begun within a narrow window during infancy, a child could be raised as either gender and grow up to be that gender. Gender was merely a social role in Money's theory, and here, he had a ready-made twin study with which he could prove his theory. Money was already well regarded as a pioneering sexologist. According to Colapinto, Money "coined the term *gender identity* to describe an inner sense of a person's sense of himself or herself as male or female" (p. 25). Money was confident to the point of arrogance when interacting with peers. America was poised for a sexual revolution, and Money wanted to lead the charge. When defending Money's tendency to speak bluntly about sex, Psychiatrist Fred Berlin, another sexologist, told Colapinto, "he thinks it is important to desensitize people in discussing sexual issues. . . . John is an opinionated person who isn't looking necessarily to do things differently than the way he's concluded is best" (p. 29).

At Money's behest, surgeons at Hopkins performed a clinical castration on Bruce, who was by then just shy of two years old. They also constructed a shallow neo-vagina, in anticipation of a full vaginoplasty to be performed when Bruce was around 14. Hormone replacement with synthetic estrogen would begin when Bruce was 11 to begin feminization. The Reimers assumed this was treatment; they were not informed that their children were to be used as research subjects. They did not understand Money's notion of the "gender identity gate" (pp. 32–34), which would close when Bruce was between two and one half and three years old. Socializing a child into a gender role had to begin early, so there would effectively be no recollection of their biologically assigned gender. Nor did they understand the treatment their son was receiving had only been performed on children with intersex conditions, or birth defects. In 1967, informed consent had not yet become codified in medical practice.

After the castration, Money met with the Reimer's and outlined the "treatment plan." They were to rename Bruce with a girl's name, dress him like a girl, treat him like a girl, give him girl's toys, and so forth. This would begin Bruce's socialization to becoming female. Also, there was to be regular follow-up visits so that Money could assess his subject's progress. He also wanted Brian to participate in yearly follow-up visits for purposes of comparison. The Reimers renamed Bruce as Brenda. In Money's notes, he would refer to the twins as John and Joan. Until recently, one approach to treating children with gender nonconforming behavior, or for children who report symptoms of gender dysphoria, had been to coercively coach parents to leverage gender-conforming behavior in their children. The World Professional Association for Transgender Health holds that such treatment is not ethical and does not work (Coleman et al., 2012, p. 16).

The next 12 years were brutal for the Reamers. Brenda resisted every step of the way. She insisted on wearing boy's clothes and wanted to play boys' sports, engage in rough house and the like. She was unruly at school and got into frequent fights. Colapinto wrote that eventually, Brenda was accepted into a clique of "misfit tomboys" (p. 124). Moreover, Brenda came to loathe the visits with Money. She did not understand that she was a research subject and did not understand the need for, nor want, surgery. Money began presenting the case of John and Joan in professional circles, to great acclaim. What he presented were lies: he falsified data and hid the truth about Brenda's fierce resistance.

Brenda spent most of that period seeing various psychiatrists and child guidance professionals. They thought they were working toward helping Brenda accept herself as female. Brenda wanted none of it, until she met a psychiatrist that broke from the traditional, Freudian psychoanalytic stance, widely utilized at that time in history. Over time, Brenda began to open up about her extreme aversion to all things female. Meanwhile, John Money was making a name for himself presenting the successful case of the boy who was raised as a girl. The BBC showed interest in highlighting the case on television, but they sensed there was something wrong. Two journalists from the BBC managed to locate the Reimers, who agreed to speak with them. During the 12-year period, Brenda did try hard to think and act like a girl (whatever that meant), but it just didn't work. The older she got, the more she was a target of bullying and harassment. Not being able to tolerate his child's distress any longer, Brenda's father told Brenda the truth about his birth. Similar to Robert Stonestreet, Brenda may have *wanted* to believe what he was told, and trust medical authority, despite *knowing* something was wrong.

The BBC investigation began the downfall of John Money. As news about the case circulated, Milton Diamond, MD, a psychiatrist who also specialized in issues around sexuality and gender, and who had consulted with Brenda's psychiatrist, took notice. He had long suspected that Money had falsified data. Diamond was no ally of Money to begin with; they were rivals, academically. He did not believe Money's theory that "social learning overrides biological imperatives in the shaping of human sexual identity" (p. 205). It took Diamond many years, but with help from the BBC and Brenda, and in collaboration with a colleague, he was able to document the errors made by Money and help Brenda move forward. The case got media attention, which allowed Colapinto to write the Reimer's story. By the time he met Brenda, she had transitioned back to male. Brenda renamed herself

David, began taking masculinizing hormones at age 15, and underwent corrective surgeries to address the deleterious impact of synthetic estrogen on his body. David remained close with his family, who were very supportive, and continued his productive therapy with his psychiatrist. He understood what caused his parents to make the decisions they made and did hold a grudge against them. Colapinto documented David's account of his father's revelation:

> He just started explaining, step by step, everything that had happened to me. He told me I was born a boy, and about the accident when they were trying to circumcise me, and how they saw all kinds of specialists, and they took the best advice they had at the time, which was to try to change me over. My Dad got very upset,
>
> Colapinto added that David stated, "I was relieved . . . suddenly it all made sense why I felt the way that I did. I wasn't some sort of weirdo. I wasn't crazy."
>
> (p. 180)

Once David's story was revealed, he entered a relatively happy period. He even found love and got married. Sadly, however, his history of trauma got the best of him and his brother. After Colapinto's book was published, Brian became estranged from his brother. He was diagnosed with schizophrenia and committed suicide by overdose in 2002. David continued to struggle with depression and traumatic stress. He made several suicide attempts. In 2004, three days after his wife asked for a divorce, David shot himself and died.

When I first read Colapinto's book in 2000, I experienced a kind of epiphany. It occurred to me that David Reimer's experience was a *reverse-proof* that gender is something we can know without taking our anatomy into account. David Reimer felt he wasn't Brenda, but felt "crazy" and "weird" because others saw him as and wanted him to be Brenda. I began looking at knowledge, how we acquire it, and what we do with it. When Bruce was Brenda, he knew something wasn't right. As he got older, his lived experience was that he was male. In his case, he had been assigned male at birth and no amount of socialization, surgery, or treatment with female hormones could change that. If that was so for Bruce, Brenda, and David, then it reasonably follows that transgender persons *know* their lived experience of their gender does not match their gender assignment at birth. I began to see transgender phenomenon as just another variation in nature, not psychopathology.

My intent in describing the early work of the Brady Urological Institute and in recounting the story of David Reimer was to show how medical technology, when it is privileged by medical paternalism and not bound by ethics, can become corrupt. The staff at Brady was using their young patients as research subjects in much the same way as Money used David

Reimer and Brian Reimer. As a result of these misuses of what Foucault termed biopolitics, all three subjects lost their lives to suicide.

Medical and Information Technology in the 21st Century

As regards transgender healthcare in the 21st century, many of the medical technologies employed to help transgender persons become who they know themselves to be have not changed very much since they were developed in the 20th century. Surgeries have been refined, certainly, and synthetic hormones, put into use in the middle of the 20th century, have much utility for transgender persons. The difference now is that those technologies are used as voluntary treatments to help people who want and need care. One reason for this new paradigm is internet technology which helps patients to research and understand what is involved in transitioning medically. Also, internet technology helps younger people to learn about their lived experience at much younger ages than ever before. As Peterson posited, transgender children and adolescents are not new. The difference is, they are now telling us first about who they are, rather than having their bodies changed without their assent because of a paternalistic desire for normalcy (and the fallacy of a true sex), no matter how well intended.

So, how do they know their gender? Most youths today are aware of the spectrum of sexuality and gender possibilities. They see such things reflected in media and popular culture. But, how does it become self-knowledge, especially for the young person whose presentation conforms to gender norms? Most of us defend against certain awareness's until we are at a point in life when we are ready to know something. For the transgender-identified youth I see, the luxury of defenses like compartmentalization is often lost early. Some youths I have seen described the process of knowing their gender as "knowledge hatching." In the next section of this chapter, I will explore the role of information technology, and how it informs young people in equal measure as does nature and nurture.

Information Technology, Identity, and the Acquisition of Knowledge

I first encountered transgender clients when the fourth version of the Diagnostic and Statistics Manual of Mental Disorders (DSM-4) changed the diagnostic label from transsexualism to gender identity disorder. Although I knew transgender persons as colleagues, clients, and social acquaintances, I bristled at the notion of assessing a person's identity, not to mention having to decide that their lived experience was disordered. Identity as a tenet of psychology and mental health emerged in the mid-20th century. Identity's architect was Erik Erikson (Cornett, 2000). Since then, the concept of identity has been a sacred cow in the theory and practice of mental health treatments. As a clinician, I do not believe I am qualified to assess a person's identity. In fact, I am not sure that I think identity reflects anything real. Knowledge is real, and we have choice and agency about what we do with what we learn about ourselves. I am qualified to listen to my client's lived experience and help them discover who they are in all of their complexities. I believe we have a self, and that we are made up of many parts, as Richard Schwartz tells us in his Internal Family Systems model (Schwartz & Sweezy, 2019). I am also committed to the social work principle that we are persons-in-environments. Individuals, myself included, often identify with a variety of beliefs and communities. We have many commitments and projects. My wish for all persons is that we can freely present various aspects of ourselves in any number of social environments, without being hampered by identity labels. What follows is another look at identity as a construct, from an ethical and philosophical perspective.

Why examine the idea of identity, an idea which has been widely accepted since the mid-20th century, in a chapter about technology and the shaping of the self? Because in the age of the internet, identities have become digitized. Instead of helping young people discover who they are experientially, by interacting with the world in an analogue way, young people find themselves dangling over a sea of discreet, online categories from which to choose. No longer is the search for self about *who* a young person is, but now the search is about *what* a young person is. Identities represented online became more salient to them. The politics of identity are stronger than ever. At times I fear we lose sight of the person when we accentuate primary identities because primary identities involve stereotypes, labeling, and in many cases, performance. Social work emphasizes personhood and the dignity of the individual. Identity categories, after all, can dilute individuality and threaten self-determination.

As a therapist, one of my commitments is to help persons of any age get to know themselves and connect more deeply with their individual selves. In the years before the internet, group therapy was particularly rewarding. Adolescents had the opportunity to use group as a way to connect with peers and learn about who they were becoming. Many of the adults I saw in groups lived lives characterized by isolation and disconnection. Group therapy gave them a safe and regular place to give and receive support and forge connections. Once the internet took hold, interest in group-work waned. For my gay clients, the internet replaced gay social spaces as they began meeting each other through the use of applications. Overtime, I felt unmoored as a clinician. I began to examine the concept of identity and began to question its utility. The work of Kwame Anthony Appiah began to inform my clinical work from a philosophical perspective regarding personhood.

For much of his academic career, the work of philosopher Kwame Anthony Appiah has been about identity: it's meaning, what ethics apply, it's primacy and mythology. In *The Ethics of Identity* (2005), Appiah carefully builds the argument that we sacrifice individuality when we define ourselves according to one, primary identity; he also believed that we risk diminishing our autonomy when we become committed members of a group that endorses a belief system around a primary identity, be it sociocultural, sociopolitical, or any orthodoxy. Appiah examined individuality and autonomy through the lenses of enlightenment era philosophers such as the utilitarian John Stuart Mill, the deontologist and transcendental individualist Immanuel Kant, and those whom they influenced. Arguably, their ideas are the foundation of our nation, as well as our ethics as social workers, and healthcare ethics in general (Beauchamp & Childress, 2013; Reamer, 2018).

Appiah appreciated the idea of intersectionality (2018, pp. 19–20). A person's sense of self embodies many aspects of experience: heritage, belief, gender, ethnicity, nationality, and so forth. Appiah himself embodies intersectionality. As a person, he can claim multiple national heritages, Western as well as African acculturation, and a gay relational identification (his website states he is married to a man). Recent literature from transgender and transgender-allied researchers endorses intersectionality as a way to understand the complicated tasks of developing and integrating the myriad of ways transgender persons experience their gender-related sense of self and how it interacts with other life dimensions (Kuper, Wright, & Mustanski, 2018, p. 437). There are many ways to be one, or more things, intertwined. Those ways are influenced by the other characteristics and qualities held and experienced by that person, and their interactions with the world. Individuality and authenticity are principal facets of personhood. They interact with, and are impacted by, the social environment. Such tensions are at the core of social life. It is possible that embracing a politic of identity as enthusiastically as we have done has diluted the value of individuality and autonomy. If so, this may have contributed to the politics of division which we are faced with currently.

Philosophers and ethicists acknowledge how our desire for a life informed by a unified, moral philosophy is thwarted by the reality of life in a contemporary, secular Western society. Bioethicist H. Tristram Englehardt, Jr., writes:

> The modern philosophical hope, despite such difficulties, has been to discover a general communality of persons. This communality has been sought through discovering a canonical, content-full morality that is more than procedural, one that should bind moral strangers, members of different and diverse moral communities. We should be able to discover a content-full secular morality . . . that can reach across diverse communities of religious and ideological belief.
>
> (1996, p. 6)

Englehardt writes about the notion of moral friends and moral strangers. We can be moral friends if we share enough moral content (beliefs) such that conflicts can be resolved, or if we can collaborate in whatever manner is best for broader social life. Moral strangers share little, if any, common moral beliefs. Obviously, relations between moral strangers can be far more difficult (1996). Perhaps, we make others into moral strangers too easily. Functionally, we have created a demand for people to align themselves with one side or another; moderates are to be distrusted. If strangers and friends become dichotomous sets, then we miss opportunities to discover what we have in common, and how we can work together on projects of mutual relevance.

Englehardt determined that a content-full, unified morality is not possible in a postmodern world, whereas Appiah believed in cosmopolitanism, or, living as citizens of the world. But not the kind of cosmopolitanism associated with urban elites. According to Appiah, "the roots of the cosmopolitan I am defending are liberal: and they are responsive to liberalism's insistence on human dignity" (2005, p. 267). Here, Appiah is referring to classic liberalism and, as such, is a moral friend of social work values. In fact, philosopher Maurice Hammington considers Appiah and social work pioneer Jane Addams to share a similar cosmopolitan view of the world. He posits that although they share a common tenet, their vision of a just world needs to be informed by care as well as proportion (Hammington, 2007). Care, which is a relatively new ethic in and of itself, often leads to curiosity. Care in this sense is not paternal or oppressive. Rather, it emphasizes interdependence among persons that supports self-determination and autonomy (Meagher, 2004). If care was normative, concerns about persons would matter and we would pay attention to, and support, each other as individuated persons with non-enmeshed concern and care (Held, 2006). Curiosity is an important part of a cosmopolitan world view. Appiah's view of human dignity and the worth of persons does not fall neatly into categories such as moral strangers and moral friends. He argues that divisions, such as what we are experiencing in today's sociopolitical arena, are themselves a problem (2018, pp. 103–104).

Appiah's 30-year project on identity, it's nature, and why it seems to matter now has its roots in his intersectional experience as a person with a Ghanaian father, a British mother, and as a product of an upper-class education and upbringing. He also happens to be gay, but rarely leads with that part of his identity. Throughout his life, he has noticed how people react to his appearance. In the United States, he is Black. In Europe, he is African. Then, there is the question of his voice: his accent can be heard as British. He identifies with his Ghanaian self as strongly as he identifies with being a philosopher on the faculty of New York University.

For Appiah, cosmopolitanism involves two practices. One is valuing all human life, even if it is the life of a stranger. The second is having curiosity about the culture which produced someone. He also asserts that such curiosity can result in a respect for variety, but the goal is not a love of variety, which is a stereotype of cosmopolitanism. Rather, "every society should respect human dignity and personal autonomy" (2005, p. 268). Personal autonomy is what creates variety. There are many ways to participate in a culture or society without having to sacrifice authenticity and individuality. Nor do people have to engage in competition regarding the prominence of their identities.

Appiah agrees that the concept of identity, as we know it presently, emerged as a social construction in the middle of the 20th century. He too cites developmental psychologist Erik Erikson as the first to designate identity as something essential to a sense of one's self (2018 pp. 3–4). However, Appiah rejects the notion that there is anything essential about identity. He believes that identities can be lived in more than one way:

> If essentialism is a misstep in the realms of creed, color, country, class and culture, as it is in the domain of gender and sexuality, then it is never true that identity leaves us no choices. The existentialists were right: existence precedes essence. . . . But the fact that identities come without essence does not mean they come without entanglements
> (2018, pp. 216–217).

It is the entanglements that vex us in this moment in history. For example, consider the evolution of how we have constructed sexual identity from sexual orientation. An orientation may be understood as essential because of the strong biogenetic relationship between orientation and experience. Until homosexuality was removed from the Diagnostic and Statistics Manual of Mental Disorders in 1973, heterosexuality was considered the norm. If a person presented as homosexual, they were thought to be ill, since they deviated from the norm. The gay rights movement, which began in the mid-1950s, gained currency. In the latter half of the 20th century, homosexuals became persons with gay or lesbian identities, deserving of the same rights as their heterosexual counter parts.

Over a relatively brief period of time, "being gay" became associated with any number of norms, values, and mores to replace the stereotypes bestowed upon the gay community by nongay people. A close look at those norms, values, and mores reveals some entanglements. Basically, the gay rights movement appeals to a Western paradigm of identity. In the United States particularly, gay identity can be seen as a primary type that ought to warrant celebration, not simple acceptance or tolerance. As a type, it seems to appeal to white, educated, urban, progressive, middle-class persons. A semiotic look at the website for the Human Rights Campaign (HRC.org) can be read as such, although admittedly, that interpretation may be subjective. Nonetheless, the HRC has commodified gay life by selling gay-branded clothing, mugs, and accessories. The HRC calls it shopping for equality. What could be more neoliberal than turning an identity category into a brand?

Transgender-identified minors began being referred to me in 2008, several years after such referrals to gender clinics in the Netherlands began to see an increase (De Vries & Cohen-Kettenis, 2012), and one year after Dr. Norman Spack's gender clinic in Boston saw an increase (Spack et al., 2012). Gender clinics provide a full array of transgender healthcare services at one facility. If there is no gender clinic in a particular region, services are provided through a network of qualified mental health providers, endocrinologists, and surgeons. Such is how my practice functions. Interestingly, the rise in referrals to gender clinics and individual practitioners coincides with Apple releasing its first iPhone in 2007, followed by Google's acquisition of Android in 2008. These events created a sea change in how young people could search for data: they could use their phones like a computer. Moreover, search speeds, boosted by artificial intelligence technology, began improving toward the end of the first decade of the 21st century (Dreyfus, 2008, pp. 125–127). I cannot help but wonder if there is some kind of correlation between information technology reaching critical mass by the start of the second decade of the 21st century and the simultaneous, measurable increase in referrals of transgender minors to clinics and specialists.

Typically, the standards of care of the World Professional Association for Transgender Health (WPATH) are followed when minors are the patient. More recently, an informed consent model has been utilized for those over 18 seeking treatment with gender-confirming hormones because treatment with hormones is partially reversible. Since the Affordable Care Act was passed, allowing private and public insurance plans to cover gender-confirming surgeries, many hospitals have established transgender surgery centers. Previously, many surgeons who specialize in gender-confirming surgeries operated on a fee for service model. For many transgender patients, the costs were just too prohibitive. The expansion of available transgender surgery programs, coverable by insurance, has made needed care more available in a timely manner, but it also functions to commodify transgender healthcare. Because surgeries are fully irreversible, surgery centers follow the WPATH standards, which require two letters of referral from qualified mental health professionals, from one who knows the patient, and from one who does an independent evaluation. In a comprehensive gender clinic, teams exist to provide everything from assessment to treatment.

The transgender minors I see present in three basic ways. The first group presents with symptoms of insistent and persistent gender dysphoria, over a consistent time frame. Changing the diagnostic label from gender identity disorder to gender dysphoria was an attempt to address concerns from transgender healthcare specialists and transgender activists that labeling a person's lived experience as a disorder would stigmatize and pathologize. Dysphoria is a term in medicine that is attached to phenomena that is not necessarily pathological but causes sufficient distress which can be alleviated by medical intervention. Youths who live with dysphoria are often in a great deal of distress and frequently misdiagnosed with labels such as major depression or bipolar mood disorder. They may engage in self-harm and be admitted to an inpatient psychiatric hospital, where they will be prescribed medications that do not address their symptoms. Mood dysphoria is simply one of a cluster of symptoms that make a diagnosis of major depression. Mental health professionals see the dysphoric mood in young person, but rarely dig deeper.

Many of the youths I see come to me after several failed inpatient treatments and failed intensive outpatient aftercare. They try to tell their care providers about their gender dysphoria, but their complaints are dismissed. Many are on cocktails of various psychiatric medications with negative side effects and little efficacy. By then, their parents are desperate. They are appropriately concerned, open but cautious. When I can provide the right education and gain the parent's trust, I'll make a referral to a pediatric endocrinologist. If parents' consent to treatment with gender-confirming hormones, things change for the better. More than a few of my young clients have been able to be successfully weaned off of their psychiatric medications. Their moods improve because gender dysphoria responds to treatment with gender-confirming hormones (Allen et al., 2019).

The second group presents with some distress, but they lead by identifying as transgender. WPATH agrees that gender dysphoria and a transgender identification are distinct, and both deserve medically necessary treatment (Coleman et al., 2012, pp. 4–6). The tension around how gender dysphoria and transgender identity plays out among transgender youths, which will be explored shortly. If a young person presents as transgender, but has little if any dysphoria, the assessment is still the same, and treatment recommendations are the same as for the first group. Assessment involves questions about how they experience their bodies. Both the dysphoric and less than dysphoric groups experience specific conflicts with their bodies, which can be addressed medically. The difference for the second group is they have to acquiesce to a label they may not want. However, in the new reversion of the International Classifications of Disease (ICD-11), gender dysphoria has been categorized as a condition, not a disease, under the "sexual health" category. While that goes further to depathologize transgender phenomenon, it may create a dilemma in the United States because access to healthcare interventions under our system requires presence of a disease.

The third group presents as gender nonbinary. Their lived experience of their gender is fluid, and they can present in a variety of ways. For example, they can simply dress and present androgynously. Others can present in a variety of colorful and creative ways, playing with gender. The latter group sometimes alarms parents or authorities. If they are content with themselves, I do not see a role for mental health treatment, unless there is a co-occurring condition that needs attention. In *The Gender Creative Child*, psychologist Diane Ehrensaft writes about a similar triumvirate, which she refers to as apples, oranges, and fruit salads in an acknowledged and respectful nod to Queer culture (2016).

Fruit salads are relatively new. They are not "either/or, but instead, all and any" expressions of gender (p. 74). Ehrensaft believes that transgender, or gender creative youth, is the result of nature, nurture, and culture. I contend that at present, culture cannot come into play without information technology. Culture has a strong impact on gender nonbinary youth. They encounter culture in the online world they frequently inhabit. Apples reflect a prototypical transgender trajectory. As such, nature is a strong influencing factor. Those are the youths who tend to live with insistent dysphoria. Oranges have less conflicts with their bodies. They may identify as transgender, and their gender expression may serve more of an exploratory purpose. With youth like these, the role of the clinician is to help them explore who they are.

The first thing I want to learn about my young transgender clients is how they discovered their lived experience of their gender and at what point did it become knowledge. Did they have a prior, internal ongoing feeling of something being wrong or different? Did they see something in the media or in culture that got their attention? Or, perhaps they met a transgender person and they felt some kind of connection. I'll start the interview by asking directly, "how did you find out about yourself?" The answer is always, first and foremost, the internet. This response implies disconnection, as transgender youth are encountering their experience not through analogue relationship and interpersonal connection, but through digitized information technology. This brings to our attention two important information technology variables. One is the nature of information technology's impact on knowledge acquisition, and the other is the impact of information technology on how we define ourselves. In looking back on 12 years of working with transgender youth, I have seen an evolution in how these two variables express themselves.

In *The Internet of Us*, Michael Patrick Lynch discusses what makes knowledge complex. His minimal definition of knowledge involves, "having a correct belief . . . that is grounded or *justified*, and which can therefore guide our action" (2016, p. 14). But how is a belief grounded? Lynch suggests three ways in which our beliefs can be grounded. First is by having reliable sources. These resources typically are from texts written by experts and good Internet resources. Second is through our lived experience, which helps us to possess reasons-for. Third, we need to have an understanding, be it from intuition or reasoned discourse (p. 15). Lynch states that "understanding is what we have when we know not only the what but the why" as well (p. 16). Digital sources are good at providing us with facts, but it has little utility regarding helping us to understand more. We need to interact with the larger world and with others. This is where clinical work comes in: in addition to having what and why at our disposal, understanding helps us to know which questions to ask our clients (p. 16). When we ask the right questions, we help them deepen their understanding of their lived experience. We become experts on our clients in order to help them become experts on themselves.

Lynch might agree that his term, "google-knowing," is how transgender youths gather information about themselves (pp. 21–40). But, as he points out, "greater knowledge doesn't always bring with it greater understanding" (p. 6). That's where we come in as clinicians. My young, transgender-identifying clients come to me with knowledge about gender dysphoria, what is involved in transitioning medically and legally, and what kinds of social transition options exist. Because they have information, they may think they understand their situation. But they need an interaction with a specialist, followed by interactions with their families, in order to truly know their situation and their options.

Sam's Story: One Transgender Boy's Experience

Sam was assigned female at birth, and throughout his childhood, he was labelled as a tomboy. He played sports, hung out with his brothers and their friends, and was generally accepted as "one of the guys" until puberty hit, and hit him hard. Sam's breasts developed quickly and were noticeable early. He wasn't rejected, but his place in the social order changed. Boys were less likely to involve him in after school football games or explorations in the woods nearby. Sam told me, "I could just tell I wasn't as welcome. It felt like I had to stay with the girls instead." He did not want to do that. Instead, he slowly began to isolate. His hair was always cut short, and he cut it shorter in an attempt to mitigate the growing sense of revulsion he felt about the changes in his body. His first period was awful for him, "like not the kind of period that all girls hate—this was like I was in some kind of horror film." By the time he had his third menses, Sam was visibly distressed. His hygiene got worse and he gained weight. His mood was visibly dysphoric.

Alarmed, his parents took him to their pediatrician who recommended him to see a psychiatrist to be evaluated for depression. Sam was able to tell the pediatrician he was having problems with menstruation. In an act of beneficence, the doctor started him on continuous birth control to arrest his menses cycle until his mental health could be assessed.

The birth control worked. With Sam's periods halted, his mood improved somewhat. The psychiatrist did not recommend medication, but referred Sam to a clinical social worker for talk therapy. Sam continued to isolate and became curious about why puberty was so difficult for him. Also, he was aware that he was attracted to girls, but not for socializing. In his words, "I wanted to be with a girl like a guy could." Assuming he might be lesbian, he began using YouTube to learn about gay women. He was intrigued, but he did not feel the clips he watched "spoke" to what he was experiencing. He turned to google to address his larger concern. Among his first search queries was "how to stop puberty." This search took him to a number of sites about a condition known as "precocious puberty," in which a child begins showing signs of pubertal at age 8 or 9. Sam was disappointed—he was too old to be considered as having precocious puberty. But the treatment for the condition, which involves hormone blocking medication, did interest him. He followed a few links and found a site for a hospital-based gender clinic.

Sam had never heard of such a place. He was intrigued, continued reading, and started searching for sites where he could learn more about transgender people and gender dysphoria. Sam could relate to gender dysphoria—when he was reflecting back on his process of learning about himself, Sam told me, "gender dysphoria isn't the same as depression. It doesn't happen until you are reminded that your body is wrong. For me, it's always worse when I shower or have to take my binder off at night."

Sam continued to use the Internet to acquire more knowledge and to understand himself. He learned a great deal about what is involved in transitioning medically. Sam's initial interest in taking hormone blocking medication evoked a fantasy of having control over his body. When he started reading about the use of gender-confirming hormones, he realized his body could truly be reshaped. He used "gender euphoria" to describe how he felt when he realized his body could physically change into something more congruent with how he felt. Sam was learning about the Dutch Protocol (De Vries & Cohen-Kettenis, 2012). Developed in the Netherlands in 2000 for use with children with gender dysphoria, it is an endocrinological technology that suspends puberty to allow time for the child, the parents and physicians/clinicians to determine whether the child is transgender. The medications are known as Gonadotropin Releasing Hormone analogues, and they have a variety of applications, including precocious puberty. Essentially, they block the production of targeted hormones (estrogen or testosterone). Unlike treatment with gender-confirming hormones, blockers are full reversible. They are ideally administered during tanner stage 2, just before puberty begins to take a heavier toll. Tanner stages are not age related, but are based on where a young or preadolescent's development is. Generally, stage 2 occur around ages 11–13, when testicular volume in boys is beginning to increase, and when breasts in girls are starting to bud. The protocol was developed in response to the increasing numbers of younger patients being referred to gender clinics in the Netherlands. These children were in great distress, but the thinking, even in the late 20th century, was that children could not have a gender identity disorder. The Dutch Approach created time for the child or preadolescent to be followed, without imposing the burdens of puberty on the young patient. After several years of treatment with blockers, they would be discontinued. Puberty would recommence, and gender-confirming hormones could be prescribed so the youth could have a puberty that was consistent with how they experienced themselves and at a developmentally corresponding time (De Vries & Cohen-Kettenis, 2012).

Sam was using the internet in two ways. One, he was learning about how medical technology could help him. Second, he began watching YouTube videos of young people chronicling their transitions. This allowed him to experience the narratives of other transgender youths. Sam also found TrevorSpace.org, a safe and respected online resource for LGBTQ young people aged 13–24. Sam found it to be a gentler and more respectful site than places like Tumblr or Reddit. As Sam said to me, "I really don't like all the political stuff on the other sites. Users get into fights with each other over things like are people who say they are non-binary really trans, or does someone have to suffer with dysphoria to be considered really transgender. I use the internet for information, I'm not really all that interested in having an online social life or support."

Anthropologists Nikolas Rose and Carlos Novas characterize what Sam was doing in this way:

> Over the last decade, the Internet has come to provide a powerful new way in which those who have access to it, and who are curious about their health or illness, can engage in this process of biomedical self-shaping. But a key feature of the Internet is that it does not only give access to material disseminated by professionals, it also links an individual to self-narratives written by patients or caregivers.
>
> (2004, p. 14)

Rabinow and Novas are referring directly to the relationship between information technology and medical technology. Sam was acquiring knowledge in what Lynch described earlier as google knowing. While that met Lynch's minimal definition of knowledge, he also points out that as persons who are trying to both know and understand, we can't do it all on our own or in a vacuum. We need experts and specialists. That's where we come in as social work clinicians (pp. 34–35).

As Sam continued his explorations online, he began to feel a mixture of, what he called, "hope and dread." Hope for getting his embodiment where he needed it to be, but dread that it might not happen for a long time. Sam shared this with his clinical social worker. She believed that his next best step was to talk with his parents. To her credit ethically and clinically, she contacted me for advice on how to proceed. She knew Sam would be asking for medical interventions and a legal name change before he turned 18. He was 15 then and could not imagine having to cope with dysphoria for three years and still maintain good grades. She observed that Sam's family seemed to have settled into a homeostasis characterized by an implied "don't ask don't tell" contract. As long as Sam's grades were still good, his parents would not worry openly about how much time he spent alone in his room. His hygiene had improved, and his menses cycle was, except for some spotting, under control. His therapist, seasoned as she was, had never worked with a transgender-identified youth as closely as she had with Sam. They did have a good therapeutic alliance and Sam felt she cared about him.

I agreed that his parents should be involved and encouraged her to coach Sam about what to tell them, when to tell them, and how to tell them. Afterward, I could get involved as a family therapist and case manager. Sam could continue his work with her, and she and I could collaborate. I call my approach transgender-specific assessment, case management, and counseling. Since gender dysphoria is not a psychopathology, talk therapy usually does little to help unless the clinician can provide education, referrals, and resources. When minors are the focus, I always work with their parents.

Sam's mother called, saying that she got my name from Sam's therapist after Sam told her about his gender identity. I explained that I'd like to start by meeting with Sam and both parents. I asked her to describe how Sam told her and his father about his gender. She told me it was in writing and that Sam "must have done a lot of research." She added that she and her husband suspected Sam was lesbian, "which would have of course been fine." But this, she told me, caught them both off guards. "Welcome to the 21st century," I jokingly quipped. If they laugh, I consider it an indication that they had the capacity to think more expansively. Fortunately for Sam, his mother laughed.

Sam and parents met with me for an extended first session. I split the time into thirds. First third was with the three of them, which gave me an opportunity to join with them and get a sense of their dynamics and a sense of which parent held the most power. In work with transgender youth, it is important to connect with that parent because they typically have the final say over a referral to an endocrinologist. The second part I met with Sam, just to get a feel and a read of what kind of teenager he was. I explained to him that my job was to earn his trust and that of his parents. I also told him that despite my being a certified gender specialist, I would not "play the expert card" on his parents. He would have to work, with my help, to get them to a place of understanding. He agreed, another good sign. I met with all three of them again for the last third of the session, discussed policies regarding confidentiality as it works in family therapy, and told them I'd like to meet with Sam individually next, followed by a session with both parents.

Sam was immediately likeable, a teenager with a combination of smarts and maturity. He told me about his Internet research, and I asked him a series of questions about his body. Adolescents who live with gender dysphoria tend to have certain preoccupations regarding their embodiment. Furthermore, they do not want to talk about them unless they have to access transgender healthcare. Sam seemed at ease, he could tell that I had mileage with transgender youth. As Lynch pointed out, when trying to understand, it is important to know which questions to ask. When Sam opened up to talk about living with breasts, the main focus of his dysphoria, he held back tears. He revealed that he has a chest binder about which his parents are unaware and that binding was becoming painful. I asked him what he hoped would happen, assuming the family work was successful. Ideally, he wanted a double mastectomy (top surgery) first. He knew that the World Professional Association for Transgender Health's Standards of Care stated that top surgery could occur prior to treatment with gender-confirming hormones (Coleman et al., 2012, p. 59). He conceded that would be a "long shot" right now because he was 15, but he'd "happily settle" for hormones and being able to bind with his parent's knowledge and understanding. He added, "I want them to use the proper pronouns and call me Sam. I also want my name change before I apply to colleges. It will make things easier." Playing out a hunch, I asked him if he would like to attend a support group for transgender teenagers. His response was emphatic: "no way! To be honest, I don't like that label. I'm not a transgender. I'm a guy. I just want to be who I am, I don't want to be labelled. I don't feel a need to be around other teens like me. No clubs for me, thank you." My hunch was that Sam would abjure a transgender socialization because he wasn't needing an identity. He wanted his body to be congruent with what he knew about his lived experience.

Sam is emblematic of many male-identified transgender youths with whom I've worked. Their bodies are their problem, and they want to use medical technology to correct a mistake they believe was made by nature. Generally, they do not agree with my position that nature does not produce mistakes, only variety. Easy for me to say. I don't live in a body that feels alien to me. In the passage that follows, Gill-Peterson seems to agree with Sam's desire for technical change without having to accept an identity label:

> For example, sex reassignment surgery—or, indeed, all desired surgeries, whether deemed "elective" or "medically necessary"—are a participation in the body's open-ended technical capacities, the ways in which its physical matter, biological systems, and affective components exceed conscious will through receptiveness to change as difference, as *nonidentity* (emphasis mine). The intervention of the surgeon's technologies is not opposed to the body's systems but rather informs and is informed by them. Hormone therapy, likewise, is a participation in the technical capacity of the endocrine system. The difference between synthetic hormone therapy and the endocrine system's autonomic functioning is that hormone therapy involves a subject's technological intervention upon its own body.
>
> (2014, p. 407)

Sam also was expressing some of Appiah's concerns regarding the essentialism of identity. Sam knew from information technology that he needed help from medical technology. As Lynch might concur, engaging with his therapist, his parents, and me, as a specialist, allowed Sam to take the factual knowledge he acquired and bring it to a new level of understanding and ultimately, the shaping of an authentic self.

The session with Sam's parents was useful. They had appropriate skepticism and concerns about Sam and asked some good questions. His parents presented as fairly traditional people. They both worked for the State government. Sam's father was in an accounting position; his mother was an administrative assistant. They had two sons and had a lot invested in Sam as their only daughter. Both teared up when admitting to a sense of loss. They were well aware that Sam had become a loner, for the most part. They missed the feeling of togetherness the family once had. One of their biggest concerns was his use of the Internet. They did not trust the Internet as a source of good information. I explained to them that most people use the Internet to learn about a wide variety of topics. From what I could tell, Sam was using reasonable sources. I suggested they watch some YouTube videos and TrevorSpace with him. Perhaps, I told them, it might help them if they spent some more time together. Additionally, I told them about some recent research on how transgender youths use the Internet for support and information. The study found that the Internet, with sites like TrevorSpace, could be a safe space for transgender youth, which may not be available to them in their offline lives, and for some, lifesaving (Austin, Craig, Navega, & McInroy, 2020). Another study found that information regarding transgender healthcare could be unduly complex and written in an equally complex manner, beyond what the National Institutes of Health recommends (Cook et al., 2017, p. 370). They showed me the letter Sam wrote. Indeed, he had done a great job comprehending complex information.

The subject of treatment with gender-confirming hormones did not come up. I wanted more time with Sam to assess how much he knows and to help him prepare for sessions with his parents. At that time, I couldn't tell whether his parents would attempt to "filibuster" his transition. Some parents and some providers will collude in an attempt to put off a medically necessary treatment which could provide relief (Healy & Allen, 2019). His parents did ask if I was certain that Sam was male, and they wanted to know how I knew. Of course, I cited my years of direct clinical experience and the transgender-specific education I underwent to get my certification. I also told them about Occam's Razor, the notion that when in possession of all the relevant facts, the simplest conclusion was most often the correct conclusion. My physician told me he was taught in medical school that "if you hear hooves galloping up behind you, don't turn around and expect to see a unicorn."

Sam's parents turned out to be extremely supportive of Sam and his transition. At first, they showed resistance to treatment with gender-confirming hormones, but not outright refusal. Sam was able to begin hormone treatment when he was 16, and top surgery was set for the summer between high school and college. He continued to bind. His parents struggled with the name change and pronoun usage, but Sam was patient. The last time I heard from, he began college after a gap year. He used the year to make sure his legal identity was fully changed, and he wanted more time to masculinize. He entered his freshman year, in his words, "as a guy."

The one issue that his parents could not fully grasp had to do with the role of the Internet and information technology. They didn't use any social media and didn't spend much time online. I think they were surprised at how much—and how quickly—things changed while they were busy working and raising their family. In the following passage, Gill-Peterson describes the tension between life before and life after the Internet and its impact on young people's knowledge of their bodies:

> In the era of the Internet, the tensions between that history and the discourse on children's sexuality have become quite visible: children try to leverage their minimally implicit agency by making their bodies the grounding of a social world on- and offline. Parents and schools, in turn, try to contain and return those bodies to the proper pedagogical spaces negotiated long before the Internet, the school and the family home. The result is a persistent unruliness that can only be neutralized to the extent that the actual social worlds of children are covered over by adult fantasies of what they look like.
>
> (Gill-Peterson, p. 125)

Peterson's observation confirms my hypothesis that the nature–nurture dialectic has been complicated by technology. One hundred years ago, children and adolescents had little to no agency over their bodies due to a lack of access to knowledge regarding their embodiment and its meaning. They were at the effect of medical professionals who made decisions about their bodies without their assent. Biomedical ethics, informed consent, and patient autonomy did not inform medical practice until much later in the 20th century.

Today, young people can use information technology to not only gain knowledge about their bodies but also discover a wide range of possible identities. When used wisely, as Sam did, technology can help us to shape authentic selves. But, this is only the beginning of the 21st century. We are likely in a very clumsy phase of learning how to use the new knowledge available to us. In order to use it effectively, we must also understand it, and what it portends. Our relationship to information technology at this moment in history is perhaps akin to what was the Brady Institute's relationship to their medical specialty one hundred years ago. Both epochs were characterized by well-intended eager enthusiasm, but lacked a full understanding of what new technologies can do in the absence of a suitable ethical framework. But, we are in the 21st century now, with more enlightened ethical paradigms available to us. Medically, I'm confident that we have learned from the mistakes of the past as regards gender and youth. This is hopeful and very human. We often learn from mistakes as we move forward. When it comes to how we use information technology, we likely have room to grow. Sam's use of the internet suggests we can use information technology to help us shape an authentic, fully expressed self.

Close Reading Questions:

1. How has neoliberalism affected medical ethics?
2. Healy writes that "Children whose genitals are ambiguous, or whose reproductive organs are undeveloped are diagnosed as having disorders of sexual development. Such children were referred to the Institute. Most of the children seen at the institute were white, and benefitted from white privilege. They were 'promised alteration and normalization through medical intervention,'" whereas children from the poor, African-American families in Baltimore were regarded as being "difficult" and treated as "disposable' research subjects" (p. 79). Which key words strike you about this example?
3. How does our suicide awareness help to change the DSM and policies for trans people?

Prompts for Writing:

1. Provide a timeline of egregious misuses of medical technology. Write about one that affects you most utilizing Healy's references for more context.
2. Look into the case of the Reamer twins and journal your reaction. How was David Reimer's experience "a *reverse-proof* that gender is something we can know without taking our anatomy into account"?
3. What do you notice about Healy's therapeutic alliance with Sam? What would you take from Healy about working with this population into your own practice?

References

Allen, L. R., Watson, L. B., Egan, A. M., & Moser, C. N. (2019). Well-being and suicidality among transgender youth after gender-affirming hormones. *Clinical Practice in Pediatric Psychology*, 7(3), 302.

Appiah, K. A. (2005). *The ethics of identity*. Princeton: Princeton University Press.

Appiah, K. A. (2018). *The lies that bind: Rethinking identity*. London: Profile Books.

Austin, A., Craig, S. L., Navega, N., & McInroy, L. B. (2020). It's my safe space: The life-saving role of the internet in the lives of transgender and gender diverse youth. *International Journal of Transgender Health*, 21(1), 33–44.

Beauchamp, T. L. (2006). The right to die as the triumph of autonomy. *Journal of Medicine and Philosophy*, 31(6), 643–654.

Beauchamp, T. L., & Childress, J. F. (2013). *Principles of biomedical ethics*. New York: Oxford University Press.

Brody, H. (1992). *The healer's power*. New Haven: Yale University Press.

Chin, J. J. (2002). Doctor-patient relationship: From medical paternalism to enhanced autonomy. *Singapore Medical Journal*, 43(3), 152–155.

Colapinto, J. (2000). *As nature made him: The boy. Who was raised as a girl*. New York, NY: HarperCollins.

Coleman, E., Bockting, W., Botzer, M., Cohen-Kettenis, P., DeCuypere, G., Feldman, J., . . . Zucker, K. (2012). Standards of care for the health of transsexual, transgender, and gender-nonconforming people, version 7. *International Journal of Transgenderism, 13.*

Cook, J. A., Sasor, S. E., Deldar, R., Poh, M., Momeni, A., Gallagher, S., . . . Chu, M. W. (2017). Complexity of online gender confirmation resources surpass patient literacy. *International Journal of Transgenderism, 18*(4), 367–371.

Cornett, C. (2000). Ideas and identities: The life and work of Erik Erikson/identity's architect: A biography of Erik H. Erikson. *Clinical Social Work Journal, 28*(1), 123.

Corrigan, O. (2003). Empty ethics: The problem with informed consent. *Sociology of Health & Illness, 25*(7), 768–792.

De Vries, A. L., & Cohen-Kettenis, P. T. (2012). Clinical management of gender dysphoria in children and adolescents: The Dutch approach. *Journal of Homosexuality, 59*(3), 301–320.

Dreyfus, H. L. (2008). *On the internet.* London: Routledge.

Ehrensaft, D. (2016). *The gender creative child: Pathways for nurturing and supporting children who live outside gender boxes.* New York: The Experiment.

Engelhardt, H. T. (1996). *Foundations of bioethic* (2nd ed.). Oxford University Press. Retrieved from https://newsroom.wakehealth.edu/News-Releases/2014/04/Laboratory Grown-Vaginas-Implanted-in-Patients-Scientists-Report

Friedman, D. (1991). Should medicine be a commodity? An economist's perspective. In *Rights to health care* (pp. 259–305). Dordrecht: Springer.

Ford, K. K. (2001). "First, do no harm": The fiction of legal parental consent to genital-normalizing surgery on intersexed infants. *Yale Law & Policy Review, 19*(2), 469–488.

Gill-Peterson, J. (2014). The technical capacities of the body: Assembling race, technology, and transgender. *Transgender Studies Quarterly, 1*(3), 402–418.

Hacking, I. (2002). Inaugural lecture: Chair of philosophy and history of scientific concepts at the Collège de France, January 16, 2001. *Economy and Society, 31*(1), 1–14.

Hacking, I. (2006). *Making up people: Clinical considerations.* London: LRB.

Hamington, Maurice (2007). Care Ethics and International Justice: The Cosmopolitanism of Jane Addams and Kwame Anthony Appiah. *Social Philosophy Today* 23 (2008), 149–160.

Haslam, N. (2016). Concept creep: Psychology's expanding concepts of harm and pathology. *Psychological Inquiry, 27*(1), 1–17.

Healy, R. W., & Allen, L. R. (2019). Bowen family systems therapy with transgender minors: A case study. *Clinical Social Work Journal,* 1–10.

Held, V. (2006). *The ethics of care: Personal, political, and global.* Oxford University Press on Demand. 98 Madison Ave # 8, New York, NY 10016.

Jonsen, A. R. (2004). The history of bioethics as a discipline. In *Handbook of bioethics* (pp. 31–51). Dordrecht: Springer.

Katz, A. L., Webb, S. A., Macauley, R. C., Mercurio, M. R., Moon, M. R., Okun, A. L., . . . COMMITTEE ON BIOETHICS. (2016). Informed consent in decision-making in pediatric practice. *Pediatrics, 138*(2).

Knapp, S., Handelsman, M. M., Gottlieb, M. C., & VandeCreek, L. D. (2013). The dark side of professional ethics. *Professional Psychology: Research and Practice, 44*(6), 371–377.

Kuper, L. E., Wright, L., & Mustanski, B. (2018). Gender identity development among transgender and gender nonconforming emerging adults: An intersectional approach. *International Journal of Transgenderism, 19*(4), 436–455.

Lynch, M. P. (2016). *The internet of us: Knowing more and understanding less in the age of big data*. New York: WW Norton & Company.

Meagher, G. (2004). Modernising social work and the ethics of care. *Social Work & Society*, *2*(1), 10–27.

Meaney, M. J. (2001). Nature, nurture, and the disunity of knowledge. *Annals of the New York Academy of Sciences*, *935*(1), 50–61.

Pellegrino, E. D., & Thomasma, D. C. (1993). *The virtues in medical practice*. Oxford: Oxford University Press.

Rabinow, P. (1997). *Ethics, subjectivity and truth: The essential works of Foucault 1954–1984* (Vol. 1). New York: The New Press.

Rabinow, P., & Rose, N. (2006). Biopower today. *BioSocieties*, *1*(2), 195–217.

Reamer, F. (2018). *Social work values and ethics*. New York: Columbia University Press.

Rose, N., & Novas, C. (2004). *Biological citizenship*. Retrieved from http://eprints.lse.ac.uk

Schwartz, R. C., & Sweezy, M. (2019). *Internal family systems therapy*. New York: Guilford Publications.

Sherry, J. L. (2004). Media effects theory and the nature/nurture debate: A historical overview and directions for future research. *Media Psychology*, *6*(1), 83–109.

Spack, N. P., Edwards-Leeper, L., Feldman, H. A., Leibowitz, S., Mandel, F., Diamond, D. A., & Vance, S. R. (2012). Children and adolescents with gender identity disorder referred to a pediatric medical center. *Pediatrics*, *129*(3), 418–425.

Szasz, T. S. (1960). The myth of mental illness. *American Psychologist*, *15*(2), 113.

Verhaeghe, P. (2014). *What about me?: The struggle for identity in a market-based society*. London: Scribe.

5 Connection and Separation Reconsidered

Challenges and Opportunities in the New World of Digital Communication

Wendy Winograd

Pre-reading Questions:

1. What do you know about modern attachment theory? Do you think that technologically mediated communication allows for the full experience in creating and maintaining human attachments?
2. How do you think that videoconferencing helped and/or hurt people's mental health during the pandemic? What do you think has been lost from human interaction with the proliferation of technologically mediated communication?
3. What feelings do you have about your own cell phone? How do you think your use of the phone affects the quality of your relationships?

As I was preparing to write this chapter, thinking about the cases, pondering my own use of technology, and wondering about the impact of the pandemic on my work and my writing, I had the following dream.

> I was walking with my dog, Molly. We came upon a dumpster along the side of the road, and I knew that there was something in there that I had lost, that I had to find. I realized that it was Molly's leash. Leaving Molly, I climbed up into the dumpster, where I found a deep pile of blankets. No sign of the leash. I tried to lift the blankets, still looking for the missing leash, but they were too heavy. I looked down and saw that Molly was walking around the dumpster and in the road. Worried that she may be hit by a car, I called to her. "Sit, stay by me." She stopped for a moment and then continued to prowl around the dumpster. Realizing that I was not going to be able to lift the blankets and find the leash, I climbed down and called Molly to me. She was safe. I was relieved. She came, and we walked together. I was slightly anxious that she might dart away to chase a squirrel, but I also marveled at how she was actually staying by me, as I had commanded.

While technology was conspicuously absent from my dream (I carried no phone, and the dumpster was filled only with blankets), the themes of my dream communicated the conflicts and tension that lay beneath the surface

DOI: 10.4324/9781003270225-5

of my work with patients in the vignettes that I was intending to elaborate for this chapter. The leash, a symbol of connection, was lost. The lost connection left my dream self with anxiety as I searched, knowing that Molly was free and could move further away from me, perhaps into danger. The leash represented safety and attachment but at the same time contained and constrained Molly. Perhaps unaware of the possible danger, she was enjoying her newfound freedom off the leash. The blankets may also have represented warmth, safety, and containment, and at the same time were too heavy to move, frustrating me from accomplishing my aim, to find the leash, and perhaps even leaving me with a claustrophobic feeling of being stifled or suffocated. At the conclusion of the dream, Molly agreed to "stay by me." Untethered by the leash, she chose to walk alongside of me, and we were connected but free, together but apart. A wish come true?

Introduction

Drawing on theory from psychoanalysis, modern attachment theory, and communication and media studies, this chapter will examine the experiences of clinician and patient as they navigate the therapeutic relationship that is increasingly impacted, interrupted, and mediated through technology, while focusing on themes of connection and isolation, attachment and separation, love, and loss. Looking at my work with two patients, a midlife career professional woman about my age and a late adolescent boy, I consider the various ways in which technology both facilitates and impedes connection, in an attempt to complicate our understanding of the importance of embodied, in-person relationships. I ask if attachments can be formed and maintained without physical presence and proximity and also what, if anything, is lost, particularly in terms of unconscious right brain to right brain communications.

John Bowlby (1988), credited with the development of attachment theory, argues that human beings seek attachments, not only in infancy, with caregivers, but throughout life, particularly in situations of danger. Supported by empirical research conducted by Mary Ainsworth, Blehar, Water, and Wall (1978), attachment theory teaches us that while the details of particular attachment styles may be learned, the need to seek attachments is biologically preprogrammed and serves a survival function. Departing from Freud, Bowlby posits that attachment is its own drive, distinct from feeding and sex. More important for my exploration here is Bowlby's assertion that attachment is predicated on *proximity*. In his words, "Attachment behavior is any form of behavior that results in a person attaining or maintaining proximity to some other clearly identified individual who is conceived as better able to cope with the world" (pp. 26–27). Building on Bowlby's original theory, modern attachment theory (Hill, 2015; Fonagy, Gergely, Jurist, & Target, 2004) and infant research (Beebe & Lachmann, 1994; Beebe & Lachmann, 2003; Trevarthan & Aitlen, 2001; Tronick & Reck, 2009) add that our ability to regulate emotional states depends upon a base of secure early attachments. Schore's (Schore, 2011, 2014) right brain to right brain communication theory can be understood to elaborate theories of emotional regulation through attachment by grounding them in contemporary understanding of complex neurobiological functions. Can such communication occur when mediated by technology? Is physical proximity, as Bowlby thought, necessary for the development of healthy attachments? If a healthy attachment has already been established, can it be maintained through a synchronous video connection? What was happening to our attachments and ability to emotionally regulate when are connections became challenged by the need to isolate to stay healthy during a pandemic?

Before the pandemic, some psychoanalysts were beginning to experiment with teletherapy, sometimes to provide continuity of treatment in times of relocation or travel. Some utilized phone or video sessions to continue to see patients when they themselves traveled. Many psychoanalysts and researchers disparage the widespread use of technology, both in and out of the consulting room. Bailey (2015) offers a dire picture of the negative impact of technology, arguing that the "highly addictive nature" of the internet and social media "reduces our ability to delay and strikes at the heart of our capacity to reflect on experiences. Interpersonal object seeking is exchanged for electronic object seeking" (p. 18). Her words are reminiscent of others who bemoan the use of technology by children and adults alike, predicting a dire future world populated of characterologically disordered individuals who have lost the ability to connect and relate. Turkle's (2015) research documents the short circuiting of empathy in the presence of technology. Turkle argues that the development of empathy requires human interaction, embodiment, and the attempt to understand another's subjectivity and observes that children and adolescents growing up today are more connected to their digital devices, which cannot really listen, than they are to one another.

Other psychoanalysts promote the advantages of technology, arguing that it is a useful tool not only in teaching (Scharff, 2015b) and clinical consultation (Wanlass, 2015) but also in psychotherapy (Scharff, 2015a; de Setton, 2015; Bakalar, 2015; Sehon, 2015). These clinicians maintain that all of the psychoanalytically understood clinical manifestations of treatment—the presence of the unconscious, transference, countertransference, projective identification, defense, resistance, and enactment—are functioning, observable, and utilizable whether the treatment is held in person, on the phone, or by videoconferencing.

Technology Enters the Consulting Room

Even before the pandemic, technology was entering the consulting room in the form of the ubiquitous cell phone. Phones would buzz, and patients, unable to ignore them, looked quickly to check the message or notification, then looked back. But in that brief moment, a connection was broken, a thought paused or lost. I often wondered how was these micromoments were affecting the nature of my connection with my patients and the meaning of our work together. Sometimes, I would comment. Other times, I accepted the power of the phone. A patient would apologize and remark that she needed to keep the phone on because there might be an emergency with her child. Old enough to remember how we managed such emergencies before the cell phone, I thought about the irony that our connection could be disrupted by the need to maintain a connection with someone else not in the room.

In considering the impact of such experiences on the nature of identity, Christopher Bollas (2018) reflects on lunch with friends in a café. He notices that members of the group drop in and out of the conversation as they become engaged by something or someone else on their phones. He argues

> In attempting to map the psychological territory, it is helpful to divide in relationships now being lived into the 'actual' and the 'virtual'; those relations we are having in real time with actual living people versus those we are having in cyberspace
>
> (pp. 50–51)

In this world, Bollas suggests, the self is essentially altered.

> In many ways in the course of a day, we associate with one another, but when we abandon actuals to talk to virtuals we are momentarily dissociated . . . This is an important function in the new world: we split the self into the associating self and the dissociating self . . . Dissociation *precedes* acts of engagement because decades of dissociative activity have become part of an adaptive mental structure
>
> (p. 55)

Seen from this lens, my acceptance of my patient's momentary dissociations to "check" her phone represents my collusion with her in the split self-model of identity that Bollas proposes. I wonder if I am supporting a pathological self-state or allowing her to function effectively in the world in which we live. Are selves changing to adapt, as Bollas suggests, or are we experiencing a deeply felt sense of loss, one that may even evoke symptoms of trauma? To what extent should we, as psychotherapists, be challenging the increasingly pervasive role that devices play in our daily lives?

The advent of text messaging offered a new means of communication between therapist and patient, one that, again, offered convenience and ease while at the same time resulting in loss: loss of the tone of voice, loss of the immediacy of a response. I told myself that I would only use text messaging for "business," such as setting or changing an appointment, and never for clinical matters. So when a patient sent me a long text with concerns that her daughter may be depressed, I picked up the phone and called, pleased with myself for refusing to allow a conversation so important to be conducted over text messaging. But who is to say that setting or changing an appointment is not a clinical matter, is not important? The more I allowed for communication through text message, the more I was seduced into the convenience of it and, at the same time, struck by a vague sense that something was lost. I wasn't receiving all the information that I might have been. The connection was weaker. I became slightly more distanced from the real.

The pandemic and concomitant quarantine brought these matters into sharp relief. When I moved my practice online, my patients and I were relieved and grateful that we had means to continue our work. At the same time, we immediately became aware of the many losses associated with the technologically mediated connection. At first, I experienced significant anxiety that the technology would fail. What would it mean about our ability to maintain our alliance if we were cut off by a failure of bandwidth or poor internet connection? I felt responsible to ensure that the internet—our technological equivalent of a leash—was healthy and secure. Not infrequently, glitches in the videoconferencing software intruded into our time together, throwing us off course and impacting our intimate connections. As time went on and we adjusted to the occasional disruption, my patients and I together recognized and mourned other losses.

We hadn't realized the significance of the sacred space that the office had become (Boulanger, 2013). Since my office is in my home, I remained in that same space and in my same chair, a comfort to some of my patients, who expressed pleasure in seeing me there. And yet, the same space was completely different without the patient's embodied presence. We noticed and grieved that together. We also began to realize that the beginnings and endings of sessions felt abrupt. Prior to the pandemic, my four-year-old grandson had taught me how important it was for him to be the one to end our video calls. If I accidentally pressed the end button, he would fly into a rage or crumble in sadness and tears and, within a few moments, I would receive a call back with a request that he end the call. And so when I moved to online sessions, I ceded control of the endings to my patients. Click. The session is over. It felt abrupt. I began to wave goodbye at the computer screen as patients prepared to end the session. Lost were moments that extended the connection before the door finally closed. "I'm just going to use your bathroom before I leave." "The rain stopped just in time." "See you next time." "Have a nice weekend."

Patients began to notice that they missed the drive to the session, when they would allow a reverie to prepare them for our time together, or drive home, when they continued to think about what we had talked over. Instead, they would likely be thrust into another video call for their work or right back into interactions with their family members, or to face the isolation of living alone in a pandemic. In addition to the lost time for reflection,

I imagined that they were also mourning the loss of our embodied presence together in the office. The proximity that Bowlby (1988) knew was key in attachments was missing, a palpable absence. While these losses were at times sad and even painful, I found comfort in the fact that they confirmed my belief that there is something essentially human about our embodied experience and about physical proximity to others, something that has not been supplanted by our technological devices. While some writers (Verhaeghe, 2015; King, 2016) opine that the very nature of the self or identity is altered by our use of technology and that relationships with real human beings are being replaced by relationships with technology (Turkle, 2011), the very present and real experience of the loss of physical presence made me hopeful that perhaps our attachments do, after all, as Bowlby believed, rely on physical proximity, and embodied relationships with others cannot be replaced by technologically mediated communication.

Deborah

I had been working with Deborah for nearly 15 years when moved to online sessions during the COVID-19 quarantine. She had initially come to therapy due to a crisis in her marriage which ultimately led to a divorce. Deborah's vulnerability in the face of a ruptured attachment was palpable in the room as, through tears and a broken voice, she described feeling as though she could not hold herself together; she was falling apart. In fact, this was not true. After her husband left, she continued to function effectively in her job, manage her household, and remain connected with her youngest child, who was still finishing high school. Her feeling, though, spoke to the vital significance of attachments that keep us *feeling* protected, safe, and as though we can go on (Bowlby, 1988; Fonagy et al., 2004; Hill, 2015). My feeling when I was with Deborah, either in person or when she would call me on the phone during this crisis, was that I was wrapping a blanket around her to hold her together. I was becoming an attachment object for her, one who could provide her with enough of a sense of safety that she could regulate her emotions and, in Winnicott's (1965) terms, feel protected in "going-on-being" (p. 86). While Winnicott was describing the capacity to go on being as it develops in the maternal/infant surround and while the existential capacity to go on being begins in infancy, as Bowlby (1988) points out, human beings need attachments to provide safety throughout life, particularly in times of threat or danger. In Deborah's case, the danger of being separated from her husband and being alone threatened her sense of stability and amplified her need for the safety of a proximate attachment object. There were no interruptions when we were together; rather, my office was a sanctuary, a private space where our relationship deepened without intrusions from the outside world. And while we never outgrow the need for others, as we are social beings who co-regulate emotions (Beebe & Lachmann, 2003; Fonagy et al., 2004; Hill, 2015), it was our work together in regulating Deborah's emotional states that allowed her, incrementally and over time, to use our relationship to build the ego strength needed to regulate her own emotions, even in times of stress. It is impossible to know for sure if this could have happened had we not been in person, but neurobiology (Schore, 2011, 2014) suggests not.

In the early phase of treatment, Deborah looked to others, including me, for answers to her own dilemmas. Often, she would bring an email that she intended to send, asking for my take on it. Should she send it? Should she revise it? What did I think? We talked about how emails and written letters were different but the same. We explored her wish that I tell her what to do, and over time, she would preface her request for advice, smiling, and saying, "I know you aren't going to tell me what to do, but . . ." We would sit together pondering her desire to communicate effectively, to be seen and known, not to be misunderstood, and she increasingly grew to trust her own voice. Her growing confidence and sense of self-worth ultimately resulted in a promotion to a managerial position at work where she oversaw several employees. I observed as she deftly and proudly handled difficult conversations at work, gaining the respect and admiration of her colleagues. Her requests for my opinion or advice came less frequently as she tuned into her own feelings and thoughts and began to advise herself.

As our connection deepened, Deborah and I were unwittingly drawn into an enactment that challenged her trust and her growing experience of being seen and valued by me. Enactments, once understood as impasses in the treatment, often seen as the result of the therapist's own acting out, are now increasingly understood as inevitable behavioral manifestations of projected or dissociated unconscious implicit relational patterns (Bromberg, 1998; Ginot, 2009; Schore, 2011, 2014). Ginot links enactments with empathy, arguing that "nonconscious ongoing emotional communications are relevant to both enactment and empathic reactions, uniting them, through their capacity to viscerally and affectively know the other" (p. 291). Therapist and patient together participate in the unfolding of an enactment, which can be affectively challenging for both. Ginot stresses the importance of the therapist's ability to create a space to reflect on the enactment, thus bringing its projected parts into conscious consideration. Such reflective processes when shared with the patient provide the opportunity for psychic growth and change.

Deborah arrived at my office, which is in my home, to find the door locked. Puzzled and confused, she stood for a moment and then began to walk away. Assuming that I had left the door open, I was waiting in my office for Deborah's arrival. It was not typical for Deborah to be late, so I walked into the waiting area and realized that I had inadvertently locked the door. When I opened the door, she turned, and I saw the tears in her eyes. "I don't know why I'm crying," she commented. "I assumed that I had the wrong night." I noted that her session had been at this day and time for quite a long time now and invited her in. As we explored the feelings that were stirred up by my mistake, a very old memory emerged. Deborah recalled being locked out of the house when she misbehaved. She knew that she was not yet 4 when this happened, as the family had moved when she was 4 and this was at the old house. Together we observed how frightening that must have been for a toddler and recognized that she had, in that brief moment, felt punished by me and frightened of being banished from my office. Had I unconsciously locked her out on purpose, I wondered? Did we cocreate a repetition of a very old dynamic in which connections felt violated by an angry parent and in which a frightened child was plagued by guilt? What was my role in this unconsciously co-created scene? On retrospect, I reflected on my own feelings of being an outsider in my family of origin. It seemed that I was participating in the recreation of a shared trauma and that the enactment served to solidify a growing identification that I felt with Deborah, one hitherto unacknowledged. Together, we had enacted a scenario which allowed us to reflect together on themes of disconnection—of being an outsider—and of the repair of a connection momentarily lost. While this enactment did happen in the context of our in-person engagement, I wondered if that were necessary. While Ginot (2009) stresses the significance of the mirror neuron system, and thus in-person, embodied experience, in facilitating such kinds of affective and nonconscious communications, Novick (2020) argues that all the elements of psychoanalytic treatment, including projective identification, countertransference, and enactment operate whether in person, online, or on the phone. I did not know then that years later, in the midst of a global pandemic, Deborah and I would have our chance to test out Novick's ideas.

A few years later, Deborah got her first smartphone, offering countless new avenues for connection and communication, but also for failed connections and miscommunications. Initially, she left it in the car, but before long, it made its way into my office. Both Deborah and I, about the same age, grew up long before the era of the smartphone, and we shared a fascination and love of all that technology offered. We considered the pros and cons of a phone call, a text message, an email, concluding that it was a benefit to have all modes of communication available. She told me with great pleasure about a family text group that had been set up between her three adult children, her ex-husband, and her, and how it had facilitated healing in their relationships in the aftermath of the separation. Together we observed that communication with her ex-husband proceeded slowly, first at a distance, through email only, then through texting, and finally, with phone calls, suggesting that a return to some sort of intimacy was managed in steps and facilitated by the more distant mode of communication that email provides.

At the same time, however, several problematic consequences of the opportunities for communication that the smartphone and social media offered began to emerge, both inside and outside the consulting room. Deborah made use of Facebook to connect with old friends in faraway places.

That was gratifying and pleasurable for her. However, she had many experiences on Facebook with one of her daughters that made her feel isolated, lonely, and left out. King (2016) explores how the dynamics of shame are transformed by social media. Noting that shame is based on an experience of being seen (or unseen) by the other, King looks at how the gaze of the other may be transforming the experience of shame in digital relationships. While shame binds us to others—our experience of shame is intrinsically a social one—it has the potential of negatively impacting self-esteem. Not infrequently, Deborah's daughter would post photos and descriptions of experiences in which Deborah was notably absent or she would find out about an important occurrence in her daughter's life that others knew about long before Deborah did. The experience of being outcast is an inherently shaming one, and Deborah felt such shame acutely. While she knew that these were indirect communications of anger on her daughter's part, she nevertheless struggled with detrimental impact these shaming experiences had on her self-worth. Moreover, she couldn't understand what motivated them. I also understood her daughter's posts as hostile expressions of rejection and framed them in part, at least, as normative expressions of a desire to separate. It was becoming clear that managing the narcissistic injuries of motherhood when adult children separate was becoming complicated by technology. Deborah was privy to more in her daughter's life than she would have been before Facebook and thereby more subjected to the hurt and shameful feelings activated by being excluded. Learning something through a Facebook post puts distance between the moment when it was learned and the moment, often much later, when she could actually talk about it with her daughter. Opportunities for intimacy—even difficult ones—were short-circuited. Lost was body language and the tone of voice.

In our work, Deborah became increasingly apt to "check" her phone during sessions. Initially, after looking at the vibrating phone for a text of voicemail message, she would apologize for the interruption. After a while, though, it seemed she had simply accepted these interruptions as normal. A classically psychoanalytic perspective on Deborah's phone use in session would probably interpret it as a resistance to deepening treatment or a defense against an uncomfortable or painful feeling that might be arising during the session. While that may have been accurate at times, I also wondered if a broad-based social change in the way we are relating to one another was afoot (Bollas, 2018). I struggled with my feelings about how to address the presence of the phone in our sessions. At times, I felt irritated at Deborah for prioritizing someone else. I felt set aside. I wanted to say something. At the same time, I worried that I may risk making Deborah feel criticized for being impolite or rude while I may appear oblivious to the new way people are relating and a kind of socially agreed upon protocol that it's "okay" to look at your phone. I began to resent the microintrusions, a split second here or there, but just enough to shift attention and dilute emotional intensity.

Indeed, King (2016) theorizes about how the internet creates a lack of boundaries and divided attention and seems to conclude that we have been irrevocably altered in terms of what we need and that the ubiquitous use of digital communication results in "disrupted attentiveness and communicative withdrawal" (p. 80). She suggests that "the gaze of the other in its physical immediacy is becoming less significant" and that "this logic of *being absent in the presence of others* penetrates even deeper into our intimate relationships that require sensual attentive presence" (p. 81). My experience with Deborah causes me to question King's implication that our use of digital media in relationships is causing a *fundamental change* in the human condition. While I am wrestling with my own feelings that something is lost when Deborah brings her phone into the consulting room, it is not presence. Presence remains. Breaks in attention are troubling, for sure, but the power and importance of the therapeutic bond feels as important as ever and is based upon our intersubjective, embodied presence, one most likely rooted in the neurobiology of attachment and the implicit and unconscious communication that forms the basis of relationship (Winnicott, 1963a, 1963b, 1965, 1971; Schore, 2011, 2014; Fonagy et al., 2004).

Another consequence of the smartphone and social media was the sheer volume of communications that Deborah found herself receiving. She was certainly not alone in having to manage so much information that it threatens to overwhelm the ego. During the years after she began to use the smartphone, Deborah became increasingly frantic, and at times, it felt as though she were regressing. Perhaps, she had. She was attempting to manage a daily barrage of text messages from her brothers, over her parents' care, from her children, over all matter of developments in their lives, and from colleagues at work, demanding immediate attention. A common aspect of the information age, this flood of information, to which we are all subject, for Deborah resulted in symptoms of anxiety and depression: insomnia, tearfulness, and anxiety attacks. At times, it was hard for me to remember the progress we had made earlier in the treatment; I began to feel as though I was failing Deborah, a feeling that I came to understand as a projection of her own feeling that she was failing to manage the sheer volume of information she felt obligated to process and respond to. Deborah took up yoga and meditation, and our work began to focus on how she could slow down. Responsibilities to her job and family made that difficult, if not impossible.

Still we persisted, and I tried to keep in mind my conviction that the best way to regulate emotion was to mentalize (Fonagy et al., 2004). Mentalization, or reflective function, requires slowing down and providing the space to think about our wishes, intentions, hopes, and fears—in short, the contents of our minds. Psychotherapy provides that space. We began to reflect not only on the traditional themes of her treatment—that her overly critical mother had left her easily wounded by criticism, that her tendency was to turn away from conflict rather than face it head on with an expectation that she could manage her feelings about it, that she struggled to say no to anyone for anything—but also on the role of social media and technology in contributing to her growing feelings of being overwhelmed. We could begin to talk about the way her phone, when it buzzed, both satisfied her need to connect with others but also interrupted and diluted our work. She wrestled with her need to look at the phone and became curious about what she might be avoiding with me when she would do so. Then, the nation was beset by the shared trauma of the coronavirus, our state went into quarantine, and I moved my practice online.

As with most of my patients, Deborah moved to an online teletherapy platform with apparent ease. Over 60 and with an underlying health condition, Deborah took the COVID-19 warnings seriously and quarantined religiously. She also began to work from home. Her comfort with technology made the logistics of the move to teletherapy straightforward. When we began, I wondered if I would feel as connected as with our in-person sessions. The experience of shared trauma (Boulanger, 2013), in some ways, deepened my connection with all of my patients, and Deborah was no exception. This was, however, a somewhat uncomfortable sort of intimacy, not only because I, too, was quarantined, worried about my health, worried about my loved ones, and making significant adjustments to the way I conducted my everyday life—from shopping, to bringing in my mail, to wearing a mask whenever I left my house. The sharing itself was uncomfortable. When Deborah spoke about how she got her groceries, I was thinking about how I got mine, and it felt like a strange role reversal to be hearing about a new delivery service for groceries in our county. Prior to COVID-19, Deborah was asking for my advice; now I was taking advice from her! My thoughts about what she would say were also changing. Deborah was clearly concerned about my health, perhaps emotional as well as physical, as every session began, "How are you, are you okay?" In other times, I would have wondered with her about her concerns about me and what they might be suggesting about her state of mind and her transference to me. I might have wondered if she were relating to me as she did to her sick mother, if she were worried that I might someday reject her, or if she had guilt about some deeper wish that she could reject me. Now, however, I took her inquiries at face value. Of course she was concerned; at any time, anyone of us could contract COVID-19.

It is possible that not being together in the room exacerbated such concerns. Can we truly tell if someone is okay when we are seeing them online? What signals are missing? I wondered if she felt the absence of unconscious communications, implicit messages. I wondered if I would miss them as well. What about being in the physical presence of another would be missed? These are hard questions to address or to talk about, as such unconscious or "right brain to right brain" (Schore, 2014) communications are nonverbal. Working online, although we do "see" the other, is largely a verbal exchange. While we imagine that we are making eye contact, in fact we are not, and our brains are working overtime to try to bridge the gap between that imagined experience and the reality (Murphy, 2020). Quoted in Murphy's *New York Times* article, "Why Zoom is Terrible," information technology professor Sheryl Brahnam explains that many of the facial expressions that unconsciously contribute to our awareness that we are communicating are obscured on video. Moreover, as my patients and I observed to one another, we are not able to see most of each other's bodies. We have all become a conglomeration of talking heads. In the early weeks of the pandemic, I worried about what would be missing. Something indeed was missing. At the same time, though, I began to realize that some of the nonverbal and unconscious communications miraculously made their way through cyberspace. During one session, I found myself looking at the clock repeatedly. It seemed as though the clock wasn't moving. The session wasn't boring, nor was I particularly tired, so I thought for a moment about the sensation that time was standing still. Could it be a communication from Deborah? I asked, "Do you wish you could stop time?" She replied instantly, "Yes! I wish I could turn it back." She had been talking about regrets that she had about her relationship with her mother and a wish that she could resolve them. Her mother, suffering from dementia, was in a nursing home that had been locked down, and Deborah had not been permitted to visit since before the state quarantine. My reverie was, after all, related to Deborah's thoughts and feelings. I had had experiences such as this in my office and always assumed that they relied on physical proximity. Now, I was experiencing them online.

This uncanny moment with Deborah complicated my understanding of the nature of embodiment and the need for physical proximity. While I don't think there is any doubt that we rely on physical presence in infant and early childhood development (Winnicott, 1965), I wonder now if we can, once we are adults and somewhat autonomous, communicate unconsciously, even when geographically separated. Is the computer image and voice enough? Is a voice on the phone enough? Before COVID-19, I would have thought not. One of the lessons of quarantine was that we human beings are so eager to connect that it seems we can communicate nonverbal, unconscious thoughts and feelings with voice and computer-generated faces alone.

Leo

To what extent can an app supplement or even replace a human relationship in an individual's ability to regulate emotion? What happens to our sense of embodiment when an app begins to feel like an extension of the self? Is it possible to construct and inhabit an identity using technology when real relationships have failed? Unlike Deborah and me, who grew up without a cell phone, indeed without a computer at all, Leo had had a cell phone since third grade. He was perfectly at home relating to others via text message, video chat, and Instagram. Could that be enough contact? Would that satisfy someone of Leo's generation? Or could he be wishing for, actually need, an embodied experience of intimacy?

Through an object relations lens informed by Winnicott (1958, 1963b) and Ogden (1992), MacRury and Yates (2016) argue that the cell phone functions as a transitional object in transitional space and, as such, offers potential for the expansion of imagination and creativity, as well as connection, and the risk of facilitating a pathological relationship to the outside world. They suggest that the modern world is a place in which we have lost the ability to mourn and are often engaged but not connected; in such a world, the use of the phone reveals an anxiety about the loss of connection and an attempt to recover a deeper engagement or intimacy with others. That said, some may be using their phones defensively, avoiding the messiness and conflict associated with true intimacy. In discussing the contradictory uses of the phone, they say "The mobile forms for us, we suggest, a powerful unconscious representation of connection and disconnection, one that evokes thinking, analysis and commentary and conveys feelings that are redolent of the *Zeitgeist*" (p. 44). In other words, the mobile phone, in that it can facilitate intimacy and (often at the same time) disrupt it, is a very powerful force that serves both a need for intimacy and the defense against it. In their words, "the mobile phone becomes emblematic of and a useful way to think about our ongoing experience of connection and disconnection within the social world" (p. 53).

The excitement that surrounds cell phone use, including its addictive quality calls to mind Fairbairn's (1986a, 1986b) exciting object, fascinates and seduces one, but ultimately disappoints. Leo's attachment to his phone and to the many apps he has downloaded and uses compulsively suggests its role as a Fairbairn's exciting object. He keeps hoping for a connection that will soothe his disabling anxiety but ultimately fails to find that in the phone. Retreating defensively from relationships in person with real people into the digital world of his phone offers a constant promise of relief that never comes. Its existence on the boundary between connection and disconnection or attachment and autonomy (King, 2016) provides a seemingly perfect but ultimately inadequate compromise for Leo, confirming my felt sense that as human beings we need something more, something perhaps ineffable or not even verbalizable but present in the embodied relationships with others.

I first met Leo about a year after he stopped attending school. He was 16. His parents had reported to me that every effort they had made to get him to go back to school had failed; when they tried, he cried hysterically and wouldn't leave his bed. They had tried several other therapists, had enrolled him in an intensive outpatient program, and finally had taken him to a long-term psychiatric facility. A few weeks in, he decided it was unhelpful, and his parents had agreed to bring him home, against the advice of the staff there. Now he was home again and refusing to leave the house. Leo had been diagnosed with type 1 diabetes when he was in first grade, and, although his condition was controlled, he refused routine checkups. Despite suffering from a toothache, he hadn't been to the dentist in nearly two years. I wondered with his parents how they would be able to get him to come to my office. They assured me that he had attended sessions with his prior therapists and wanted to come. We agreed to twice weekly psychoanalytically oriented therapy.

My initial meeting with Leo's parents led me to expect a dour, ornery adolescent, perhaps wearing black and looking forlorn and lonely. It was therefore a surprise when Leo came bouncing into my office for his first appointment. He was polite, outgoing, and open. While I sensed that something may be hidden, I was also aware of how engaging and talkative he was. At times, I wondered if he fooled me into thinking that he trusted me and was telling me everything while in fact he was privately guarded and cautious. I struggled with a vague sense that I was being had and, at the same time, a desire to trust Leo, and I wondered if my ambivalence was a reflection of his own. He recounted the history of his therapeutic encounters and related his difficulty attending school as if it puzzled him. "I really want to go to school. I really do. I just can't. It's the same with the doctor. I know I need to go, and I really do wish I could. But I just can't." When I asked what he thought might be getting in his way, what he might be afraid of, he could not say. For a few months, he chatted about friends he used to have, when he could still go out, and he expressed his disappointment that he could no longer be engaged socially, all the while apparently accepting that this was just the way it was. He just didn't understand it.

When I tried to explore feelings about his diagnosis of diabetes, he assured me that it was "no big deal." He wasn't concerned about it, nor had it ever bothered him to be different. When I asked if something had happened at home or at school that caused him to be unable to go, he couldn't think of anything. When I tried to probe about the dynamics with his family when he refused to get out of bed, he matter-of-factly told me of the scene that he would cause. Sometimes, they would plead with him. Other times, they would rage at him. And still other times, his mother would dissolve into tears and bemoan the fact that she had failed as a mother. Leo felt guilty about that, and when I asked if he ever got angry at them, he denied it, saying that he was just not an angry person. Once, when he was talking about his own wish to have a family, he commented that he wouldn't raise his children as he had been raised. He noted that his parents were not disciplinarians. "Mind you, I like it that way. I'm grateful that I can pretty much do what I want. But I wouldn't raise my children that way." I wondered, "Why, if it works so well for you?" As often happened with Leo, he couldn't really say why. He just knew that he would not give his children as much freedom as he had been lucky enough to have.

Leo challenged my ability to keep control of the treatment. I found myself making adjustments to the way I would customarily work. Leo was insistent that I do not speak with his parents. So, afraid of defying Leo, I rarely spoke with his parents. He was 16, and on the verge of independence, so I rationalized to myself that perhaps my role was to facilitate a separation and that keeping a clear boundary with his parents might in fact be therapeutic anyway; I thereby gave in to his wishes. At the same time, Leo was not functioning well, and I knew that his parents needed to be more involved. They struggled to set limits with Leo, and I found that I did as well. Leo managed to keep us all under his control, as if he were the parent and we the children. On the occasions when I did speak with Leo's father or mother, usually around a missed session, I had the opportunity to gently challenge them to be more insistent with him. Their response revealed their feelings of helplessness, even weakness, buttressed by the excuse that they didn't want to make Leo feel guilty. In time, I began to recognize that I was reluctant to challenge Leo's parents just as they were reluctant to challenge Leo. We were all caught in an enactment of sorts, in which, on the surface, it seemed that Leo's parents and I were frightened to trigger Leo's anxiety when in fact, Leo was making us too anxious to help him contain it.

As I was beginning to understand that Leo's anxiety was, at least in part, related to his having too much power in the family, I thought his use of technology was a means of containing the anxiety, thereby sidestepping the adults in his life who had failed him. King (2016) wonders about how the construction of self is significantly altered by a digital gaze and by parents who may be more engaged with their digital devices than they are with their children. She notes that in cases where the indifference of a parent overly engaged in his/her phone will engender in the child feelings of rejection and insecurity, leading to compensatory grandiosity and pseudo-independence. Could Leo's power and pseudo-independence stem from a failure of embodied mirroring? Had his phone become a substitute parent, mirroring his experience and identity in ways in which his parents could not?

Leo discovered a number of apps that functioned to organize and bind his experience as well as occupy his mind with countless details that served to hold his anxiety at bay by keeping disturbing thoughts and feelings out of awareness. With gusto and glee, he told me about his calendar app, his many task lists, and his yoga and exercise apps. He spent time in his sessions reading to me from his task lists, which were scheduled to the minute, enhanced by notifications, and detailed every moment of his daily life. He had scheduled everything from his appointments with me to the exact times when he would eat (and what he would eat), the exact times when he would brush his teeth and take a shower, and the exact times when he would practice yoga or lift weights. I began to experience his apps as a kind of extension of his mind, a depository for all the minutiae that he used to avoid the more difficult experiences that he wished to forget. It was during this phase of our work that I realized that he was, after all, hiding the more important causes of his distress, not only from me but from himself. I felt stuck. I felt rejected. I knew Leo felt stuck. I expected he felt rejected. I struggled with my fear of being pushed aside in favor of smart phone apps until I recognized it as a projection of Leo's feelings about having been pushed aside himself. While I had concerns that Leo would abandon me—stop treatment—I began to wonder if Leo was also worried about abandoning me or being abandoned. Indeed, I began to surmise that his parents' inability to care for him adequately was most likely experienced as an abandonment, even as he praised his parents for their care. I didn't yet know the full origin of these fears. Neither did Leo.

Until he was willing to talk about feelings other than his anxiety and until he was willing to think more deeply about what was beneath the panicky feelings he so frequently experienced, we would remain stuck. We talked about the stuckness and also about what needed to happen to move us forward. Leo was obstinate; he knew that I believed that talking about it was the only way he could really get relief, but he refused to let me in.

Then the coronavirus pandemic put us all into quarantine. Working online with Leo was, no doubt, more comfortable for him. He expressed that it was a relief not to feel pressure to leave his house. Since the pandemic, that seemed like a healthy, rather than pathological, stance to take. His parents stopped trying to get him to go to the doctor, return to school, or come to my office. His life could be totally conducted from the safety of his bedroom, online. He was protected from the embodied experience that physical presence offers, an experience that he said in words that he wanted but one that he avoided at all costs. Paradoxically, though, our relationship deepened. At first, it was a hint here or there. Leo would be recounting his schedule for the day and then pause to mention that he had felt panicky the night before. When I probed, he demurred. "I don't want to talk about it. Please don't ask me." Sometimes he would offer me a bone, "I will talk about it, someday. I hope that is sooner rather than later. I just can't now. I might have a panic attack if I do." I began to wonder what he was keeping from me. Although Leo presented himself as someone comfortable with adolescent experimentation with marijuana, alcohol, and sex, his extreme social avoidance made me wonder if there were a hidden trauma. He usually denied the existence of any precipitating event, but ever so infrequently he would hint that there was something, something he would tell me about sometime in the future. For now, he kept it secret.

I experienced a push and pull from Leo. At this point, Leo was working with me three times weekly, and he periodically asked for an additional session—the pull. At the same time, I felt him pushing me away with his calendar and task obsessions and with his outright refusal to talk about what he believed was the source of his anxiety. But I also felt that something was shifting. I began to ask him what it was about our relationship that prevented him from disclosing his fears. He began to talk about not wanting to burden me, not wanting to burden his parents. Being close, he told me, means you might hurt someone. What I had also come to sense was how much Leo had been burdened by having to manage things on his own, without needed structure and containment that his parents failed to provide.

At the same time, his success in managing anxiety with an app perplexed me. I thought of it as a grandiose defensive feeling that he needed no one. Along with Winnicott (1963a, 1963b, 1965, 1971), Bowlby (1988), Hill (2015), and Fonagy et al. (2004), however, I believed that physical proximity, face-to-face mirroring were essential to affect regulation. How, I wondered, can this happen with an app?

Then, about six weeks into quarantine, Leo called me in between sessions. This was the first time he had ever called me. The apps failed him, and he sought a human connection to regulate his anxiety. He was very agitated and told me that he had had a fight with his father. He had discovered that his father had lied about something, and he had become enraged. The lie was a silly one, and I couldn't really fathom why his father would have lied. It was quite clear that this small lie was not the source of all of Leo's intense rage, rage so intense that it scared him. Could this rage be about the burden he felt because his father had been unable, in Leo's words, to "discipline" him? More likely, I thought, the lie might be a screen for a more serious betrayal, one that was unspeakable or, perhaps, unknown to Leo. The call between sessions marked a turning point in our relationship. Leo turned to me for help regulating affect that had been disturbed by the conflict with his father. In the midst of our separation due to the pandemic, we were becoming close. Surprisingly to me, however, the deepening of our connection, the mirroring I was providing that led to greater affect regulation was all happening online!

When our work had begun, a little over a year before this phone call, I felt as though Leo related to his smart phone as an extension of his own body, seeming to prefer the comfort it would offer to any comfort from me. Prior to this moment, Leo used his phone to soothe himself; he managed his fears of intimacy, in part by agoraphobic behavior, but also by substituting technology for human contact. Something in our relationship had shifted, however. Perhaps, I thought, relieved and validated at the same time, technology is not enough. Relationships—embodied, messy, with the potential to hurt and burden but also with the potential to soothe and comfort—were necessary after all. Leo was getting to that.

The revelation of a family secret brought all of these dynamics to the fore and brought to light a significant source of Leo's anxiety. During the pandemic, Leo's father, who suffered from depression, became increasingly depressed and took to his bed. In his typically parentified role, Leo began researching (online) for a therapist for his dad. He tried repeatedly to get his dad to agree to start online therapy and, at one point, even contacted a therapist and made his father an appointment! His father refused. One night, after his father hadn't left his bed in over a week, Leo and his mother threatened to call 9–1–1. At that point, Leo's father confessed that he had been having an affair with another woman for several years and that he was struggling with their separation due to the pandemic. He was, he said, terribly guilty and sorry.

Enraged and frightened, through tears, Leo reported this to me in our next session. He wished and feared that his father would move out. While Leo had not consciously known of his father's infidelity, he did, after all, know (Bowlby, 1979). This was not the secret that Leo consciously held from me but rather an unthought known (Bollas, 1987) that left him anxious and upset without knowing why. Once we could think about it together, its hold on Leo's emotional state was loosened. The process of mentalizing what was now known, of being able to reflect and consider how it had affected things over a period of years, provided relief from anxiety. Together, as Leo and I talked and talked about the range of feelings—from anger, despair, betrayal, hurt, and even relief to know—we were co-regulating Leo's affect. While he still turned to technology at times, to a yoga or meditation app or to go through his calendar and organize his day, Leo began increasingly to use his time with me to manage and tolerate feelings he was now able to recognize and own. As with Deborah, I found myself surprised by the extent to which our relationship could function so effectively through cyberspace. At the same time, work with Leo demonstrated the need for true human connection and concern, qualities that an app could not provide.

Conclusions

The intersection of technology with the human challenges of being in relationships while feeling separate characterizes the tensions inherent in the two case vignettes offered here. Our human need for attachment and connection, increasingly understood as stemming from the intersection of neurobiology and psychology, is, it seems, both facilitated and hindered by our growing use of technology to communicate and connect.

Deborah's use of the therapeutic alliance with me served as a necessary attachment that facilitated emotional regulation. One could interpret the expression of her need as a wish for reattachment through a leash, or umbilical cord, and it could be seen as regressive—a wish to return to the womb. However, Bowlby (1988) and modern attachment theorists Fonagy et al. (2004) and Hill (2015) remind us that it is a mistake to assume that our needs for attachment are regressive. Rooted in our neurobiology (Schore, 2011, 2014), they are lifelong and form the basis for our capacity to regulate—a function that, although we increasingly do autonomously, requires relationships throughout life. Deborah's use of technology was likewise complicated. Social media allowed her to titrate intimate relationships, manage connections with friends and family far away, and continue in therapy during a pandemic. Social media also resulted in deeply shaming experiences that threatened her sense of self-worth.

Seduced by the idea that his phone could offer him connections that terrified him but that he craved, Leo compulsively sought apps to organize his experience and decrease the felt threat of in-person engagement. Indeed, he attended his online appointments with me more regularly, and our work deepened. At the same time, however, Leo's experience, always felt less than what he craved, and the phone provided an inadequate compromise for Leo. In the end, the phone apps failed to contain his anxiety as well. As our connection deepened, even as it was conducted online, Leo turned to his attachment with me for emotional regulation. Phone apps alone had failed him.

Of course, human connections have been aided by technology since the advent of writing. However, with the introduction of digital media, the speed and nature of technologically mediated communication has changed dramatically. Technology has facilitated communication and allowed relationships, including therapeutic ones, to be sustained and even developed through a pandemic that necessitated quarantine. People are able to be in communication and connection with loved ones who are not physically present. However, as Bollas (2018) observes, the omnipresence of devices that connect us with virtual others are, in the end, diluting the relationships we have with actual others.

In preparing my thoughts to write this chapter, my dream functioned as a kind of reverie (Levine, 2012; Civitarese, 2013) that facilitated the representation of my thoughts about my patients' and my own challenges to stay connected while feeling free. The dream material came to me in a pre-technology form; the experience with Molly, my dog, was embodied and steeped in physicality. I climbed onto a dumpster, attempted to heft heavy blankets, never found the leash, and ended up walking side by side, together but untethered. If the leash could be seen as an umbilical cord between Molly and me, it had been cut, and yet, our attachment remained strong and functional as Molly did not run away.

Is it the case that an embodied experience of physical presence is necessary for the development of an attachment that offers sustained, contained, and regulated affect? My dreaming self seems to say yes. However, work with Deborah and Leo suggests that perhaps the answer is yes and no. On the one hand, conducting online therapy during the pandemic taught me that Novick (2020) was, in many ways, correct that psychoanalytic processes such as transference, countertransference, projective identification, and unconscious communication can transpire through cyberspace. And yet, at the same time, when I consider the therapeutic work done through video conference, I am left with a vague sense of loss and disappointment that seems to reflect the absence of embodied connection and which leads, at times, to profound experiences of loneliness. The physical presence of a caregiver in an infant's life is necessary for the initial development of a secure attachment for sure; as we grow increasingly autonomous, however, our attachment system continues to rest on a neurobiological substrate. In the end, person-to-person unconscious communication must be weakened and thinned out when we are not in person together. The intensity of our connections is inevitably diluted by the microintrusions caused by checking in with a virtual other. Needs for connection and autonomy exist in tension.

At times, connection can feel overwhelming and stifling; other times, autonomy is fraught with anxiety and loneliness. Finding the right balance is key to managing life's challenges with emotional equilibrium intact.

Close Reading Questions:

1. Identify two quotes that illustrate Winograd's ambivalence and conflicted feelings about the use of technology in psychotherapy? What are your feelings about technology and psychotherapy?
2. What can you conclude about Winograd's assumptions about the curative factors in psychotherapy from the following quotes about attachment, relationship, and mentalization?

   • "My feeling when I was with Deborah . . . was that I was wrapping a blanket around her to hold her together."
   • "And while we never outgrow the need for others, as we are social beings who co-regulate emotions (Beebe & Lachmann, 2003; Fonagy et al., 2004; Hill, 2015), it was our work together in regulating Deborah's emotional states that allowed her, incrementally and over time, to use our relationship to build the ego strength needed to regulate her own emotions, even in times of stress."
   • "Mentalization, or reflective function, requires slowing down and providing the space to think about our wishes, intentions, hopes, fears—in short, the contents of our minds. Psychotherapy provides that space."

Prompts for Writing:

1. Using attachment theory as it is explicated in Winograd's work, write about your work with a patient. What is the nature of the attachment between you and your patient? How do you understand its role in helping your patient?
2. Winograd's work with Leo involves keeping and revealing secrets. Write about the role of a secret in your own life or in your work with a patient.
3. Develop your own theory of attachment as affected by telehealth and teleconferencing. Reflect on your ability to truly engage with and trust others through the screen.

References

Ainsworth, M. D., Blehar, M. C., Water, E., & Wall, S. (1978). *Patterns of attachment; assessed in the strange situation and at home.* Hillsdale, NJ: Lawrence Erlbaum.

Bailey, B. (2015). The impact of electronic media and communication on object relations. In J. S. Scharff (Ed.), *Psychoanalysis online 2: Impact of technology on development, training, and therapy* (pp. 15–28). New York: Routledge.

Bakalar, N. L. (2015). A baby saved: A mother made. In J. S. Scharff (Ed.), *Psychoanalysis online 2: Impact of technology on development, training, and therapy* (pp. 195–208). New York: Routledge.

Beebe, B., & Lachmann, F. M. (1994). Representation and internalization in infancy: Three principles of salience. *Psychoanalytic Psychology, 11,* 127–165.

Beebe, B., & Lachmann, F. M. (2003). The relational turn in psychoanalysis: A dyadic systems view from infant research. *Contemporary Psychoanalysis, 39,* 379–409.

Bollas, C. (1987). *Shadow of the object: Psychoanalysis of the unthought known.* New York: Columbia University Press.

Bollas, C. (2018). *Meaning and melancholia: Life in the age of bewilderment.* New York: Routledge.

Boulanger, G. (2013). Fearful symmetry: Shared trauma in New Orleans after hurricane Katrina. *Psychoanalytic Dialogues, 3*(1), 31–44.

Bowlby, J. (1979). On knowing what you are not supposed to know and feeling what you are not supposed to feel. *Canadian Journal of Psychiatry, 24*(5), 403–408.

Bowlby, J. (1988). *A secure base.* London: Routledge.

Bromberg, P. M. (1998). *Standing in the spaces; Essays on clinical process, trauma, and dissociation.* Hillsdale, NJ: The Analytic Press.

Civitarese, G. (2013). The inaccessible unconscious and reverie as a path of figurability. In H. B. Levine, G. S. Reed, & D. Scarfone (Eds.) *Unrepresented states and the construction of meaning: Clinical and theoretical contributions* (pp. 220–239). London: The International Psychoanalytic Association.

de Setton, L. S. (2015). Is there a difference between telephone and in-person sessions? In J. S. Scharff (Ed.), *Psychoanalysis online 2: Impact of technology on development, training, and therapy* (pp. 173–184). New York: Routledge.

Fairbairn, W. D. (1986a). A revised psychopathology of the psychoses and psychoneuroses. In P. Buckley (Ed.), *Essential papers on object relations* (pp. 71–101). New York: New York University Press.

Fairbairn, W. D. (1986b). The repression and the return of bad objects (with special reference to the "war neuroses"). In P. Buckley (Ed.), *Essential papers on object relations* (pp. 102–126). New York: New York University Press.

Fonagy, P., Gergely, G., Jurist, E., & Target, M. (2004). *Affect regulation, mentalization, and the development of the self.* New York: Other Press.

Ginot, E. (2009). The empathic power of enactments; the link between neuropsychological processes and an expanded definition of empathy. *Psychoanalytic Psychology, 26*(3), 290–309.

Hill, D. H. (2015). *Affect regulation theory: A clinical model.* New York: W. W. Norton & Company, Inc.

King, V. (2016). "If you show your real face, you'll lose 10 000 followers"—the gaze of the other and transformations of shame in digitalized relationships. *Communication and Media, XI*(38), 71–90.

Levine, H. B. (2012). The colourless canvas: Representation, therapeutic action and the creation of mind. *The International Journal of Psychoanalysis, 93*(3), 607–629.

MacRury, I., & Yates, C. (2016). Framing the mobile phone: The psychopathologies of an everyday object. *Communication and Media, XI*(38), 41–70.

Murphy, K. (2020, April 29). Why zoom is terrible: There's a reason video apps make you feel awkward and unfulfilled. *New York Times.* Retrieved from www.nytimes.com/2020/04/29/sunday-review/zoom-video-conference.html?referringSource=articleShare

Novick, J. (2020, April 1). *Case presentation with an adolescent.* Best Practices in Distance Analytic Treatment for Continuity with Children and Adolescents: An Emergency Response Mini-Course in Technology and Ethics During the Novel Corona Virus (COVID-19) Pandemic. Zoom Course. Bethesda, MD: International Psychotherapy Institute.

Ogden, T. H. (1992). *The matrix of the mind: Object relations and the psychoanalytic dialogue.* London: Karnac Books.

Scharff, D. (2015a). Occasional telephone sessions in ongoing in-person psychoanalysis. In J. S. Scharff (Ed.), *Psychoanalysis online 2: Impact of technology on development, training, and therapy* (pp. 163–172). New York: Routledge.

Scharff, D. (2015b). Teaching psychoanalytic psychotherapy and infant observation by video link. In J. S. Scharff (Ed.), *Psychoanalysis online 2: Impact of technology on development, training, and therapy* (pp. 133–144). New York: Routledge.

Schore, A. N. (2011). The right brain implicit self lies at the core of psychoanalysis. *Psychoanalytic Dialogues, 21*(1), 75–100.

Schore, A. N. (2014). The right brain is dominant in psychotherapy. *Psychotherapy, 51*(3), 388–397.

Sehon, C. M. (2015). Teleanalysis and teletherapy for children and adolescents? In J. S. Scharff (Ed.), *Psychoanalysis online 2: Impact of technology on development, training, and therapy* (pp. 209–232). New York: Routledge.

Trevarthan, C., & Aitlen, K. J. (2001). Infant intersubjectivity: Research, theory and clinical applications. *Journal of Child Psychology and Psychiatry, 42*, 3–48.

Tronick, E., & Reck, C. (2009). Infants of depressed mothers. *Harvard Review of Psychiatry, 17*(2), 147–156.

Turkle, S. (2011). *Alone together: Why we expect more from technology and less from each other.* New York: Basic Books.

Turkle, S. (2015). *Reclaiming the conversation: The power of talk in a digital age.* New York: Penguin Books.

Verhaeghe, P. (2015). On the new discontents of civilisation. *Journal of the Centre for Freudian Analysis and Research, 26*, 70–89.

Wanlass, J. (2015). *The use of technology in clinical supervision and consultation.* London: Karnac.

Winnicott, D. W. (1958). The capacity to be alone. *The International Journal of Psychoanalysis, 39*, 416–420.

Winnicott, D. W. (1963a). The development of the capacity for concern. *Bulletin of the Menninger Clinic, 27*, 167–176.

Winnicott, D. W. (1963b). From dependence towards independence in the development of the individual. In D. W. Winnicott (Ed.), *The maturational processes and the facilitating environment* (pp. 83–92). New York: International Universities Press.

Winnicott, D. W. (1965). *The maturational processes and the facilitating environment.* New York: International Universities Press, Inc.

Winnicott, D. W. (1971). *Playing and reality.* London: Tavistock Publications.

6   The Disembodied Self and the Future of Psychotherapy

Michael Jarrette-Kenny

Pre-reading Questions:

1. How has your relationship with technology impacted your relationships and informed your attachment experiences with those closest to you? How has it impacted your relationships with strangers?
2. How has technology impacted your ability to focus and attend to your environment? Do you ever feel like you are not part of reality?
3. How does your online persona differ from your conception of offline self? Do you feel that boundary between your online self-blurring? Or do you sense more of a chasm between online and offline realities? Which one is "more real"? How much time do you spend in one world versus the other?

"Just let me show you one last thing."

Before I can respond to her, the phone is out, and I am left as a spectator in the therapy session. My patient sits enraptured like a child opening presents on the couch before me, the faint glow of the smartphone's luminescence encircling her dazed and expectant face. Despite my protests, she starts scrolling through her meticulously choreographed, online life: the romantic interests, the likes, and the unfriended hecklers whom she cyberstalks with feigned disinterest through the Instagram accounts of acquaintances. There is even a soundtrack as she plays the songs that she sends back and forth flirtatiously, the lyrics pregnant with all of the implications of her undeclared longings. All the while, it is not the content, but the tool that dominates the exchange, a not so silent partner in the transactions between patient and therapist.

As for myself, despite my misgivings about her phone, there is the lurking presence in the back of my own mind; the unanswered emails awaiting me between sessions, the strange phantom vibration of the smart phone in my coat pocket, ignored but somehow demanding a response. These interlopers have invaded the therapeutic experience for good or ill as text messages and videos testify against our children and spouses, ambiguously urging us into

DOI: 10.4324/9781003270225-6

confrontations with strangers or into misunderstandings with well-meaning loved ones. They judge and criticize us anonymously as we go about our quotidian tasks, an invisible audience which may know us better than we know ourselves, tracking our shopping preferences and heart rates, even the frequency of our footsteps and sleep cycles.

Many therapists I know have watched this process unfold with a mixture of uneasiness and helplessness, taking their cue from theatrical performances, announcing before the session that all devices must be switched off. A small few have embraced it as an opportunity, while others have continued to ignore the presence of the technological third party.

This chapter concerns the current and future impact of technology on psychotherapy and the experience of selfhood. Recent events have moved the practice of psychotherapy toward a model of disembodied interaction; that is engagement with a clinician via text messages, audio and video messaging. Apps such as Talkspace and Betterhelp have become popular alternatives to traditional psychotherapy based on factors such as reduced cost and accessibility. Despite their popularity, these services have been far removed from the mainstream of mental health treatment, relegating teletherapy to a small corner of the psychotherapy world. These alternative services began to develop prior to the 2020 global pandemic alongside the loosening of existing restrictions on the use of telehealth for providers in all mental health settings, thus initiating a nationwide experiment in the provision of these services to the general public. As social distancing and shelter in place restrictions were enacted across the United States, these services emerged as the only option available, prompting the question of how these methods relate to the more traditional modes of in-person psychotherapy. Clearly, as these developments have demonstrated, it has become important for social workers and therapists to adapt to and be responsive to this radical restructuring of the field. More than this, it forces us to question the impact of the medium of technology upon the central message of the psychotherapeutic endeavor.

Our experiences of self and others are increasingly mediated by the world of screens, a place which has promised a freedom from the constraints and inhibitions of the body. But has the use of technology to address issues related to this disembodiment merely reinforced the very problems that it attempts to redress?

Your Brain on the Internet

Nicholas Carr, author of *The Shallows: What the Internet is doing to our brains* (2020), notes the effects of internet technology on the experience of conducting research, particularly in regard to focus and concentration. Citing Mary Anne Wolf, author of *Proust and the Squid* (2010), he addresses how the way we read and gather information online has impacted our ability to concentrate and has rewired our brains. He places this in a historical context citing Socrates' lament of how writing would impact our ability to remember things and the effects of the typewriter on the philosopher Friedrich Neitzsche's style and later works, while discussing the other unforeseen benefits that have arisen from various technological developments.

The obvious truth that Carr elucidates, whether citing the effects of timepieces and cartography on our experience of space and time, or search engines and word processors on writers and readers, is that the tools we utilize shape and mediate our experience of the world. While I might lament these developments, and in my reading habits prefer print media to the screen, at this point, my preferences feel obsolete.

I can already see the impact of technology on my younger colleagues and patients, not simply in terms of how we interpret information but in our social interactions and communication skills. Research by Horvath et al. (2020) suggest that there is "preliminary evidence suggesting addiction-related differences in neural processes in the context of smartphone use," results which question "the harmlessness of smartphones, at least in individuals that may be at increased risk for developing addictive behaviors" (p. 6).

Of course, these effects are not limited to the manner in which we read and write. Just as cistercian monks' rigid adherence to prayer times may have inadvertently lead to the development of wrist watches and our current slavery to clocks and efficiency, in a similarly circumstantial way, the smartphone and computer may have stumbled in and upended the therapy couch.

M.I.T. professor Sherry Turkle, an early advocate of technology who in recent years has become one of its staunchest critics, has authored a series of books addressing the impact of technology on our social functioning. In an interview, she recounted a conversation with Sara Konrath, a researcher who upon noting the decline in empathy scores among college students, set about designing an empathy app.

> In this, Konrath followed a common impulse—if technology got us into a problem, technology will get us out of it. We're all tempted by this idea. But I believe it's a myth that takes us away from the obvious—we are the empathy app! This simple truth should place the practitioners of empathic listening, of quiet space and self-reflection, at the center of today's most important cultural conversations. But I see too many therapists held back by a crisis of confidence about their core beliefs in the power of words and relationships.
>
> (Turkle, 2016a November–December,)

This power of words and relationships for which Turkle advocates intrinsically involves the unmediated presence of the human, not simply what is said but the things not said, the silent engagement of another attentive being, responsive, occasionally at odds with us, misunderstood and potentially misunderstanding, but willing to repair misattunement and ruptures in the connection.

Konrath, the researcher Turkle mentions, has since extended her inquiries beyond empathy to other areas of interpersonal functioning, noting similar changes in levels of narcissism and in adult attachment style. While not all of these changes can be attributed to technology, they happen to coincide with the increasing popularity of social media.

> The emergence of these forums in the late 1990s coincides with the rise in Dismissing attachment styles among American college students, and the innovations in social networking soon thereafter may have accelerated these changes throughout the 2000s.
>
> (Konrath, Chopik, Hsing, & O'Brien, 2014, p. 13)

More specifically, in relation to social media, higher levels of use "were associated with poorer sleep quality, lower self-esteem and increased anxiety and depression" (Woods & Scott, 2016, p. 19). Similarly, a study conducted by the University of Pennsylvania randomly assigning undergraduates to limit access to social media (Facebook, Instagram and Snapchat) "showed significant reductions in loneliness and depression over three weeks compared to the control group" (Hunt, Marx, Lipson, & Young, 2018, p. 751). Increasingly, despite the unprecedented connectivity we have established between our online selves, our actual lives have become lonelier and more isolated.

This fact has become increasingly evident to me in my work with people who have suffered from traumatic early life experiences, particularly at the hands of abusive or neglectful caretakers. How does the experience of traumatic attachment affect changes in the emotional state of internet and smartphone users? Is therapy diminished by the digital world, that is, through video and text? These questions will be explored through a discussion of three composite cases where problematic attachment patterns and trauma histories have converged with technology in unexpected, complicated ways. In addition, I will use first person accounts from practitioners and clients of app-based therapy services culled from a variety of online sources, examined through the lens of modern attachment theory and phenomenological psychopathology.

From the Disembodied Self to the False Self

The phenomena of disembodiment, "the transcendence of body constraints in cyberspace" (Kang, 2007, p. 475), presents a number of issues in regard to individuals who suffer from mental health issues. Recent neuroscience challenges the previously dominant cognitive paradigm which has relied upon the metaphor of computer information processing in understanding the ways in which human beings think and navigate the world (Wilson, 2002). In particular, the embodied basis of emotions in the development of consciousness as elucidated by neuroscientist Antonio Damasio (1999) suggests a mechanism by which our internal representations arise from bodily sensation and in turn become an object to themselves. Damasio notes:

> As the representations of the body grow in complexity and coordination, they come to constitute an integrated representation of the organism, a proto-self. Once that happens, it becomes possible to engender representations of the proto-self as it is affected by interactions with a given environment. It is only then that consciousness begins, only thereafter that an organism that is responding beautifully to its environment begins to discover that it is responding beautifully to its environment.
>
> (p. 284)

The body then is the foundation of our experience of consciousness, a "map" of one's engagement with the world which then becomes an object of reflection. If this is the case, then in a very real sense our ability to think and navigate the world is based on this foundation of bodily experience. According to his somatic marker hypothesis, this bodily experience (fluctuations in heartbeat, muscle tone, etc.) function as the foundation of emotional responses which in turn guide us in our ability to make choices among competing alternatives. Damasio's case studies of individuals whose brain injuries impair their ability to feel illustrate that in the absence of emotion, we are unable to manage even the simplest task without becoming paralyzed with indecision.

Now that we have established the relevance of the body to our mental functioning, where exactly is the body when we are online, and what are the implications for our engagement with the world when it is left behind?

Psychiatrist Thomas Fuchs (2014) utilizes the case of mental disorders in order to challenge cognitive explanations of interpersonal development (namely the means by which we develop a conception of others having minds like our own). He suggests that prevailing theories of autism and schizophrenia are based on theories of mind which stress the failure of mentalizing, that is, the nature of the dysfunction is conceptual (a purely cognitive account based on faulty capacity for reading other minds), whereas the phenomenological account focuses on the embodied nature of mind and the notion of these disorders arising from more fundamental disturbances in embodied interpersonal functioning. This disturbance in intersubjectivity occurs on various levels (primary—imitation of others by the infant and patterns of interaction on an implicit level including affective attunement, secondary—where the individual begins to develop a conception of others as intentional agents, and tertiary—the ability to flexibly alternate between perspectives of ourselves and others as mental agents) with consequences ranging from failures in interpreting social cues or as seen in psychotic states, profound confusions of self and other (what Fuchs' refers to as transivitism). He notes that individuals with these disorders often attempt to compensate through a process of over mentalizing, suggesting that the notion of defective cognitive modules contradict the actual compensatory efforts of high functioning individuals (such as the case of Temple Grandin) who suffer from those disorders.

In a separate paper, he further extends the individual's embodied experience to their ways of living/being with others and the surrounding environment. He traces back this idea of lived space to Kurt Lewin's topological "field psychology," a concept later revived in ecological models of understanding the mind (a conception close to social work's person in environment ethos). Lived space is conceived of as "the totality of the space that a person pre-reflectively 'lives' and experiences, with its situations, conditions, movements, effects and its horizon of possibilities—meaning the environment and sphere of action of a bodily subject" (Fuchs, 2007, p. 426). One's lived space is seen as dynamic and shifting, particularly in interactions with others. This notion essentially states that the person is not a dualist product of mind and body, but a dynamic system that does not exist as separate from the world but as integrally related to it. "Who am I? is inseparable from the question, 'What is the world like in which I live?'" (pp. 427–428). Individual psychopathology in this view is regarded as "a narrowing or deformation" of lived space. But what exactly is the lived space of cyberspace? How does the nonspace of the digital realm (or to put it another way, the simulation and text-based experience of screentime) and the interpersonal dynamics within these environments act to constrict or impoverish an already curtailed horizon of possibility? Certainly in some sense, the very premise of information technology is on expansion. Freed from the strictures of geography, we are able to join and connect with people across the planet. Yet in another sense, we aren't going anywhere. How does the physical/spatial dimensions of social media affect its inhabitants? Perhaps by removing people from environments that reinforce pathology, we force them to relate to the world in a different, more adaptive fashion. An individual whose physical environment is impoverished can gain instant access to a nearly infinite library of information and knowledge. A lonely or physically disabled person can instantly speak or communicate with an understanding therapist or commiserate with a group of like-minded friends. By the same token, if the lived space continues or reinforces the previous dysfunctional pattern, or if they are returned to the same conditions that produced illness, then we should expect the pathological situation to continue or worsen. In the following cases, I will explore the ways in which this lived space intersects with complex trauma and disorganized attachment.

Kathy

I don't know what is wrong with me? When he doesn't respond, I just start to lose it. Kathy, a recently divorced nurse, spent most of her off time obsessing about the various romantic interests she has cultivated through her nearly constant presence on social media and dating sites. Intensely focused on winning over her potential partner, her warm and responsive demeanor drew in many interested, eligible suitors. However, as time progressed, these promising beginnings would invariably disintegrate, the involved parties declining in status from idealized "soulmates" to "narcissistic assholes" within a span of a few weeks, sometimes within a matter of minutes. Often during her therapy session, these vitriolic outbursts against the offending male would culminate in a monologue devoted to her feelings of self-loathing. These sessions would often end with a tearful demand for me to "be honest" and answer definitively the question lingering behind this vicious cycle;

Is it me? It has to be me. This keeps happening to me wherever I go. So it must be me doing it.

When she had first come for therapy, she was in the process of ending her marriage to a man she had met in college. Her husband had been pressuring her to attempt to have a child, though due to a medical condition, conception would have been difficult if not impossible. In any case, such attempts seemed ill advised given the state of her marriage and her husband's abusive nature. Many of our early sessions had centered on domestic violence and codependency issues. Despite the abundant evidence of her husband's abusive tendencies, she was dumbfounded by his uncaring attitude and general mistreatment of her since their marriage three years earlier. Everyday she would wake up into a world of imagined sweetness and light, only to have this idyllic vision brutally dispelled by the grim reality of the person she was actually living with. This injustice seemed particularly egregious when compared to the rarified universe in which her Facebook friends resided.

Everybody else seems to be living these perfect lives. I keep trying to keep up. I don't understand; what's wrong with me?

As a result of this sense of inadequacy, she carefully staged and produced an almost unrecognizable public version of her life on Instagram and Facebook, curating this sanitized version, leaving out the hours of despair, the weekends spent lying in bed or obsessively scrolling through her "friends" similarly imaginary lives. In person, she had to bring the pictures to life, spending most of her money on designer clothes and other props such that she was in serious financial trouble. All of these aspects of her real life were hidden well behind what she referred to as "her mask," the sunny smile she used to conceal her true feelings.

While this experience of falsity had existed in Kathy prior to any significant involvement in the online world, her experiences on Facebook had greatly complicated and amplified these preexistent tendencies.

Gil-Or, O., Levi-Belz, Y., and Turel, O. (2015) discuss this relationship between online self-presentation through the lens of Winnicott's concept of the false self, noting that

> the false Facebook-self is driven, in part, by shortcomings in one's personality, which may relate to his or her upbringing and the consequent social traits he or she has developed. Specifically, false Facebook-self is

enhanced when self-esteem and general authenticity are low, and these traits tend to be lower among individuals with avoidant and anxious attachment styles.

(p. 8)

From the outset of her treatment, it was clear that her masochistic engagement with violent, abusive partners, and deep feelings of defectiveness were related to the abandonment she suffered as a result of her parents' drug abuse and mental health problems. Deeply ashamed of the chaos she was experiencing at home, she learned to disguise her true emotions.

I've always had to pretend: people would always be asking me what was wrong when I was a kid . . . almost like they could see everything that was happening on my face. So I learned to fake it. You just keep smiling even if all you really want to do is scream and cry.

★

She had come to therapy with great reluctance, a sense that it was somehow an admission of failure, that she had become like her parents before her, dysfunctional. Therapy was for people who were too weak to deal with their problems on their own.

I've always dealt with things myself. She looked up briefly and turned to stare out the window at the wooded area behind the parking lot. A moment later a chime emitted from her phone brought her back to it.

You can't trust people, she added in a matter-of-fact tone, still scrolling down the page.

I asked her how she had come to feel that way, asking her gently to put the phone down for a moment. She sighed and set it down on the arm of the couch with the screen facing up, her hand absentmindedly caressing the surface as she closed her eyes again and began to speak.

I don't know, I guess it's always been like that. When I was a kid my parents were always fighting in front of us, me and my little brother. Mom was always too messed up to take care of him, so I would make him dinner and help him get ready for school in the morning. The worst would be when my Dad got home and saw that she hadn't done anything but sleep all day. The day he left, he was beating her up so badly, I thought he was going to kill her. I got in between them and started calling him names and hitting him. I mean, I might as well have been a mosquito. He turned around

She paused as if feeling the blow heading toward her again, pursuing her into the present.

And he hit me so hard in the face that I flew across the room. This huge 200 pound man hit a 12-year-old girl like that, like he was hitting a grown ass man. That's what I can remember. I feel like he must have given me brain damage or something. My brother talks about when we were kids, and I feel like I wasn't even there.

Her voice trailed off into a whisper. Later she described these moments, hearing the words and wondering at her distance from them, experiences as remote as something she saw on T.V. a decade earlier. She swallowed hard and looked down at the ground, talking more to herself than to me.

Anyway, if you can't trust your own parents, who can you trust?

Soon after the incident she had described, she was removed from their custody and along with her younger brother, began living with their grandmother. While this arrangement provided a more secure environment than her parent's home, her grandmother was emotionally remote if not overtly abusive. A strict catholic, she inculcated in her granddaughter a sense of guilt regarding her sexuality and fear of divine retribution for her "sinful nature." (This fear of damnation remained a potent trigger for her current anxieties, particularly in relation to her marital indiscretions, her panic symptoms being perceived on some level as a punishment from God.) As a teenager she began to experience the beginnings of her mental health issues, attempting to regulate her anxiety and depression through a variety of self-damaging/parasuicidal behaviors (cutting, bulimia). Perpetually locked in her room for hours for minor transgressions, she would spend hours in a trance-like reverie, dreaming of an ideal world beyond the prison of her bedroom, a harbinger of her experiences to come. Despite these setbacks, she was able to find solace in school and excelled academically, graduating from a university and taking a job in N.J. (far from the rural mid-western community in which she had been raised) soon after passing her nursing licensing exams. Her religious faith and her need to care for her younger brother were identified as the major reasons she had not, despite persistent feelings of hopelessness, acted on her suicidal impulses.

In response to the lack of emotional connection in her home life, she began a series of extramarital affairs, first with a doctor that she worked for, then branching out to random men from dating sites. Her marriage eventually came to an end as a result of the infidelities. Following the divorce, her online dating life became more chaotic, moving from anonymous "Tinder hookups" to various websites geared toward the fetish/BDSM community. Her interest began to escalate beyond mere curiosity to the point where she began meeting men through the site, resulting in several incidents where she was raped and nearly killed. She hesitated to call the situations rape, though it seemed clear from her description that the result of the interaction went far beyond the parameters of the consensual.

I can't really say whether it was or wasn't. I mean, the lines are so blurred.

Disconnected Selves

A persistent theme in these early sessions with Kathy was a sense of feeling stuck in a recurrent pattern of behavior, of wanting desperately to be loved and cared for, yet choosing relationships in which this hope was impossible to realize. The dysfunctional relationship is predictable if unfulfilling, while a healthier relationship is felt to be frightening, evoking intense anxiety at the thought of rejection or abandonment. On another level, it may illustrate the fundamental situation of a child who cannot exist independently and must rely on whatever semblance of parental authority is available to them. As Blizard (1997) notes, "When a child is dependent on a parent or care-taker who is abusive, the child is confronted with a terrible dilemma. How can the child maintain attachment to a person who is necessary for survival but also threatens the child's psychic and bodily integrity?" (p. 1). By attaching either to unavailable married men or to the idealized fantasy figures she met online and with whom she communicated almost exclusively through text, the delicate balance of closeness and distance could be maintained, at least for a time.

Another factor which asserted itself fairly early in the treatment process was the experience of dissociation, most prominently in reference to the indistinct memories of her violent childhood. Dissociation can be defined as "An experienced loss of information or control over mental processes that, under normal circumstances, are available to conscious awareness, self-attribution, or control, in relation to the individual's age and cognitive development" (Cardeña & Carlson, 2011, p. 251). A distinction can be made between ordinary dissociative processes (such as reading a book or being absorbed in a movie) that are common among the general population and pathological dissociation, which involves a more fundamental and pervasive disruption in consciousness and experience. This type of dissociation, more common among victims of trauma, "entails a division of an individual's personality, that is, of the dynamic, biopsychosocial system as a whole that determines his or her characteristic mental and behavioral actions" (Nijenhuis & Van der Hart, 2011, p. 418). Reviews of the literature of the past 25 years indicate that dissociation is highly related to traumatic experience and the development of post-traumatic stress disorder (Carlson, Dalenberg, & Mcdade-Montez, 2012, p. 487).

Beyond the issue of trauma-related dissociation is the relationship between dissociation, attachment style, and problematic internet use. Craparo (2011) notes that "Significant correlations exist between IUAD (Internet Use, Abuse, Dependence.), alexithymia, and dissociation" (p. 1051). In the same article, he speculates that "Internet addiction could represent a psychic retreat necessary to modulate the painful emotions in a subject with an insecure attachment" (p. 1056). In effect, the addictive, obsessive behavior represents an adaptation or coping mechanism for the survivor of abuse, an attempt to self soothe in the absence of the responsive, validating presence of another human being. The detachment of the online world mirrors the devil's bargain children of abusive caretakers must make to simultaneously attach and not attach. Further, in the absence this intersubjective context (the validating other), the meaning of these internal emotional experiences remains ambiguous and confusing.

Alexithymia or "lacking words for emotions" is "associated with difficulties in identifying, analyzing and verbalizing feelings, constricted imagination, and a concrete, externally oriented way of thinking" (Mei, Xu, Gao,

Ren, & Li, 2018, p. 1). In the context of internet use, we can return back to our earlier discussion of Damasio's somatic markers. Human beings develop their capacities for trusting their emotional responses from validating interactions with significant caretakers. In the absence of these relationships, the individual lacks awareness of these emotional guideposts that allow us to interact with our environment and with others in a meaningful way. The trance-like engagement with screens might act in concert with Kathy's other dissociative symptoms, her confusion of fantasy with reality, feelings of depersonalization and emotional disconnection.

The culmination of these violent interactions with online predators provided the return to the body in the same manner as her earlier self-injurious behaviors had, embodied in the experience of pain, a flesh and blood human being instead of being a depersonalized ghost. Soon afterward, the feeling of bodily engagement would give way to one of self-disgust. The fantasy engagement with an idealized other existing in the nonspace of web pages and text messages must inevitably be supplanted by the embodied and disappointing reality of the brutal sadist in a cheap hotel room.

Ron

Ron continues to palm his smartphone throughout the session staring at the last text message suspended in anticipation, waiting for the response. Beside the words is the time stamp, expanding from "now" into minutes and hours, reminding him how long ago the message arrived, traveling invisibly through space to sting its eager target. He disengages and goes back to whatever it was he was doing (in this case talking about his perfectionism), conscious of the device resting beneath his hand, waiting for the comforting buzz or the chirping cartoon noise that signals the arrival of the weightless cargo that will free him from the mounting tension in his chest, the message from his loved one (in this case his wife) or from work (his boss whose resemblance to his cold, absentee father can cause panic symptoms at the least signal of displeasure). At other moments, it's a thumbs up or liking of his latest post, the symbolic stroke from the all-powerful mother that symbolizes that he will be ok. The scene evokes the Still-Face Paradigm introduced by Tronick, Als, Adamson, Wise, and Brazelton (1978), the mother attentive and engaged suddenly deadpan and unresponsive, while the child escalates from panic to disengagement. It is no wonder that high scores on the adverse childhood experience scale (ACES) predict significant increase in one's risk of later addiction: "Each of the 10 categories of ACES was associated with a 2- to 4-fold increase in the likelihood of illicit drug use by age 14 and increased the risk of use into adulthood" (Dube et al., 2003, p. 567). More often than not, the surrogate mother is a candy bar or prescription pain killer. For Ron, this surrogate mother was his smartphone.

The birth of his first child coincided with a period of increasing difficulty in his fairly new marriage. As he began to be relegated to a secondary position in the relationship due to the demands of childcare, feelings of abandonment, and rejection from his own childhood began to surface. Working mostly from home, he often resorted to online activities to relieve stress, like winning and losing money on online poker tournaments and frequent visits to internet porn sites. I began to see him after a period of mania where his wife became aware of his frequent losses and his lack of interest in her sexually.

In a subsequent session, we explore the broader family dynamics underpinning his obsessive tendencies, his father's repeated admonitions to not upset his alcoholic mother and his mother's eventual death from a drug overdose. The disconnect from the parent is then in turn reinforced by a new dependency, on a surrogate mother made of silicon.

I'm diagnosed Bipolar, I don't know how many years ago, probably 15 now, but when I look back over my life umm. . . . I've been suffering from depression since I can remember. Definitely began having difficulties in sixth, seventh grade, in middle school, like middle school was a disaster.

I just didn't. . . . I just wasn't fitting in anymore. Having friends became very difficult, like I didn't. . . . It was almost like I didn't get kids my age, and it only got worse.

In response to his increasing sense of isolation, he spent most of his time in front of his playstation by himself, much to the chagrin of his parents, particularly his mentally ill mother.

The two people who have always been the biggest pain in the ass in my life have been my mother and my father and I think. . . . I think mostly about my mother, but the older that I get and things that went on with her and the way that she behaved and the way that she behaved towards me.

My mother was never diagnosed with anything but she was herself in therapy for years. She was very smart, very charming, very funny and the kind of person who, you know, she was probably more entertainment to her therapist than anything else. She would go in and would be very clever and be very, you know, smart about what was going on in her life. She should've been a comedian is probably really what she should have been, but unfortunately she had never found that path but was. . . . Knew enough to say all the right things that made her sound together and on top of it without ever actually getting to the bottom of anything.

It was chaotic, but not daily chaotic. Like when it was. . . . When everything was on good terms, it was fantastic. But, the slightest little thing that could go wrong . . . you know like. . . . It was very much an environment of control. And I guess as long as she felt that she was in control everything was fine, but the second that there was. . . . It was sort of like, as long as I was being a good little boy everything was great. I was the greatest kid who ever lived. I was respectful, oh you're so wonderful, you're smart and funny etc. But, the second . . . the second that I showed any measure of independence or, you know, an opinion that didn't go exactly the same, you know like. . . . The second I sort of stepped out into anything that would make me my own, like you know, individuate me in any way, that was when the hammer of control had to come back down.

In the aftermath of his mother's suicide, the matter of what could have been done to intervene in her lifelong trajectory remains unclear. The need for self-preservation when one's parent is unable to tolerate attachment appears to preclude the level of engagement necessary to provide assistance.

I'm not saying that a person like that can't change or that therapy can't whatever. I'm saying that you are not that person. (What) you need to do is to get the fuck away from them. Because, at least from my own experience even looking back, I don't know what I would've done, had I done it differently, that would've changed anything. Like I wasn't gonna sit down and be like "Mom, how have you been? Come on, talk." like. . . . She was what she was, and if anyone might have been able to help her, it definitely wasn't me, because I wasn't. . . . I was barely in a position to even help myself. Like what I had to do was get away from her. She was . . . she was rough. When I was a kid . . . a little kid, we still lived in P——, so I couldn't have been older than third grade, because that was when we moved. I was trying . . . she had this little plexiglass thing, it was like a cube, and it was sitting next to the refrigerator and I needed to get, I don't know what it was, probably a box of cereal or some shit that was on top of the refrigerator. So I stood on this thing trying to get it and it broke. And she fucking lost her shit, I mean lost her shit, to the point where she was like, "You break my stuff, you think can $%&$" whatever. She actually took my fucking teddy bear, Bosco, I still remember. . . . I can still see it, and fucking held a knife to his throat, said she was going to cut the head off the teddy bear. During another argument over her doing something equally as ridiculous and, this was a rare moment of, you know, looking through the eyeglass, or I should say, honesty on her part, where she said, "The reason that I did that to you was because I was trying to push you away, because I know you're better off without me." If I put the rest of my life through that filter, things start to make sense a little bit. Yeah, because there was a lot of that kind of you know, "You're the greatest boy on earth, you are so wonderful, you're this, you're that . . . to "You're so ungrateful, blah blah blah" you know like there were very many nights where, for no reason that I understood, she would suddenly be standing in the doorway of my bedroom, waking me up to just have 45 minute or hour long rant, just telling me "how terrible I was and how everybody says it, and she always defends me. But, you know, she thinks that obviously they're right." I mean, just ridiculous shit.

In Ron's case, it seems inevitable that growing up in this inconsistent environment of alternating praise and devaluation would result in the development of mental health issues.

For Ron, at least to some extent, attachment experiences with treatment providers allowed some healing of these parental ruptures to occur.

Right after my mom killed herself, I went to this woman—who was my mother's therapist for a little while, just cause I, you know, knew her. Well, I wanted to understand, but also it was like I needed to talk to somebody and . . . she was safe. I knew her, and it was also, she knew the whole family. . . . I could almost speak to her like I would to an aunt or a friend, and like I didn't have to do a lot of explaining, "well, this is family history and this is" My mother had been going to her for years. She knew my aunts and my grandmother, you know like. I didn't have to explain anything.

Emotional attunement between therapist and patient seems to be a critical component of effective care in crisis situations. Yet, it often appears that the implications of attachment are of secondary importance in the realm of technology.

Disembodied Psychotherapy

In March 2020, as the number of the COVID-19 infected began to escalate, the Center for Medicare Services lifted preexisting restrictions on telehealth and began my own and many other therapists initial forays into previously uncharted territories.

The experience brought forth to me in a personal way the risks and rewards of the body that to sit across from someone and share their space is to place oneself in a position of danger and vulnerability. In a situation where a cough could expose you to contagion and banishment to quarantine there is an engagement, an undisguised unveiling of one's motives and sincerity, expressions, and gestures which disclose our intentions and unconscious conflicts against our will. And perhaps erroneously, we feel this power to read another body, to determine through the tangled hieroglyphs of furrowed brow and entwined limbs the truth of another's inner life.

Poker players search for the tells which will give away their opponents deception, while politicians claim the privileged power of their gaze to look into the soul of the dictator across from them and determine whether they will honor their agreements. Nonetheless, therapy should not be about determining through the use of Paul Ekman's methodology the veracity of our patients accounts, but of our willingness to bear witness to them, to engage in the subtle dance of emotional resonance that begins in the presence of our parents attentive gaze.

The adult just as surely as the child needs the felt presence of another being. As Dreyfus (2008) notes in his discussion of telepresence and the phenomenological approach of Maurice Merleau Ponty, despite advances in technology, even the most sophisticated simulation of another person fails to capture the intercorporeal experience and the shared engagement with the surrounding world. Citing Harry Harlow's sadistic attachment studies of monkeys clinging desperately onto a cloth doll rather than go without a mother, one will do anything to return to engagement with another being. This vulnerable body must risk itself in the mirror of another, in the ambivalent gaze of a potential friend or foe in order to feel they truly exist. He states:

> Its ability to get a grip on things provides our sense of the reality of what we are doing and are ready to do; this, in turn, gives us a sense both of our power and of our vulnerability to the risky reality of the physical world. Furthermore, the body's ability to zero in on what is significant, and then preserve that understanding in our background

awareness, enables us to perceive more and more refined situations and respond more and more skillfully; its sensitivity to mood opens up our shared social situation and makes people and things matter to us; and its tendency to respond positively to direct engagement with other bodies; underlies our sense of trust and so sustains our interpersonal world.

(p. 70)

While Dreyfus's discussion of telepresence comes from his concerns as an educator, it is easy to see the relevance to the practice of psychotherapy. The notion that the body attunes itself to other bodies and to the risks and rewards of a shared environment brings us back to Damasio's notion of somatic markers and the role of our emotional selves in navigating our world and our relationships with other people.

A great deal of psychotherapy research seems to support the notion of the importance of relationship, beyond the numerous theoretical differences attending the various treatment modalities, suggesting that it is the common underlying mechanism which may account for the effectiveness of most successful treatment. The right brain to right brain dysregulation that occurs in ineffective parenting and which is the precursor to much traumatic experience may suggest a mechanism by which healing occurs in therapy, a collaboration between the right brain of the therapist and the right brain of the patient. Regulation theory suggests that "psychotherapy is not the talking but the communicating cure" (Schore & Schore, 2008, p. 14).

This connection between therapist and client, in essence a recapitulation of the parental bond, perhaps enables the co-construction and emergence of a healthier, more integrated "self," a process which occurs within most empathetic therapeutic relationships. It is this notion of limbic resonance which may explain the efficacy of most psychotherapeutic approaches despite their often contradictory theoretical viewpoints. In "A General Theory of Love," Lewis, Amini, and Lannon (2000) make explicit the transformative effects of relationship and its connection to psychotherapy:

Evolution has sculpted mammals into their present form: they become attuned to one another's evocative signals and alter the structure of one another's nervous systems. Psychotherapy's transformative power comes from engaging and directing these ancient mechanisms.

(p. 168)

These mechanisms may be of particular importance in the healing of trauma. Some writers have suggested that children of addicts should be viewed as cases of complex PTSD in light of the length and intensity of exposure to traumatic situations and the emotional dysregulation connected to the involvement of primary caregivers (Walker, 2009). Emotion dysregulation and dissociation, it is argued, are a consequence of interpersonal factors— in this case ineffective, abusive, or neglectful parenting. The resulting disorganized attachment styles of these children may act as precursors to the development of trauma symptoms in later life.

In the cases of Kathy and Ron, the experience of trauma and attachment style appears to be reinforced by their interactions with technology. Kathy appeared to view herself as desirable and in control when receiving praise from her online admirers, and worthless and weak when she failed to maintain their interest. This grandiosity alternates with the feeling of essential worthlessness, the "splitting" that is considered to be the central "primitive" defensive strategy of the borderline personality disorder, a tendency toward idealization and devaluation of self and others, driven by "a constitutionally determined the lack of anxiety tolerance" (Christopher, Bickhard, & Lambeth, 2001, p. 696). In Ron's case, this splitting manifested in his compulsive online behavior, the exhilaration of sexual excitement and gambling and the inevitable shame and self-punishment brought on by his inability to be present for his new family. This description overlaps with object relational conceptions of borderline personality disorder, perhaps suggesting that we reconceive this as a "disorder" of traumatic attachment. Van der Kolk notes in regard to this type of complex trauma:

> Abused and neglected children, and many adults with histories of abuse and neglect, tend to suffer from 1) a lack of a predictable sense of self, with a poor sense of separateness, and a disturbed body image, 2) poorly modulated affect and impulse control, including aggression against self and others, and 3) uncertainty about the reliability and predictability of others.
>
> (2001, p. 7)

From distortion's of self-concept (distorted self-presentations on social media) to impulsivity (addictive and self-harming behaviors) and ability to trust, all of these areas are impacted negatively by their online experiences.

Artificial Selves and the Problem of Other Minds

Yuval Noah Harrari (2016) finds that we are moving toward an era in which algorithms will be able to anticipate all of our needs in a fashion which will exceed our own level of self-awareness. That is to say, those who are able to interpret our online behaviors will have more knowledge of our needs, our preferences for mates, our diet and fitness level, our spending habits and sexual predilections, then we will, and from this aggregate data will determine the nature of our "true self." Turkle (2016b) refers to this "algorithmic self" as a transitional point by which the human becomes progressively more mechanized, the narrative of experience reduced to mere data point (p. 89). As our subjective experience of wants and desires gives way to its online shadow one may ask, what is the nature of this self being cultivated by technology, and what relationship does it bear to our ordinary conscious self? In what sense can it be claimed that this conception of self is truer and more real than that which is gleaned from our biographies and connections with those closest to us? Does our online self present a truer picture of who we are or is some fundamental aspect of personhood lost in the translation?

Long before there were personal computers, Philip K. Dick (1928–1982) explored these questions regarding the intersection between the real and simulation. A science fiction writer whose amazingly prescient visions of the future anticipated much of our postmodern malaise and who struggled throughout his life with mental health and substance abuse issues, imagined a portable suitcase-sized psychiatrist named Dr. Smile (admittedly much larger than the standard smart phone) whom his protagonist interacts with in much the same manner as iPhone users do with Siri, the digital assistant interface for the apple operating system.

Around the same period in the mid-1960s, a computer scientist at M.I.T. named Joseph Weizenbaum began to develop a computer program (Eliza) which emulated the much mocked mirroring technique developed by Carl Rogers, a rather elegant solution to the argument posed by seminal computer scientist Alan Turing (1950), namely, how can we know if a computer is conscious? The answer anticipated by Rene Descarte (1999) in his famous meditations is that we can't, just as we cannot verify the existence of another human being's consciousness. Instead of the impossible step of determining if another being is conscious, Turing proposes something he refers to as the imitation game.

> The new form of the problem can be described in terms of a game which we call the "imitation game." It is played with three people, a man (A), a woman (B), and an interrogator (C) who may be of either sex. The interrogator stays in a room apart front the other two. The object of the game for the interrogator is to determine which of the other two is the man and which is the woman. now ask the question, "What will happen when a machine takes the part of [the man] in this game?" Will the interrogator decide wrongly as often when the game is played like this as he does when the game is played between a man and a woman? These questions replace our original, "Can machines think?"
>
> (p. 1)

Essentially, we must rely upon behavioral evidence, primarily our own gut instinct to support the veracity of another subject's speech in the absence of the body, just as we rely upon the body (e.g., speech, body language and other indicators) to determine if we can trust the person we are talking to in person. We are presented with similar conundrum when we receive dubious phone calls or emails from the I.R.S. or police departments fraudulently demanding our social security numbers or money, or for that matter when reading comments from Russian bots in the comment section in a politician's Facebook or twitter page. Perhaps you have felt the peculiar frustration in those moments of signing into a website and being forced to convince them that you are in fact not a robot by repeatedly attempting to identify common everyday objects and failing miserably.

In these cases, the prevailing methodology still relies upon Turing's original thesis, subject to error and the vicissitudes of interrater reliability. The difference is that we cannot doubt the existence of a flesh and blood person standing before us in the same way that we may doubt a series of characters flashing on a screen. As one of Dick's characters says of the artificial psychiatrist "it's just pretend, to keep us from loneliness. It's alive but it's not connected with anything outside itself" (1991, p. 78).

The imitation game of online communication often appears to reinforce our sense of disconnection. Language divorced from the feedback of emotional expression can give us a variety of intense experiences, but it cannot give us the conscious attentive gaze of another living being. Even our pets provide us with this fundamental engagement that is unavailable from one's iPhone. That emotional resonance and conscious engagement are crucial factors in the development of the child's emotion regulation. In the absence of that parental presence, the child fails to calibrate its inner response to the external world and must seek out a different kind of strategy to manage its emotional life (often through compulsive behaviors of some type). Studies have shown in regard to emotion regulation "significant negative correlation with mother attachment, father attachment, peer attachment, problematic Internet use, video game addiction, and gambling disorder" (Estévez, Jáuregui, Sánchez-Marcos, López-González, & Griffiths, 2017, p. 537). Hence, the relationship between high scores on the adverse child experience scales (frequently tied to abuse and neglect by primary caregivers) and addictive behaviors as well as other adverse health outcomes (Brown & Shillington, 2017). The crucial factor of emotional attunement is muted or absent in therapies which do not include the bodily engagement with another, particularly in cases of disorganized attachment. Perhaps, it also accounts for the behavioral disconnect between our offline and online selves.

Therapy in the Time of Coronavirus

The federal government's responses to the global pandemic of 2020 was a loosening of existing restrictions on the use of telehealth for providers in all mental health settings, initiating a nationwide experiment in the provision of these services to the general public. Prior to this event, numerous arguments have been put forth regarding the ethics of implementing telehealth. Stoll, Müller, and Trachsel (2020) have conducted a survey of the existing literature on the subject noting the main arguments for (1) increased access to psychotherapy and service availability and flexibility, (2) therapy benefits and enhanced communication, (3) advantages related to specific client characteristics (e.g., remote location), (4) convenience, satisfaction, acceptance, and increased demand, and (5) economic advantages and against

(1) privacy, confidentiality, and security issues; (2) therapist competence and need for special training; (3) communication issues specific to technology; (4) research gaps; and (5) emergency issues (p. 1). Some evidence has existed for the efficacy of various types of technology-based interventions. For example, a literature review on "text messaging as a management tool for mental health has been proposed in many mental health conditions with promising results" (Berrouiguet, Baca-García, Brandt, Walter, & Courtet, 2016, p. 9). In particular, these services showed promise for underserved populations who were reluctant or unable to utilize traditional psychotherapy (e.g., home-bound individuals suffering from mental or physical disabilities (Hopps, Pépin, & Boisvert, 2003), or who live in remote locations (Dwight-Johnson et al., 2011). Despite research supporting teletherapy as a mode of treatment, therapists continue to remain skeptical about the efficacy of these approaches when compared to traditional in-person therapy. Rees and Stone (2005) have attempted to evaluate these attitudes suggesting that "psychologists' ability to judge the nature of the alliance in a videoconferencing session is likely to be biased by negative expectations" (p. 652). As social distancing and shelter in place restrictions were enacted across the United States in response to the pandemic, telehealth became the only option available for most psychotherapists, prompting practitioners to examine their attitudes and bias about these methods of treatment first hand.

When I had started to write on this topic, the most popular methods for accessing online therapy were the aforementioned app-based platforms Talkspace and Betterhelp. I had considered exploring their services as either a therapist or a patient in order to have a better understanding of the experience. A brief (admittedly biased) sampling of reddit posts and employee reviews of Talkspace managed to dissuade me from the idea.

From a user experience standpoint: app works well and is mostly intuitive, the security features are adequate and unobtrusive from using the Talk space therapy room. The service gives the user the ability to choose a therapist that matches their sex, and confidentiality is nice. Given your price tier, you can pay up to $79/wk. and receive weekly half-hour video sessions. Most common pricing is the $49/wk. plan for basic access to message a therapist.

Signing up for Talkspace is a financial risk that I cannot recommend. Coming from a long relationship with traditional therapy, I found this method to be jarring and unproductive.

From my experience, the biggest issue that I had with Talkspace is the required amount of work for you to get anything out of the therapy. Billing themselves as "therapy for the modern age" I found the service nothing but an uphill battle to acclimate to and to get even a shred of progress toward better mental health.

My therapist recommended sitting down and writing out how I was feeling daily for a half hour in the morning and a half hour in the evening. Totaling 7hrs per week writing about myself and how I am feeling. As someone who is dealing with severe depression and anxiety, I find this incredibly challenging. I hate myself, and that is a core reason why I signed up, and I can't just write to someone I don't know about how I am feeling with no context or structure. To add insult to injury after several weeks of trying to write about myself, our discussions lacked any direction to improve or discuss my problems.

This led to my second month going days at a time with nothing more than "Hello Daef I'm back on the platform today" or "I've noticed you haven't responded in a while." Respond to what? Why bother talking when the only time that I'm available you're away? My therapist never asked prompting questions beyond "how are you feeling today?" answer: not F$&%ing great that's why I signed up. Meaning most conversations would never build into something beyond a shallow introspective analysis.

I originally signed up for a once per month conference call with my therapist, but my person never reached out to schedule a time. I wasted an extra $10/wk so even if you pay more for a better experience there is no guarantee that you'll even get what you pay for. I know that you can "easily switch therapists," but they don't reimburse you for the time that you spent with the person who wasn't helping and the money you wasted on their hack job service.

I wrote this review on the brink of tears, want to know how I'm feeling? Ripped off, lied to, and screwed over. If you need therapy, I recommend trying anything else first. You probably won't get the help you need here (DaefByrns, 2019).

Therapist experiences were similarly a mixed bag; alternating between praise for the flexibility allowed by the format and irritation at the lack of support, exploitation of workers, and quality of treatment provided.

Pros

— *It has been easy to build my caseload in just a few months on Talkspace*
— *Good work for those who are in-between jobs*

Cons

— *I've had problems with live videos and clinical emergencies and didn't have access to help until 1–2 days later.*
— *The pay is low for the amount of time you put in. Talkspace estimates you are spending 10 minutes a day with a client. This is not realistic if you are providing a good clinical service. Most of my clients are very engaged and I am giving them at least 30 minutes a day, but only getting paid for 10 minutes. When you get paid at the end of the month, it is disheartening to see how little you make given a high caseload.*
— *They keep track of client attrition and your percentage monthly. I have had two clients transition to in-person therapists with my help and because they left, this reflects negatively on my attrition rate. It seems unethical to keep a client in online therapy when they would benefit from in-person therapy, but this is the message that I'm getting from Talkspace.*
— *The advice they give on how to give online therapy is a little bit funny to me. They seem to promote the use of smiley faces and soft therapy practices. Often clients do appreciate a therapist who is willing to challenge them* (Anonymous, 2020).

While I was considering these matters, the coronavirus pandemic arrived in the United States and I, along with all of my clients, received the firsthand experience of teletherapy I had been seeking.

★

I lost everything. I didn't even get to post a single picture.

A month into the quarantine Kathy reached out to schedule an appointment. She wept openly as she described the frenzied efforts to gain access to her phone and all of the pictures stored there after the apple store declared that it was damaged beyond repair and all its contents lost. By her response, it was as if she had not only lost the images of the life events chronicled there, but lost the experiences themselves. It was a loss that distracted her from the unfolding chaos of the post COVID-19 world.

I wanted to call you. I knew you were having remote sessions but I just couldn't bring myself. I'm on the computer all day and I just can't stand it, seeing myself on the screen. When I notice it sometimes I push the computer back. I think about how ugly and fat I look. Her voice trailed off as she appeared to be lost in thought.

When do you think they are going to open the office again? I told her that the facility had not decided on a date yet, but that it was not likely to be happening any time soon.

I miss being there with you. It feels like there is something missing. I mean I see you but the office is like this safe place. Not that my house isn't a safe place it's just. I feel like . . . even though you're there and I can see you I feel alone. I don't know if I'm making any sense. Then I started to feel like so much time had passed, that you would be mad at me for not calling the office back. I was so worried about it. You're not mad at me right?

Ron by contrast felt comfortable enough with the virtual, perhaps too comfortable, feeling more than ever the inexorable pull of the screens in response to the overwhelming demands of emotionally connecting with his anxious wife and child. He remained sequestered on the upper floor of his house, safely barricaded from the cries of his young child.

I feel like life has stopped, like there isn't any point. I have this long list of things to get done and I get so overwhelmed with it that I just shut down and hours go by. Then it's like a race to get things done and my mind starts racing. I get so angry at myself that I just give up and the next day it all starts all over again. When I come down she seems so angry and resentful, I know I should care but I just feel so depleted that I just give up and shut down.

Through the Looking Glass

As we move increasingly into the mediated landscape of the digital age, the tools that we have evolved over eons that have allowed us to communicate and interact have been curtailed, shaped into a narrower, more ambiguous form. The computer and smartphone become portals where we leave behind our physical selves. The felt sense of being situated in a particular place and time becomes secondary, even incidental to our existence. Divorced from the body, freed from the inhibitory strictures, and engagement with the bodily foundations of emotions, the mind spins tirelessly down the rabbit hole (as both Kathy and Ron could attest).

The information and emotional resonance provided by the bodies of others through the eyes, through postural and vocal cue, analytically reduced to the symbols of language are freed from the risks and rewards of physical interactions and thus prone to misinterpretation and disconnection. As Fuchs (2005) notes, "the bodily schema serves as a virtual model for simulating one's own future actions as well as for understanding the actions of others" (p. 103). Severed from this age-old engagement with the physical, have we lost the bodily basis of our experience of empathy? Researchers have noted the phenomenon of online disinhibition, how the act of being online facilitates behavior ranging from benign disclosures of personal information to "rude language, harsh criticisms, anger, hatred, even threats" (Suler, 2004, p. 1). Some have suggested that these behaviors reveal evidence of the uncivilized reality beneath the veneer of civilization.

Human beings, like our primate cousins, are supposedly hardwired to be social beings, to respond to the suffering of others. When this capacity fails, it calls into question fundamental aspects of our self-concept. From a neuro-scientific perspective, questions of this hardwired empathic response inevitably involve discussion of mirror neurons. Mirror neurons have cropped up everywhere in recent years, from possible explanations for autism to explanations for how the brain maps our bodies. In a famous experiment, researchers were able to eliminate phantom limb pain in some amputees using a mirror in order to trick the brain into thinking the missing limb was still there, indicating the possible role of visual feedback in the development of the phenomena (Ramachandran & Rogers-Ramachandran, 1996). Of relevance to our discussion is the supposed role of mirror neurons in empathy. Most individuals have had the experience of wincing in pain when witnessing another person hurting themselves. Imaging studies of psychopaths' response to visual triggers for empathy suggested that they do not respond as strongly to such cues. However, when instructed to empathize, the subjects' scans were comparable to "normal" individuals, suggesting that there is a volitional component to perceptions of empathy (Meffert, Gazzola, den Boer, Bartels, & Keysers, 2013). In effect, we all are able to turn off or modulate empathy when we want to, as evidenced by our differential empathic responses to strangers and our close friends and family members. In regard to mirror neurons, does the type of mirror matter? To take an example from, the current awareness among the general public regarding the long history of oppression of black Americans and the growing popular support of Black Lives Matter is in no small measure due to the evidence of our sense experience, the excruciating horror of seeing video footage of unarmed black men being murdered. To see is to imagine or assume the perspective of the other. As human beings, we spend an inordinate amount of our lifetimes watching other human beings and vicariously experiencing their lives. Since visual feedback seems to be implicated in the mirror neuron system and by extension our experience of empathy, does the absence of an actual body before us divorce us in some fundamental way from empathic engagement with another? What if that body is a flat image on a screen, or an imagined body summoned by a text message?

Returning to Fuchs phenomenological perspective, in his paper "The Virtual Other" (2014), he explores virtuality and its relationship to empathy, elucidating certain aspects of intersubjectivity which are pertinent to our questions regarding teletherapy and the impact of technology on the experience of the self.

Primary empathy in his view is based on intercorporeality and intersubjectivity, that is, it represents a type of embodied knowledge gleaned in our interactions with other human beings. As in my earlier discussion of the role of attachment in emotion regulation, the bodies and emotional states of ourselves and others are engaged in constant interplay, such that this emotional resonance allows us to participate in a somewhat direct fashion in their joys and sorrow in an unconscious prereflective fashion.

> Other forms of empathy such as extended empathy (that which refers to an imaginal assumption of the perspective of others), and Fictional empathy (empathy directed towards non existent, fictional objects or beings such as characters in a novel) require an explicit, cognitive operation, namely, the conscious envisioning of the situation of the other, which often employs information about him that one could not infer directly from the situation at hand. Also, it involves an imaginative operation, that means, a transposition into an 'as-if' scenario (i.e. as if I were the other) which transcends the bodily or physical level.
>
> (2014, p. 158)

Fuchs theorizes that as one moves further away from the corporeal to more disembodied forms of interaction that the imaginal quality of interaction is heightened, making our exchanges more prone to error, shifting the quality of communication with others from genuine connection toward a kind of self-involved engagement with one's own projections.

This type of situation arose in my work with Alice.

Since reports of the first cases out of China started to appear in the evening news, Alice had become increasingly paranoid. Unable to arrange transportation to my office for sessions and with her escalating medical complaints, we had been unable to maintain her treatment. With the advent of teletherapy, however, we were given the opportunity to reconnect in a manner that had been impossible given the prior constraints on telehealth.

I can't seem to ever get comfortable.

Fidgeting constantly, Alice struggled to concentrate throughout our sessions. Several years earlier, she had fallen ill with a bout of spinal meningitis. While she had recovered after a brief hospitalization, she had become immobilized with a host of other maladies. As she had become more homebound, she became more obsessed with a series of online relationships, some of which went on for years. She would form friendships in online support groups for people suffering from depression and anxiety. Inevitably these exchanges would escalate to unwanted romantic attachments, where she was overburdened with the needs and demands of these insensitive, self-centered men.

Can't they see that I have my own problems. I just pull away, and they get more insistent. Eventually, they give up and stop talking to me. They accuse me of being heartless. But once they stop talking to me, I can't stop thinking about them. I keep wondering if something happened to them. I'll go on their friends' pages looking for signs of them. It's just so frustrating.

Our discussions eventually returned to the fact that she very rarely had any kind of direct communication beyond text messages and emails. Aside from pictures on a website, there was very little substance to the people she communicated with. Often they would simply exchange banal platitudes or emojis while playing online games. Only one had ever spoken to her on the phone and then only to ask her to send him money under dubious circumstances.

While initially the option of teletherapy was helpful in allowing us to continue treatment, it presented a number of challenges. Her preference for telephone calls as opposed to the face-to-face contact allowed by FaceTime reinforced one of Alice's core conflicts, a failure to engage with the other as a person, projecting and misreading the intentions of others. Our sessions became lengthy monologues rather than true interactions. In the absence of visual cues, active listening on my part would often be misconstrued as disinterest or boredom. At my suggestion, we returned to facetime sessions as a way to reassure her that I was present and engaged with her. We were able to process this earlier skepticism in light of her conflict laden relationships with her critical and rejecting father, the prototype for her similarly anxiety provoking and frustrating relationship with her online boyfriends.

Conclusion

Despite these caveats regarding teletherapy, as I write in the midst of the COVID-19 pandemic, it remains the only type of therapy that I am able to provide. For my existing clients that I have seen for years, the imaginative jump from face to face to phone call often feels indistinguishable from the experience of having them in my office; the nuances of their speech patterns and facial expressions are easily summoned in my imagination (despite the likelihood of miscommunications and projections). For others, video conferencing has been helpful in preserving some aspect of the face-to-face engagement of in-person therapy. For new patients, the weirdness of conducting assessments and establishing rapport in the online medium has thrown me back into the awkwardness of my first years as a therapist. Given the unprecedented circumstances in which we are providing treatment, it is difficult to discern how much of my experience of teletherapy is unique to the circumstances of the pandemic or will continue beyond it.

Online forums like Reddit have provided many observations from therapists and patient's alike regarding their experiences. For myself, I remain
ambivalent, at once grateful that I am able to provide support for my patient's
during a challenging historical moment and frustrated by the limitations of
the medium. As one patient states in a reddit thread on teletherapy:

> *Before I delve into this, I just want to say that I know I'm very lucky to be able
> to continue my therapy with everything that's been going on, and that many
> people aren't as fortunate. I get that, but
>   I freaking HATE teletherapy.*

> *I'm sure this has been discussed to some degree here, so pardon me, but does any-
> one else feel like they're almost . . . keeping a lot of things to themselves, like "on
> hold" until their in-person sessions resume? I've been doing 1–2x weekly 30 minute
> phone sessions with my therapist since I'm not comfortable with webcam, and I find
> I dread them. Keep in mind that I LOVED therapy before all this started. I'm
> missing my connection to her that can only be had in person* (mnbell2013, 2020).

It seems inevitable that therapy will eventually move further and further
into the online medium and into the complications of disembodiment, perhaps eventually being provided by online chatbots or some next generation
version of Apple's *Siri* or Amazon's *Alexa*, relegating in-person therapy to a
historical curiosity or perhaps a service, like classical psychoanalysis, available to a rarefied few who can afford it. Will the convenience and attentiveness of a personalized app, attuned to the nuances of our unconscious
online selves prove sufficient to allay our worst tendencies or will it merely
reinforce our sense of isolation and disconnection? It will remain for us to
see what will be gained and what may be lost in translation.

Close Reading Questions:

1. How is the self-defined by the author and in what sense can it be
    disembodied?
2. In what ways does our experience with screen time mimic or relate to
    the experience of dissociation described in cases of complex trauma?
3. In a clinical context, how might technology complicate emotion regu-
    lation or addictive behavior in individuals with traumatic attachment
    experience?

Prompts for Writing:

1. In what ways may issues of race, gender, sexual orientation, and political
    affiliation be subverted or complicated by the use of disembodied forms
    of communication?
2. How does Alan Turing's "imitation game" relate to the experience
    of doing psychotherapy? Is there something beyond language and

simulations of conversation or could a sufficiently convincing construct perform the same healing function as a skilled psychotherapist?

3. How has technology impacted social workers' capacity to establish therapeutic rapport? Write about a case in which you felt the medium impacted your experience of working with a client. How has it complicated our ability to screen for symptoms of acute and post-traumatic stress?

References

Anonymous. (2020, February 25). "Keepings changing, don't have live help for therapists (for both clinical and IT), low pay" glassdoor. *Glassdoor, Inc.* Web, Online Forum Post. Retrieved from www.glassdoor.com.hk/Reviews/Talkspace-Reviews-E1284778.htm

Berrouiguet, S., Baca-García, E., Brandt, S., Walter, M., & Courtet, P. (2016). Fundamentals for future mobile-health (mHealth): A systematic review of mobile phone and web-based text messaging in mental health. *Journal of Medical Internet Research*, 18(6), e135.

Blizard, R. A. (1997). The origins of dissociative identity disorder from an object relations and attachment theory perspective. *Dissociation*, 10, 223–229.

Brown, S. M., & Shillington, A. M. (2017). Childhood adversity and the risk of substance use and delinquency: The role of protective adult relationships. *Child Abuse & Neglect*, 63, 211–221.

Cardeña, E. B., & Carlson, E. B. (2011). Acute stress disorder revisited. *Annual Review of Clinical Psychology*, 7, 245–267.

Carlson, E., Dalenberg, C., & Mcdade-Montez, E. (2012). Dissociation in posttraumatic stress disorder part I: Definitions and review of research. *Psychological Trauma: Theory, Research, Practice, and Policy*, 479–489.

Carr, N. (2020). *The shallows: What the Internet is doing to our brains*. New York: W. W Norton & Company.

Christopher, J., Bickhard, M., & Lambeth, G. (2001). Otto Kernberg's object relations theory: A metapsychological critique. *Theory & Psychology*, 11(5), 687–711.

Craparo, G. (2011). Internet addiction, dissociation, and alexithymia. *Procedia-Social and Behavioral Sciences*, 30, 1051–1056.

DaefByrns. (2019, June 25). My review of talkspace" Reddit. *Reddit, Inc.* Web, Online Forum Post. Retrieved from www.reddit.com/r/therapy/comments/c5af5t/my_review_of_talkspace/

Damasio, A. (1999). *The feeling of what happens: Body, emotion and the making of consciousness*. New York: Harcourt Brace.

Descarte, R. (1999). *Discourse on method and meditations on first philosophy*. Cambridge: Hackett Publishing.

Dick, P. (1991). *The three stigmata of Palmer Eldritch*. London: Vintage.

Dreyfus, H. L. (2008). *On the internet*. London: Routledge.

Dube, S. R., Felitti, V. J., Dong, M., Chapman, D. P., Giles, W. H., & Anda, R. F. (2003). Childhood abuse, neglect, and household dysfunction and the risk of illicit drug use: The adverse childhood experiences study. *Pediatrics*, 111(3), 564–572.

Dwight-Johnson, M., Aisenberg, E., Golinelli, D., Hong, S., O'Brien, M., & Ludman, E. (2011). Telephone-based cognitive-behavioral therapy for Latino patients living in rural areas: A randomized pilot study. *Psychiatric Services*, 62(8), 936–942.

Estévez, A., Jáuregui, P., Sánchez-Marcos, I., López-González, H., & Griffiths, M. D. (2017). Attachment and emotion regulation in substance addictions and behavioral addictions, *Journal of Behavioral Addictions*, *6*(4), 534–544. Retrieved June 17, 2020, from https://akjournals.com/view/journals/2006/6/4/article-p534.xml

Fuchs, T. (2005). Corporealized and disembodied minds: A phenomenological view of the body in melancholia and schizophrenia. *Philosophy, Psychiatry, & Psychology*, *12*(2), 95–107.

Fuchs, T. (2007). Psychotherapy of the lived space: A phenomenological and ecological concept. *American Journal of Psychotherapy*, *61*(4), 423.

Fuchs, T. (2014). The virtual other: Empathy in the age of virtuality. *Journal of Consciousness Studies*, *21*(5–6), 152–173.

Gil-Or, O., Levi-Belz, Y., & Turel, O. (2015). The "Facebook-self": Characteristics and psychological predictors of false self-presentation on Facebook. *Frontiers in Psychology*, *6*, 99.

Harari, Y. N. (2016). *Homo Deus: A brief history of tomorrow*. London: Random House.

Hopps, S. L., Pépin, M., & Boisvert, J. M. (2003). The effectiveness of cognitive-behavioral group therapy for loneliness via inter relay chat among people with physical disabilities. *Psychotherapy: Theory, Research, Practice, Training*, *40*(1–2), 136.

Horvath, J., Mundinger, C., Schmitgen, M. M., Wolf, N. D., Sambataro, F., Hirjak, D., . . . Wolf, R. C. (2020). Structural and functional correlates of smartphone addiction. *Addictive Behaviors*, 106334.

Hunt, M. G., Marx, R., Lipson, C., & Young, J. (2018). No more FOMO: Limiting social media decreases loneliness and depression. *Journal of Social and Clinical Psychology*, *37*(10), 751–768.

Kang, S. (2007). Disembodiment in online social interaction: Impact of online chat on social support and psychosocial well-being. *Cyber Psychology & Behavior*, *10*(3), 475–477.

Konrath, S., Chopik, W., Hsing, C., & O'Brien, E. H. (2014). Changes in adult attachment styles in American college students over time: A meta-analysis. *Personality and Social Psychology Review*, 18.

Lewis, T., Amini, F., & Lannon, R. (2001). *A general theory of love*. New York: Vintage.

Meffert, H., Gazzola, V., den Boer, J. A., Bartels, A. A., & Keysers, C. (2013). Reduced spontaneous but relatively normal deliberate vicarious representations in psychopathy. *Brain*, *136*(8), 2550–2562.

Mei, S., Xu, G., Gao, T., Ren, H., & Li, J. (2018). The relationship between college students' alexithymia and mobile phone addiction: Testing mediation and moderation effects. *BMC Psychiatry*, *18*(1), 329. Doi:10.1186/s12888-018-1891-8

mnbell2013. (2020, May 18). "I feel like I'm in "maintenance mode" until teletherapy is over"Reddit. *Reddit, Inc.* Web, Online Forum Post. Retrieved from www.reddit.com/r/TalkTherapy/comments/glv1bq/i_feel_like_im_in_maintenance_mode_until/

Nijenhuis, E. R., & Van der Hart, O. (2011). Dissociation in trauma: A new definition and comparison with previous formulations. *Journal of Trauma & Dissociation*, *12*(4), 416–445.

Ramachandran, V. S., & Rogers-Ramachandran, D. C. (1996). Synaesthesia in phantom limbs induced with mirrors. *Proceedings of the Royal Society*, *263*(1369), 377–386.

Rees, C. S., & Stone, S. (2005). Therapeutic alliance in face-to-face versus videoconferenced psychotherapy. *Professional Psychology: Research and Practice*, *36*(6), 649.

Schore, A., & Schore, J. (2008). Modern attachment theory: The central role of affect regulation in attachment and treatment. *Journal of Clinical Social Work*, *36*(1), 9–20.

Stoll, J., Müller, J. A., & Trachsel, M. (2020). Ethical issues in online psychotherapy: A narrative review. *Frontiers in Psychiatry*, *10*, 993.

Suler, J. (2004). The online disinhibition effect. *Cyberpsychology & Behavior*, 7(3), 321–326.

Tronick, E., Als, H., Adamson, L., Wise, S., & Brazelton, T. B. (1978). Infants response to entrapment between contradictory messages in face-to-face interaction. *Journal of the American Academy of Child and Adolescent Psychiatry*, *17*, 1–13.

Turing, A. M. (1950). Computing machinery and intelligence. *Mind*, *49*, 433–460.

Turkle, S. (2016a, November–December). The empathy gap digital culture needs what talk therapy offers. Psychotherapy Networker. Retrieved January 29, 2022, from https://www.psychotherapynetworker.org/magazine/article/1051/the-empathy-gap

Turkle, S. (2016b). *Reclaiming conversation: The power of talk in a digital age*. New York: Penguin.

Van der Kolk, B. (2001). The assessment and treatment of complex PTSD. In R. Yehuda (Ed.), *Traumatic stress*. Arlington, VA: American Psychiatric Press.

Walker, P. (2009). *Emotional flashback management in the treatment of complex PTSD*. Retrieved December 6, 2014, from https://www.psychotherapy.net/article/complex-ptsd

Wilson, M. (2002). Six views of embodied cognition. *Psychonomic Bulletin & Review*, *9*(4), 625–636.

Wolf, M. (2010). *Proust and the squid: The story and science of the reading brain. Thriplow*. Cambridge: Icon Books.

Woods, H. C., & Scott, H. (2016). # Sleepyteens: Social media use in adolescence is associated with poor sleep quality, anxiety, depression and low self-esteem. *Journal of Adolescence*, *51*, 41–49.

7 The Role of Technology in Community Mental Health

A Strengths-Based Approach

Zakia Clay

Pre-reading Questions:

1. What supports on a micro, meso, and macro level are needed to successfully integrate technology as a tool for client engagement in practice settings?
2. Are transference and countertransference more difficult to navigate when working in community-based outreach programs? Why or why not?
3. What are some long-term occupational stressors that may persist for frontline workers post COVID-19? What strategies can be used to overcome them?

The short, rhythmic bells of email notifications had become the soundtrack to my workday back when I worked on the front lines of community-based mental health. Long before 2020, I'd developed the Pavlovian response to automatically check my inbox each time that sound goes off. Our program had touted its ability to be accessible to those in need 24/7, 365 days out of the year. I was never without my two cell phones and a laptop, not even in dreams. I was programmed to swiftly answer an emergency on-call, get my progress notes in, and monitor units of service to ensure outcomes were being met. This level of access and expectation could be intense at times. Nevertheless, it came with the job.

Later in my career, after I'd put in too many stressful, burned out years, I tucked myself into academia. When the pandemic hit, as my department and university decided how to move forward in extraordinary times, the melody of my email notification was a welcome sound of normalcy. As I checked my email, I was surprised to see a message from a clinician I had trained months earlier. Although it wasn't uncommon for a former trainee to reach out, there was a sense of despair that was too palpable to ignore. I suggested we schedule a phone call to connect.

They expect us to go out there and care for people, but they don't even care about us.

In an instant, it was as if I was back behind the wheel driving to the next client's home. There was nothing I could say in that moment to calm Hazel's concerns. She was a newly licensed clinician working in a community-based

DOI: 10.4324/9781003270225-7

mental health program at the height of the global pandemic. I remained silent and could not find the words to respond. I began an inner dialogue and started to rehearse all of the positive responses I could give, but it would all be a lie. The idea of going out to a client's home, with no PPE, no plan of how to provide support, and no guidance from the agency was unimaginable. Still, frontline workers who provided community-based services put themselves and their families at risk to help others.

Hello, are you still there? she asked with a bit of desperation in her tone. Her voice transported me back to reality. The truth about the moment was that we were in the middle of a pandemic. I cleared my throat and half-heartedly suggested she advocate for herself and her needs. Deep down I knew it was much more complicated. Clinicians were not equipped, agencies were not equipped, and the system was not equipped to navigate what was quickly unfolding around us.

Michael Lipsky, author of *Street-level bureaucracy: dilemmas of the individual in public services* (2010), introduced the term "street-level bureaucrat" to describe public service workers like police officers, educators, social workers, counselors, and health workers. Lipsky (2010) noted,

> As providers of public benefits and keepers of public order, street-level bureaucrats are the focus of political controversy. They are constantly torn by the demands of service recipients to improve effectiveness and responsiveness and by the demands of citizen groups to improve the efficacy and efficiency of government service.
>
> (p. 3)

Frontline workers in community-based programs shoulder the burden of navigating these same complex relationships. They, too, act as gatekeepers of entitlements and wield power over a program's efficacy. Additionally, constituents expect street-level bureaucrats to marshal those who get out of order. In effect, frontline workers mediate the relationships between clients and services. Engaging in this type of street-level work, not surprisingly, results in frontline workers exercising "discretionary measures" (Lipsky, 2010). Work by Akosa and Asare (2017) asserted that "street-level bureaucrats have discretion because the nature of service provision calls for human judgement that cannot be programmed and for which machines cannot substitute" (p. 30). More specifically, policies don't account for the nuances of practice. Inevitably, despite best efforts, there will always be a situation for which a program has not planned. Frontline workers also work in demanding environments with limited resources (Lipsky, 2010; Spitzmueller, 2016). Thus, workers will be required to, at times, operate autonomously and make in the moment decisions that respond to the needs of the client system. The pandemic amplified this very fact. As stay at home orders and social distancing precautions were put in place, many programs provided little guidance, forcing frontline workers to use their discretionary power.

The sudden rise in coronavirus cases unmasked the vulnerabilities in the mental health system, specifically, community-based outreach programs (CBOP) because, historically, these programs provide services in an individual's home. In this regard, frontline workers can offer services that range from case management to therapeutic support. William C. Madsen and Kevin Gillespie, authors of *Collaborative helping: a strengths framework for home-based services* (2014), liken community-based services to a "walking and talking" approach that has adopted many traditional therapy modalities. There's something to be said about meeting with someone in their home and in the community. When clients enter the therapy room, there is temptation to come cloaked in a better version of themselves, shielding parts of their persona that they want to remain hidden from the evaluative eye of a clinician. Yet, seeing clients at home allows frontline workers the opportunity to overtly bear witness to person-in-environment. Clinicians like Hazel grow accustomed to this lateral relationship of helping that can stretch over long periods of time. While there is empirical evidence to support this type of community-based approach to mental health treatment, there is an emerging need to include more innovative interventions.

The use of technology has become ubiquitous in Western culture; however, CBOPs have only taken modest strides toward integrating technology into service delivery. Many programs have enhanced some aspects of their services through the use of smartphones and tablets. Aside from these devices, programs also transitioned to electronic health records, which has led to more efficiency in documentation. Despite the benefits of technology, CBOP never fully realized the additional possibilities the digital world could offer the field. In many ways, co-opting CBOP with digital enhancements would subvert the very essence of the service. These programs were about working alongside individuals and being in the trenches. How could this type of relationship be replicated using technology? The pandemic complicated face-to-face meetings with clients. For the first time, in-person meetings could jeopardize the health and well-being of frontline workers and clients alike, thus, forcing the use of technology and other digital innovations as the primary tool for engagement.

Despite limited guidance and training, frontline workers like Hazel had to bear the burden of enacting new ways of engaging clients using digital tools. This chapter will use the street-level bureaucracy framework to explore the existing systemic and practice dilemmas that were exacerbated by the pandemic and offer ways that technology can be used to engage clients both during a crisis and beyond. My tenure in CBOP, relationship with Hazel and role in academia, will also present a unique opportunity to examine the toll the public health emergency has taken on frontline workers and programs as they attempt to respond to client needs. Recommendations for the effective integration of technology in both policy and practice will be offered.

The Case of a Frontline Worker: Hazel

For a newly licensed clinician, managing structural conditions can be particularly challenging. In this regard, I wasn't surprised when Hazel reached out to me seeking guidance about how to manage work in the midst of COVID-19.

They're saying we still have to go out and see people, and I just her voice trailed off as if she could no longer bring herself to speak. The silence on the one end was deafening. I imagined Hazel on the other end of the call frozen in place. At this point, there were still a lot of unanswered questions about the virus. But because Hazel was considered an essential worker, she was expected to go into the office. Hazel was torn between the responsibility she felt she had to the clients, the community, her family, and to herself. Lipsky (2010) suggests:

> The processing of people into clients, assigning them to categories for treatment by bureaucrats, and treating them in terms of those categories, is a social process. Client characteristics do not exist outside of the process that gives rise to them. An important part of this process is the way people learn to treat themselves as if they were categorical entities.
>
> (p. 29)

Hazel was concerned about the clients she worked with believing that they would not be able to self-manage without her during the pandemic. Hazel, like many other frontline workers, created narratives about what it means to be a client. Albeit unconscious, Hazel relegated service recipients to their role as a client. This social construction influenced Hazel's perceptions of a client's potential and capability. In this case, the categorization of clients contributed to Hazel's increased sense of responsibility toward the clients she worked with each day. Hazel was fearful about what her absence would mean to clients.

I feel guilty for being afraid to go out, but I'm also afraid of what will happen to the clients if I don't. Hazel had convinced herself that the clients she worked with were incapable of navigating on their own. In many ways, CBOP cultivated an environment of codependence. Clients were dependent on workers; similarly, workers were dependent on clients. The very notion of clients having to self-manage was implausible. If Hazel had such low expectations for the clients she worked with, then what kind of expectations did they have for themselves?

The clients that Hazel typically served were diagnosed with severe mental illness and experienced extensive hospitalizations. Early in my career, I quickly learned that, often, the same hospital systems that are supposed to aid people in getting well are the same structures that contribute to making them ill. I still have a vivid memory of a new client, Kenny. At the time, I was a new frontline worker, charged with helping him reintegrate back into the community after a lengthy state psychiatric hospitalization. I would arrive each day at his apartment enthusiastically ready to work with him on anything from activities of daily living to developing emotional regulation skills. As each week went by, I noticed a decline in Kenny's cleanliness. What began as a subtle odor became an unbearable musky scent that greeted me at his front door during each visit. It was early in my practice career and I had not quite mastered how to address concerns around hygiene. Yet, I was left with no choice.

Hey, Kenny, I've been meaning to ask you . . . do you have everything you need to shower?

I said with a bit of unease.

Yeah, I'm good on that front, he quickly asserted.

Oh okay, well . . . umm I'm wondering how often you generally take care of those types of personal needs. I asked with skepticism.

What do you mean? He responded. I began fiddling with my hands as I often do when I get nervous and decided it was time to stop beating around the bush.

Like showering. I've noticed a smell coming from you and I'm wondering if everything is okay. I was relieved to finally say it; I was proud of myself.

I haven't showered since I got here. You never told me to. He whispered. My pride quickly turned to embarrassment. We both stared back at each other as silence filled the room. In that moment, it became clear how lengthy hospitalizations can lead to the profound deskilling of clients. In such settings, clients don't need to think about when to wake up, shower, eat, or take medication; the staff provide reminders. There is no need to manage money, cook, or clean; it's done for you. I took this for granted and Kenny did too. He hadn't showered since being discharged from the hospital because he was waiting for me to provide a prompt. I spent the next several months working to reorient Kenny to life roles outside of a client.

Lipsky (2010) would agree that systems perpetuate the social construction of being ill. Paul Verhaeghe, author of *What about me? The struggle for identity in a market-based society*, argued that the neoliberal values of the west can be toxic to an individual's mental health. Verhaeghe (2012) posited that

> An important part of any free-market process is the recruitment of customers. At present, advertising is not considered acceptable in the medical sector, but there are ways of getting around this. The trick is to convince people that they might have something wrong with them or that their health is a risk, and that they really need to take steps to protect themselves.
>
> (p. 131)

Although street-level bureaucrats like Hazel may not explicitly express doubt in the self-efficacy of clients, the sentiments are often implicitly communicated. Some clients may act accordingly, thus internalizing their "disordered" label convinced that they must engage in treatment to attain a more homogeneous identity. In this case, the embodiment of illness has created a passive relationship in which Hazel maintains a position of power and control over the individuals receiving services. The preservation of these roles is fiscally advantageous for the mental health system but presents a complicated dynamic for Hazel and other frontline workers.

Where We Started

For most of the 19th century, asylums and institutions were used to house those living with mental illness. Those deemed mentally disturbed endured segregation, neglect and harsh treatments like caging and physical restraints (Modak, Sarkar, & Sagar, 2016). During this time, Dorothea Dix became an outspoken critic against the human suffrage occurring for those being warehoused in asylums. Dix's interest in the care of patients began during a trip to Britain when she connected with members of the lunacy reform movement (Modak et al., 2016). Upon returning to the United States, Dix became a fierce advocate and lobbied for more humane treatment for those living with mental illness (Modak et al., 2016). Her commitment and tireless efforts played a pivotal role in improving patient care and ultimately led to legislative action (Parry, 2006).

By the 1950s, research pursuits were underway that began exploring the etiology and potential treatments for severe mental illness (Davis, Fulginiti, Kriegel, & Brekke, 2012). Alongside these endeavors was the rapid training of clinically licensed professionals and hope for alternative treatments beyond the confines of institutional walls. In 1954, the first psychotropic drug was introduced and began to shift the long-held belief that mental illness was untreatable (Gronfein, 1985). The ability for individuals with mental illness to better manage their symptoms through medications also helped to change public perceptions about discharging patients back into the community. Psychopharmacological interventions ultimately foreshadowed radical changes that lie ahead in mental health.

President John F. Kennedy signed the Community Mental Health Centers Act in 1963 accelerating deinstitutionalization in the United States (Davis et al., 2012). The law sparked the development of community mental health centers for individuals living with mental illness through the allocation of federal funding (Terry, Townley, Brusilovskiy, & Salzer, 2019). Aside from comprehensive community-based therapeutic options, the legislation also supported staff recruitment and training. Scholars soon began to compare institutional treatment and community-based care. The evidence found community-based care to be less costly and more effective in treating mental illness (Terry et al., 2019).

The excitement around deinstitutionalization and community-based treatment approaches eventually turned into scrutiny. While the Community Mental Health Centers Act provided the financial means to restructure treatment for mental illness, the funding was unsustainable (Blair & Espinoza, 2015). Programs were unable to provide adequate follow-up care and most importantly housing options for those being released from psychiatric hospitals with no place to live (Ray & Kanapaux, 2002). As a result, community mental health centers struggled to stay open and many individuals returned to the hospital or ended up homeless. In response to these legislative failures, community stakeholders, patients, and family members collaborated with the National Institute of Mental Health and developed the concept for Community Support Systems (Anthony, 1993). The conceptual framework for Community Support Systems identified components that were evaluated for efficacy in providing adequate community-based services to individuals living with severe mental illness. Some of the fundamental components include basic support, case management, crisis intervention, and psychosocial rehabilitation (Anthony, 1993). This new understanding paved the way for new initiatives like CBOP that focused on the delivery of recovery-oriented services.

Street-Level Work

The mist of the rain cooled my skin as I rang the bell for the third time. Some may have given up by then, but I knew better. I quickly walked to the side of the building and pressed my face against the window to try to get a glimpse inside. The room was dark, but I knocked hard on the glass in hopes that the sound would bellow throughout the apartment, alerting the client of my arrival. We spoke earlier in the day to confirm that I would be coming by, but a lot could've happened since then to distract from our weekly meetings. Just as I reached for my cell phone in a final attempt to make contact, the front door opened.

I was immediately bombarded by an intense wave of heat that seemed to magically evaporate any evidence of rain from my face. James, my client, stood shirtless and smiling.

Hey, come on in, he said gleefully. I looked over his shoulder and into his apartment in an attempt to assess the situation.

Where is your shirt and why is it so hot in there? I asked with growing concern. Even though I had been working with James for several years and had developed a strong therapeutic alliance, I always remained overly cautious during all my home visits. I was cognizant of the fact that, unless there were significant safety concerns, I met with clients alone. James was older and was becoming increasingly absent minded.

I was cold so I turned up the heat, but now I'm hot, he explained. I walked through the door into a familiar haze of lingering cigarette smoke. I began to scan the room. The living room table had a half-eaten honey bun and brown sticky rings nearby that were still glistening, likely from the coffee that spilled earlier. As we entered the kitchen, I noticed that the oven door was open despite it being on with nothing in it. When I asked James if he forgot to close the door, he explained that he intentionally heated the oven and left it open.

I told you, I was cold and the heat would've taken too long to kick on so I just used the oven like we did growing up, he said nonchalantly. I glanced at the nearby thermostat that was reading 90 degrees and encouraged James to reduce the temperature. In that moment, I knew there was no way we would have enough time to fully address the original purpose of the visit. Speaking with Hazel brought back this memory and countless others from my street-level work.

Meeting with clients in the intimacy of their home, no doubt, requires an agile approach. Workers must skillfully navigate the art of cultivating a trusting relationship without blurring boundaries. In this setting, it is not uncommon for a client to misinterpret the therapeutic relationship for friendship. Yang, Garis, Jackson, and McClure (2009) reminded us that explicit tools for establishing professional boundaries are absent in a client's home. There is no waiting area, no formal meeting room, and no visible program signage to remind either party of the professional relationship. In an in-home setting

> clients may request that the clinician engage in informal activities such as drinking tea or juice, moving chairs or otherwise adjust the environment, reading mail, etc. The intimacy may lead to more frequent offerings of food or gifts, presenting additional decision-making challenges for the [clinician] as he or she considers the context of the gift in the in-home setting.
>
> (Yang et al., 2009, p. 338)

The informality of this therapeutic milieu is fertile ground for transference and countertransference. As such, frontline workers in CBOP must remain vigilant and attend to these feelings as they arise.

Comparatively, service delivery that happens predominantly in a client's home can offer a unique opportunity for therapeutic work. Most importantly, in many ways, it's easier for frontline workers to build a rapport with clients. More often than not, clients allow frontline workers into their personal space day after day. This close professional relationship can contribute to client engagement and ultimate work toward improved outcomes.

CBOP appealed to me early on in my career because I couldn't imagine being at a job that required me to be wedded to a desk. No day was like the last; you always had to think on your feet and most importantly, be comfortable seeing people in their home. As a frontline worker, I was expected to have five hours of face-to-face contact each day. The mornings were hectic. The office was always filled with the chatter of frontline workers on the phone confirming visits with clients for the day so they could try to get organized all the while knowing frontline work never seemed to go as planned. If you were someone who needed structure and routine, then CBOP were not for you.

Most days I was so busy; I didn't have time to eat. When I did, I had to surrender to the conveniences of a fast-food drive through. The one thing that I underestimated was the amount of time I would spend in the car. I became a master of shortcuts to avoid traffic so I could make it to the next visit on time. Although being in the car so much wasn't always easy, it had its benefits. The car had a way of disarming clients. I found that even the most guarded client eventually took down a brick from their wall of defense if we were in the car going to an appointment.

Burnout

Hazel, like many other frontline workers, had fears for her own health and safety during these uncertain times. Due to the transmission capabilities of coronavirus, Hazel's concerns also extended to her family. She worried that continuing to have face-to-face visits would put her and her family at undue risk. Scholars have already begun to investigate the psychological burden of the pandemic. Shreffler, Petrey, and Huecker (2020) conducted a systematic review of the existing literature to measure the effects of the pandemic on the wellness of healthcare providers. The study concluded that frontline workers are more susceptible to distress and negative health outcomes (Shreffler et al., 2020). Of particular interest were the authors' speculation that the frontline workers who reported lower stress levels perceived more control of their situation (Shreffler et al., 2020). This was not the case with Hazel. She felt compelled to reach out to me following what she believed was her program's recalcitrance to act and put frontline workers first. She felt helpless. The program's perceived failures likely compounded the already present stressors of performing street-level work.

In 2018, the American Psychological Association pointed to research that estimated between 21% and 61% of mental health practitioners experienced signs of burnout. Maslach and Leiter (2016) define burnout as a "prolonged response to chronic emotional and interpersonal stressors on the job" (p. 351). In Hazel's case, in addition to living with mental illness, the clients she worked with also encountered a variety of adverse life experiences including trauma. Frontline workers delivering services to such populations, by nature, may vicariously take on the emotional burden of their clients which could further contribute to vocational stressors.

Research of street-level bureaucracy theory provides further insight into the toll of frontline work. Street-level bureaucrats often struggle to adequately perform their job duties due to high caseloads, rising documentation requirements, and a lack of resources (Lipsky, 2010; Spitzmueller, 2016). Despite these organizational influences, frontline workers often personalize their inability to cope with their work conditions. Lipsky (2010) explained,

> Street-level bureaucrats often experience their jobs in terms of inadequate personal resources, even when part of that inadequacy is

attributable to the nature of the job rather than rooted in some personal failure. Some jobs just cannot be done properly, given the ambiguity of goals and the technology of particular social services.

(p. 31)

Hazel seemingly personalized her apprehension to meet with clients face to face rather than acknowledging that as a system, we were not prepared to contend with all the challenges that came along with the pandemic. She feared that if the clients she worked with failed, it would be due to her unwillingness to see them. As mentioned earlier, Hazel's distress likely preceded the pandemic. Nonetheless, the state of practice was filled with disempowered clients, disempowered frontline workers, and now disempowered systems that were seemingly crippled by the pandemic. Leiter and Maslach (2005) cautioned that "when the workplace does not recognize the human side of work, and there are major mismatches between the nature of the job and the nature of people, there will be a greater risk of burnout" (p. 49). It would be critical to consider the humanity of our profession when contemplating ways to move forward and ameliorate such complex dilemmas. The absence of staying true to the foundational principles of our work could have immeasurable effects on the field for years to come.

Technology and Practice

Luckily, CBOP began evaluating ways to use digital tools to aid in service delivery. Telehealth emerged as the best solution (Torous, Myrick, Rauseo-Ricupero, & Firth, 2020). Hazel was not convinced that the use of digital tools would allow for the same type of relationship. In a later conversation with Hazel, she shared her thoughts on the move to increase the use of technology to connect with clients.

I'm definitely happy that they finally listened to our concerns. They told us to start looking at who we think is high risk and who we think would be okay with just a call. I'm not sure how many of the clients will even stay on the phone that long or even would pick up.

Her pessimism permeated through the phone. I asked her if she had other ideas on how she could still work with clients safely.

I'm not sure, but my program is looking into Zoom so we can at least see people. I just don't see how this is all going to work in the end, but I guess it's better than the alternative.

Hazel's words resonated with me. I would have been just as cynical of the plan to abruptly transition to phone calls or virtual meetings. While using technology as the primary tool for engagement seemed to be a practical solution, there were many complicating factors that needed to be considered. I thought back to the clients that I once worked with on the front lines. How would they acclimate to phone calls or Zoom?

There is a growing body of literature that has confirmed the efficacy of using technology-based interventions to deliver mental health services (Lattie et al., 2020; Lopez, Schwenk, Schneck, Griffin, & Mishkind, 2019; Richards, Simpson, Bastiampillai, Pietrabissa, & Castelnuovo, 2018). Of particular interest is a review by Lopez et al. (2019) that examined technology-based mental health treatment and its impact on the therapeutic alliance. The findings highlight that, overall, the therapeutic alliance can be successfully maintained through the use of various digital tools (Lopez et al., 2019). Additionally, Richards et al. (2018) conducted a study in which they examined the perceptions of the therapeutic alliance among patients and therapists who were engaged in traditional face-to-face treatment that included an enhanced online Acceptance and Commitment Therapy Program. A thematic analysis revealed that participants felt the therapeutic relationship was improved through the use of technology (Richards et al., 2018). As frontline workers like Hazel made the pivot toward technology-based services, the undercurrent of the digital divide emerged.

Technology has been transformative; however, its accessibility is disproportionately distributed and often excludes those with socioeconomic disadvantages. Herein lies the challenge of integrating digital enhancements in CBOP. The reality is that some clients have access to technology and some do not. More recently, digital divide scholars have gone beyond the traditional binary conceptualization of technological disparities and have embraced a more multidimensional framework (Hargittai, Piper, & Morris, 2019; Van Deursen & Van Dijk, 2019; Scheerder, van Deursen, & van Dijk, 2017). The current focus of determinants of the divide are internet access, technological skills, and outcomes (Hargittai et al., 2019; Scheerder et al., 2017).

Early scholarship on digital inequities examines the role of access. Financial resources and geography can both influence access. Many clients in CBOP are on a fixed income which can make acquiring the internet a financial hardship. An important consideration is that the financial responsibility of access increases over time. For example, the ongoing maintenance and upgrades that come with access and accompanying devices (i.e., laptops, smart phones, tablets) are inevitable. Hence, just because an individual can afford access today doesn't necessarily mean they can sustain that financial responsibility in the future. Physical location is another aspect to access. Not all parts of the world have internet connectivity or broadband capabilities. In 2018, the Federal Communications Commission noted that 31% of rural households in the United States still lacked access to broadband internet. However, internet connectivity saturation is projected to continue expanding which, in turn, broadens access (Van Deursen & Van Dijk, 2019). As individuals begin to cross the access divide, the skills to use technology become essential.

The guidance on social distancing during the pandemic has quickly delineated novice technology users from those who have acquired more expertise. Nevertheless, CBOP and other mental health providers began to transition to a prominently technology-based approach to care assuming that each client had not only the necessary equipment to facilitate virtual sessions but also the aptitude to navigate the tools. Yet, circumstances differ from client to client. These inconsistencies were something Hazel was observing as she began providing services via telehealth. In one conversation, she explained,

> *I spent more than half the meeting waiting for [client] to find a good Wi-Fi spot. The minute we got started he would get booted out. This happened several times. He finally ended up sitting in front of his next-door neighbor's house for a better connection.*

Next, she spoke about a client who couldn't navigate a virtual platform.

By the time I finally got them to log on, they couldn't figure out how to put on the audio. I was trying to read their lips while talking to them through finding the audio button to turn it on, but it was a fail. I was trying my best not to show how frustrated and annoyed I was, but I kept thinking about how many more clients I had to go through this with that day. I didn't even address the fact that their camera was pointed at the ceiling the entire time.

Recent studies indicated that individuals from a more privileged background were more technologically skilled than those that were not (Hargittai et al., 2019; Fang et al., 2019). Other contributing factors included age and educational attainment (Hansen et al., 2018; Fang et al., 2019). Combating these barriers would require a systematic approach to skills teaching that would take time and persistence. Particularly because skill acquisition in this regard is complex. Van Deursen et al. (2016) detail the second level of the digital divide, skills. Further, they make the distinction between operational skills (basic internet use), information navigation skills (the ability to explore, locate, and evaluate information from the internet), social skills (capability to exchange ideas), and creative skills (develop content and share with others). The pandemic could not accommodate a commitment to develop such a comprehensive menu of digital competencies in a short period. The US government's move to temporarily relax regulations around telehealth use were unprecedented. As a result, CBOP and other service providers acted. There was no time to determine accessibility or to examine digital competencies. Clients and frontline staff were thrusted, willingly or not, into this new digital realm of mental healthcare.

The danger in imposing digital tools on individuals who are not ready or willing is disengagement. Hazel expressed concerns for a number of clients that had seemingly "disappeared." She had no way of assessing how they were managing the crisis or what their needs were, respectively. On the one hand, Hazel's account showed a willingness of both frontline workers and clients to collaboratively navigate new digital tools. On the other hand, it also magnified how technology can disrupt the therapeutic dyad. For some, the expectation to use technology as the primary tool to receive treatment may be daunting at best. Whether actual or perceived shortcomings of technology use can be a deterrent to active participation in treatment.

According to the digital divide discourse, the third and final level focuses on outcomes. In doing so, consideration is given to the benefits of technology use (Scheerder et al., 2017). Inherent advantages of effective technology use are easy access information, social connections, better job opportunities, and overall efficiency with managing day-to-day tasks (i.e., paying bills, keeping track of appointments). As I reflected on this multidimensional conceptualization of the digital divide, I began to consider how this gap extended beyond clients. Some frontline workers also lacked the skills needed to efficiently navigate and integrate technology into services. I recalled my time working in a CBOP and assisting colleagues with what we would now consider digital basics like using text messaging and smartphone. If technology-based services were going to be a part of the new standard array of services, then providers would need to work toward improving digital literacy and skills across systems.

Changing a System

The Health Information Technology for Economic and Clinical Health Act of 2009 prompted systems to begin adopting electronic health records (Adler-Milstein & Jha, 2017). This commitment to digitization was initially incentivized by the government, but it wasn't long before providers like CBOP began recognizing the practical efficiencies technology could offer. I was a frontline worker when electronic health records were being widely implemented. I recall my CBOP planning a big roll-out, inclusive of agency-wide trainings and identified superusers who would serve as experts that could also help their peers navigate the paradigm shift. Additionally, we received agency laptops and tablets that would allow for documentation in the community. The resistance that comes with such organizational change was expected; however, the digital divide among frontline workers was significantly underestimated. While I am not the most technologically inclined, I along with many others at the agency were able to acclimate to the change relatively quickly. However, there were still a notable number of my peers who struggled with basic digital operational skills. These challenges persisted for weeks and in some cases, months. Notwithstanding the technological learning curve, all frontline workers were still expected to deliver the same amount of services. Overtime, the expectation was to increase productivity given the efficiency gains the electronic health record offered. Not everyone was able to manage the transition. Consequently, the beginning of the electronic health record in CBOP meant the end for some frontline workers.

COVID-19 reignited the move toward technology in mental health. Adopting an electronic health record seemed to be the main digital step forward. However, Hazel was able to speak to the current state of practice. Hazel acknowledged,

> *Some people couldn't understand why they wanted us to start using video with clients. Don't get me wrong, it's annoying and takes longer, but I'm realizing how helpful it is to see clients. Especially now. My agency didn't really train us on how to use Zoom or these other platforms. I figured it out eventually, other staff are still struggling.*

Hazel's account highlights the ongoing digital divide in CBOP. But these technology inequities are likely not exclusive to CBOP. Research continues to project an increase in the use of technology in the workplace warranting the swift acquisition of basic digital skills (López Peláez, Erro-Garcés, & Gómez-Ciriano, 2020). If organizations don't commit to adequate training and preparation of frontline workers, then the digital divide will widen.

Prior to the more liberal allowances around telehealth, virtual services were not readily embedded into billing structures. Lattie et al. (2020) conducted a mixed methods study with 89 clinician and supervisors that aimed to better understand frontline worker attitudes about technology. In addition, they explored barriers to successful implementation of technology. One emerging theme was related to billing structures. In particular, there was mutual concern over the lack of a billing mechanism for text messaging (Lattie et al., 2020). Participants highlighted that some clients were more engaged via text message than any other digital means. In this case, if clients and frontline workers are discouraged from texting despite its apparent positive effect on treatment, then are we contributing to a possible therapeutic impasse? Of course, there are valid concerns around the use of text messaging, but are we then basing services on available billing structures rather than what's best for the client?

Verhaeghe (2012) found that "work content is less important than whether a certain performance or activity 'counts' or not. The need to score well means that employees constantly adapt their work to reflect changes in the scoring system" (p. 137). This would suggest that frontline workers would likely only engage in using technology that resulted in positive billing. Ultimately, the productivity of frontline workers in CBOP is tied to billing. The global pandemic has further compounded fiscal concerns. Although many state mental health authorities have provided some temporary financial cover for agencies, budget concerns still remain. Lipsky (2010) reminds us that

> Established street-level bureaucracies may also attempt to increase their clientele if they perceive themselves under attack and calculate that demonstrations of significant service provision, or increase clientele,

might aid their cause. Relatedly, street-level bureaucracies may attempt to increase the number of clients when they are competing against other programs with similar objectives.

(p. 92)

The uncertainty of what lies ahead has many CBOP and other like systems carefully considering the fiscal implications of COVID-19. If programs are expected to continue offering technology-based interventions, there are additional financial considerations. For example, the proper use of technology to communicate with clients must ensure compliance with Health Insurance Portability and Accountability Act. In most cases, this requires specific devices and/or the use of applications that come at a monetary cost. Accordingly, programs will undoubtedly feel compelled to take steps they feel may put them ahead of their competitors. Trying to stay ahead of the competition often means increasing expectations on frontline workers without additional resources. On the surface, it would seem as though the pandemic has primarily had a negative impact on CBOP. Yet, many of the unexpected changes to service delivery can be a source of encouragement.

Technology Beyond the Pandemic

As the pandemic continued, many CBOP extended the use of technology-based approaches to service delivery. Doing so allowed frontline workers and clients to uncover resilience and hope for the future. In a perspective piece by Torous et al. (2020), the authors highlight the potential for use of technology beyond COVID-19,

> the field's next steps will also be critical in ensuring digital health is used today to deliver the best care during the current crisis, ready for any resulting mental health spike following the immediate crisis, and prepared to support future crises as well as care as usual.

(p. 1)

The crisis accelerated any future plans to further integrate technology into CBOP and other healthcare systems. Nonetheless, the public health emergency created an opportunity to use technology in ways that may have not been considered otherwise. The expedited implementation also confirmed not only the system's capacity to adjust but also the actors who operate within them. After months into the crisis, it was hard not to juxtapose Hazel's initial fears with her excitement of how much technology has been beneficial. I recall her boasting about how she has become much more efficient since using more digital strategies.

It's a relief not to have to spend as much time in the car anymore. I use the extra time to see more clients and actually get my notes in on time.

I was curious about how the agencies manage situations when a client is less receptive to using technology. She explained,

> Honestly, we don't push it on them. If the person doesn't feel comfortable, then we just plan to have a socially distant visit. I still try to talk to those clients about how it can be helpful to learn to use their phones better or I offer to teach them how to Zoom even if it's to connect with someone other than me.

Hazel's willingness to maintain an open dialogue with clients who express discomfort and/or an unwillingness to use technology may prove to be fruitful in the future. Fang et al. (2019) used a systematic search to explore the existing literature and focused on individual agency in information and communication technology access and use. The study found that individuals that identified as middle-aged or older adults reported a correlation between increased technology exposure and comfortability. Further, the same group attributed nonuse with lack of skills and training (Chang, McAllister, & McCaslin, 2015; Fang et al., 2019). In Hazel's case, her relaxed approach to discussing the benefits of technology may disarm skeptical clients. Those same clients may eventually be willing to use digital tools for treatment purposes with Hazel or for social connections with natural supports.

Increased use of technology also dispelled some of Hazel's preconceived notions that surfaced soon after the onset of the pandemic. Hazel seemed certain that the vast majority of the individuals she worked with would not fare well if using technology would be the main source of engagement. Yet, she eventually admitted that many clients seemed to be getting used to this new way of connecting and were opening up more. Research by Mirkovic et al. (2016) would support Hazel's account. The study examined the views of information technology among patients with chronic health conditions. Findings indicate participant satisfaction with the use of information technology in identifying and discussing personal strengths (Mirkovic et al., 2016). One important caveat was that participants recommended that technology use be structured for use at home and found that it was critical in empowering them to play a more active role in their health (Mirkovic et al., 2016). As studies continue to emerge, policy makers can more thoughtfully consider the longevity of technology-based approaches in practice.

Discussion

Hazel's case illustrates the theory to practice gaps that occur in street-level work. The pandemic only further amplified an already fragmented system. Many CBOPs endorse a mission to help disenfranchised groups; yet, their inability to adequately respond during the onset of the public health emergency unintentionally disenfranchised many of their frontline workers. Hazel described a lack of humanity, a voice unheard. Despite my tenure in

CBOP, education, and training, I too felt helpless. In many ways, we were simply actors in a flawed system hanging onto hope for the change our profession had indoctrinated us to believe in.

Through Hazel, I witnessed both the fragility and power of street-level bureaucrats.

Her apprehensions soon began to influence her perception of the clients she supported and her belief in their ability to succeed. These insecurities and client judgments could have influenced treatment decisions and approaches. Luckily, Hazel used her agency to take control of her situation by seeking help. In doing so, she steadily regained the confidence in her work that I believe could circumvent chronic burnout. Whether in the face of a crisis or day-to-day dilemmas, it is important for agencies to support frontline workers and be responsive to any concerns for safety and well-being. Hazel's willingness to reach out to me highlights the benefits of peer support, mentorship, and/or supervision. Cultivating and maintaining such relationships are crucial to the continued professional development of all social workers no matter their length of tenure in the field.

This case also illustrated the contributions technology-based approaches could have in CBOP. All too often, we wed ourselves to practice routines and learn to operate within relatively predictable systems. However, the global pandemic served as a reminder to the profession of the need to be flexible and open to innovations. While I acknowledge that technology can never replace the humanity and connection that face-to-face modalities of practice offer, they can complement already established approaches. Moreover, further research from social workers and other disciplines may yield more knowledge about the role digital tools can play and contribute to the development of enhanced-practice approaches.

Policy and Practice Considerations

Leveraging the power of technology with the needs of client systems can result in innovative approaches to care. In the case of CBOP, the use of technology in practice may have remained subordinate to traditional face-to-face therapeutic modalities if not for COVID-19. The possibilities that digital tools offer may have been overlooked. In order to fully realize the benefits of technology-based approaches in practice, policy makers and other stakeholders must acknowledge the potential for perpetuating disparities that already exist. The digital divide discourse reminds us that the intersectionality of attributes such as socioeconomics, social positions, educational experiences, and geographic location structure our knowledge, skills, and access to digital resources (Chang et al., 2015; Fang et al., 2019; Van Deursen & Van Dijk, 2019). Social workers have a history of engaging in street-level work (Lipsky, 2010) therefore, the profession is well positioned to respond to the inevitable role technology will play in practice.

In 2016, the National Association of Social Workers (NASW) leadership responded to the continued inequities by prioritizing social justice. This acknowledgment highlighted that national injustices warranted action. Relevant to this shift in focus was an emphasis on economic and environmental justice (NASW, 2018). In many ways, both areas can be viewed as gatekeepers to technology access and use.

Close Reading Questions:

1. How does the author illustrate the fragility and power of street-level workers? What text evidence does the author offer to highlight how clients and frontline workers relate to the experience of disempowerment during the pandemic?
2. What images came to your mind—and what did you feel in your body—when Clay described the case of Hazel?
3. How might Clay's identification as a woman of color affect the significance of her narrative and the ways her message might be received?

Prompts for Writing:

1. Describe ways in which frontline workers function as an extension of systems that perpetuate the social construction of illness.
2. What role does intersectionality play in structuring our knowledge, skills, and access to digital resources? What is your personal engagement with the concept of intersectionality in your own practice?
3. In what ways are frontline workers challenged in terms of maintaining empathic engagement with their clients? What strategies might street-level workers use to maintain empathy in the midst of crisis?

References

Adler-Milstein, J., & Jha, A. K. (2017). HITECH act drove large gains in hospital electronic health record adoption. *Health Affairs, 36*(8), 1416–1422.

Akosa, F., & Asare, B. E. (2017). Street-level bureaucrats and the exercise of discretion. *Global Encyclopedia of Public Administration, Public Policy, and Governance,* 1–6.

American Psychological Association. (2018, January 25). *Research roundup: Burnout in mental health providers.* Retrieved from www.apaservices.org/practice/update/2018/01-25/mental-health-providers

Anthony, W. A. (1993). Recovery from mental illness: The guiding vision of the mental health service system in the 1990s. *Psychosocial Rehabilitation Journal, 16*(4), 11.

Blair, T. R., & Espinoza, R. T. (2015). Medicare, Medicaid, and mental health care: Historical perspectives on reforms before the US congress. *JAMA, 314*(21), 2231–2232.

Chang, J., McAllister, C., & McCaslin, R. (2015). Correlates of, and barriers to, Internet use among older adults. *Journal of Gerontological Social Work, 58*(1), 66–85.

Davis, L., Fulginiti, A., Kriegel, L., & Brekke, J. S. (2012). Deinstitutionalization? Where have all the people gone? *Current Psychiatry Reports, 14*(3), 259–269.

Fang, M. L., Canham, S. L., Battersby, L., Sixsmith, J., Wada, M., & Sixsmith, A. (2019). Exploring privilege in the digital divide: Implications for theory, policy, and practice. *The Gerontologist, 59*(1), e1–e15.

Federal Communications Commission. (2018). *Broadband deployment report*. Retrieved from www.fcc.gov/reports-research/reports/broadband-progressreports/2018-broadband-deployment-report

Gronfein, W. (1985). Psychotropic drugs and the origins of deinstitutionalization. *Social Problems, 32*(5), 437–454.

Hansen, H. T., Lundberg, K., & Syltevik, L. J. (2018). Digitalization, street-level bureaucracy and welfare users' experiences. *Social Policy & Administration, 52*(1), 67–90.

Hargittai, E., Piper, A. M., & Morris, M. R. (2019). From internet access to internet skills: Digital inequality among older adults. *Universal Access in the Information Society, 18*(4), 881–890.

Lattie, E. G., Nicholas, J., Knapp, A. A., Skerl, J. J., Kaiser, S. M., & Mohr, D. C. (2020). Opportunities for and tensions surrounding the use of technology-enabled mental health services in community mental health care. *Administration and Policy in Mental Health and Mental Health Services Research, 47*(1), 138–149.

Leiter, M. P., & Maslach, C. (2005). Reversing burnout: How to rekindle your passion for your work. *Standford Social Innovation Review, Graduate School of Business, 3*(4).

Lipsky, M. (2010). *Street-level bureaucracy: Dilemmas of the individual in public service*. New York: Russell Sage Foundation.

Lopez, A., Schwenk, S., Schneck, C. D., Griffin, R. J., & Mishkind, M. C. (2019). Technology-based mental health treatment and the impact on the therapeutic alliance. *Current Psychiatry Reports, 21*(8), 76.

López Peláez, A., Erro-Garcés, A., & Gómez-Ciriano, E. J. (2020). Young people, social workers and social work education: The role of digital skills. *Social Work Education, 39*(6), 825–842.

Madsen, W. C., & Gillespie, K. (2014). *Collaborative helping: A strengths framework for home-based services*. New York: John Wiley & Sons.

Maslach, C., & Leiter, M. P. (2016). Burnout. In *Stress: Concepts, cognition, emotion, and behavior* (pp. 351–357). Cambridge: Academic Press.

Mirkovic, J., Kristjansdottir, O. B., Stenberg, U., Krogseth, T., Stange, K. C., & Ruland, C. M. (2016). Patient insights into the design of technology to support a strengths-based approach to health care. *JMIR Research Protocols, 5*(3), e175.

Modak, T., Sarkar, S., & Sagar, R. (2016). Dorothea dix: A proponent of humane treatment of mentally ill. *Journal of Mental Health and Human Behaviour, 21*(1), 69.

National Association of Social Workers. (2018). *Social justice priorities: Equity and inclusion*. Retrieved from www.socialworkers.org/Portals/0/PDF/Advocacy/Public/Social-Justice/Social-Justice-Priorities-2018-2019.pdf

Parry, M. S. (2006). Dorothea Dix (1802–1887). *American Journal of Public Health, 96*(4), 624–625.

Ray, C. G., & Kanapaux, W. (2002). *Community mental health centers at the 40-year mark: The quest for survival*. Rockville, MD: Mental Health in the United States.

Richards, P., Simpson, S., Bastiampillai, T., Pietrabissa, G., & Castelnuovo, G. (2018). The impact of technology on therapeutic alliance and engagement in psychotherapy: The therapist's perspective. *Clinical Psychologist, 22*(2), 171–181.

Scheerder, A., van Deursen, A., & van Dijk, J. (2017). Determinants of internet skills, uses and outcomes: A systematic review of the second-and third-level digital divide. *Telematics and Informatics, 34*(8), 1607–1624.

Shreffler, J., Petrey, J., & Huecker, M. (2020). The impact of COVID-19 on healthcare worker wellness: A scoping review. *Western Journal of Emergency Medicine, 21*(5), 1059.

Spitzmueller, M. C. (2016). Negotiating competing institutional logics at the street level: An ethnography of a community mental health organization. *Social Service Review, 90*(1), 35–82.

Terry, R., Townley, G., Brusilovskiy, E., & Salzer, M. S. (2019). The influence of sense of community on the relationship between community participation and mental health for individuals with serious mental illnesses. *Journal of Community Psychology, 47*(1), 163–175.

Torous, J., Myrick, K. J., Rauseo-Ricupero, N., & Firth, J. (2020). Digital mental health and COVID-19: Using technology today to accelerate the curve on access and quality tomorrow. *JMIR Mental Health, 7*(3), e18848.

Van Deursen, A. J., Helsper, E. J., & Eynon, R. (2016). Development and validation of the internet skills scale (ISS). *Information, Communication & Society, 19*(6), 804–823.

Van Deursen, A. J., & Van Dijk, J. A. (2019). The first-level digital divide shifts from inequalities in physical access to inequalities in material access. *New Media & Society, 21*(2), 354–375.

Verhaeghe, P. (2012). *What about me?: The struggle for identity in a market.* London: Scribe.

Yang, J. A., Garis, J., Jackson, C., & McClure, R. (2009). Providing psychotherapy to older adults in home: Benefits, challenges, and decision-making guidelines. *Clinical Gerontologist, 32*(4), 333–346.

8 Addressing Social Injustice in Social Work Practice

The Clinical Advocacy Model

Edith Lori Slater

Pre-reading Questions:

1. Is social justice advocacy conceptualized in mental healthcare treatment? What might "clinical advocacy" in action look like in mental healthcare? How can the social work profession best respond to the public's need for advocacy?
2. What are your personal experiences with advocating for your clients? In what sense do you feel that their needs have been neglected within the existing mental health system?
3. How might increasing awareness of one's own intersectionality facilitate social justice advocacy?

In *Social Work Speaks: National Association of Social Workers Policy Statements*, the National Association of Social Workers (NASW, 2009) emphasized that a fundamental professional value of social work is social justice, which is concerned with human rights, self-determination, the protection and safety of individuals facing imminent violent danger, and the international redistribution of resources. Concomitantly, the NASW (2009) stated that the profession's educational focus remains appropriately aligned with its rich activist traditions, which are steeped in public justice. The profession's explicit social justice values means that social workers must be sufficiently socially aware in order to combat injustices with clients while upholding human rights, self-determination, safety, access, opportunity, and empowerment. How does social justice, the profession's North Star and prescribed guiding principle, translate into clinical social work private practice?

Although it is elusive, social justice work is the path toward cultivating a fairer society. In today's society, whether we like it or not, our profession is moving toward clinical work, which should continue to include social justice work. Social workers are positioned to notice subtle and overt social inequities within systems since they work in schools, agencies, social welfare programs, nonprofit mental healthcare facilities, private practices, hospitals, and even in local and state governments. While they may see the injustices take place, there is inconsistency regarding if and how to address

DOI: 10.4324/9781003270225-8

social justice work in practice. McLaughlin (2009) reported that some social workers view social justice work as the act of influencing attitudes and judgments, while others shied away from doing advocacy work because they were weary that it would diminish a professional identity. Other social workers, according to Hare (2004), asserted that the cornerstone of social work practice is promoting social change and problem-solving in human relationships by empowering clients on micro and meso levels. Yet, Lord and Iudice (2012) reported in a study of 167 social workers in private practice that none of them identified their work as social justice oriented. The shift away from social justice work, as reported by Abramovitz (2005), was a response to the rise of psychiatry in the field. Arguably, the age-old controversy within the profession regarding the role of social justice and advocacy work in social work practice is linked to its ambiguity.

The Council for Social Work Education Standards (CSWE, 2019), NASW Code of Ethics, and the social work's mission are unequivocal regarding the profession's prescribed commitment to promoting social justice; yet, social justice work and advocacy continue to mystify many social workers in practice. With this discrepancy, some within the profession are asking: How did we get here? Morgaine and Capous–Desyllas (2015) contended that the social justice work inertia is attributable to the lack of a common understanding within the field. According to Specht and Courtney (1995), some social workers accuse others in the profession of abandoning social justice values in lieu of the status associated with psychotherapy practice, while McLaughlin (2009) reported that social workers working in agencies face limitations in their ability to focus on social justice work. Reisch (2002) asserted that the profession undeservingly wraps itself in social justice rhetoric, whereas McCauley and Moskalenko (2011) reported that social justice work is too uncomfortable because of its association to politics. Regardless of the reason, social justice work is in danger of running adrift at a time when society is entreating for more. To understand the disconnect between the profession's commitment to social justice work and the commitment to social justice work that social workers actually identify with, Slater (2020) explored if and how social workers integrated social justice work in private practice. Slater reported that even with social workers confirmed social justice values, advocacy work eluded them in practice; however, more importantly, they reported that they would likely do more advocacy if they had additional education, training, and networking to that aim. Thus, the rift between social work values and practice could conceivably be caused by a dearth of social justice and advocacy education in social work training. This rift can be reconcilable through educational requirements that include clinical advocacy competency.

The Clinical Advocacy Model (CAM) is a clinical advocacy framework that prepares social workers to *Think Big, Ask The Right Questions, and Advocate.* CAM's three-pronged approach includes the development of clinical advocacy acuity, the use of the assessment tool known as HEAL, and refinement of concrete advocacy skills. Social workers who *Think Big* must develop clinical advocacy acuity by taking active steps to become and remain self-aware in order to engage in self-reflective practice as a way of professional life that contributes to the detection of social injustice. The development of clinical advocacy acuity will aid social workers in knowing how to *Ask The Right Questions* during assessment using the HEAL intervention, a tool for presumed social injustices that arise in practice. HEAL helps social workers determine whether an issue is social justice related and how it is related to social justice; the tool also emphasizes the ways to explicitly address the topic and/or advocate by honing in on social justice issues related to Health, Economic, Academic, and Legal systems that impact mental health. With accurate understanding of an injustice in the context of the client's lived world after implementing HEAL, social workers are prepared to act. An integral aspect of social justice work insists that social workers advocate, and CAM provides social workers with concrete ways to do clinical advocacy on behalf of clients whose social justice needs are linked to their mental health. The portrait of Eylin, a composite case study, will intimately illustrate my real-life, challenging, and unrehearsed decision-making experience when social justice issues arose in clinical practice.

In the current divided political climate, there has been widespread attention paid to the proliferation of disparities within social institutions, especially as they pertain to ethnically and racially diverse groups. Reflexively, some social workers have expressed concerns regarding the neoliberal tendency in social work and whether or not the profession can meet the moment by valuing social justice in clinical practice. While the concern regarding neoliberalism within the field is real, it can only be remedied by joining all social workers through education, training, and networking to disseminate the importance of clinical advocacy in practice. Clinical social workers, with knowledge cured from people that are disproportionately impacted by inequities, can better understand the importance of ensuring access to all clients and addressing social inequities. Reimagining and strengthening clinical social work depend on the profession's dedication to preparing social workers by focusing on scholarship that hones in on social justice and advocacy competency as a way of fulfilling the profession's mission. CAM, a clinical advocacy framework, will provide social workers with the knowledge and tools to ensure that clinical, advocacy, and social justice work are all central foci in practice. Fortunately, this means that the disconnect between clinical work and the profession's overarching political context of fulfilling social justice needs is reconcilable. Clinical advocacy must be the gold standard of mental healthcare practice, not the exception.

The Divide in Social Work Perspectives

Reflecting on social justice movements of the past evinces that the profession has been shaped by and has influenced movement outcomes through its action and inaction (Ehrenreich, 2014). Some of the most significant social work movements in US history, according to Abramovitz (2005), were the Charitable Organization Society (COS) and the Settlement House Movement (SHM), whose approaches were instructed by their distinct views of social problems: While COS equated morality to self-reliance, SHM recognized that the equation is meaningless because each person does not have access to the same resources. Expectedly, the decline of COS was said to be linked to its inflexibility tied to its litmus test, which differentiated eligibility among the needy and broadened the white agenda, according to Gough (2020). The colonialist agenda embedded in the profession, as reported by Gregory (2020), continues to haunt the profession in our present-day skimming over social justice issues in practice. Wakefield (2013) reported that the long-standing tension surrounding the methodology regarding the role of clinical social workers in practice has seized attention away from mental healthcare outcomes, which has obscured the goal of promoting social justice in practice. While the influences of diverging schools of thought regarding the social work approach persist within the profession, some social workers aim to treat individuals in their environments, and others treat individuals in a bubble.

Similar to COS, the current clinical approach emphasizes the treatment of individuals. This unfortunate clinical orientation within the profession has undermined the person-in-environment perspective, which is the social work trademark. Ehrenreich (2014) reported that a preponderance of social work knowledge comes from psychology, rather than sociology, which is paradoxical because of its implicit biases. Decades ago, Northen (1982) warned of the dangers linked to generalizing a select body of knowledge, such as psychology, that lacks diversity and broadly applying it to social work practice. She asserted that psychology in social work practice reflexively attaches power to individuals who are similar to the standard's creators while simultaneously relegating all others as inferior. Early on, Northen recognized that expanding social workers' exposures to other more diverse bodies of knowledge is connected to social work practice that focuses on an individual's ecological, relational, cultural, and institutional systems, which are essential to promoting social justice. Due to the hierarchical nature of psychology, its prevalence within the field was reported by Beller (2014) to be out of sync with supporting a client's right to self-determination and alliance formation, which are hallmarks of social work. Tamburro (2013) asserted that until social work frees itself from a silo view of humanity, it jeopardizes being an instrument of the oppression it seeks to defeat. Illogically, knowledge culled from diverse groups was dismissed in dominant pedagogy, according to Bernal (2002), which undermined social justice efforts. Imagine if curated bodies of knowledge regarding mental health were diverse and included the experiences and first-hand knowledge of Native Americans, African-Americans, Latinos, Asians, and Pacific Islanders, which then were integrated into a new, inclusive psychology and woven into the study of social work specializations such as addiction, children and families, and school social work. How might the term "normal" be reinvented and how might it reshape our approach to mental healthcare? Moving social justice and advocacy education to the forefront must begin with valuing diverse bodies of knowledge and not treating them as addenda to existing knowledge. Kumashiro (2000) reported that the minimal requirements in pedagogy regarding diversity ends up alienating rather than joining, which is detrimental to anti-oppressive education. If we are too far removed from the suffering of others, according to Shepherd (2019), then we are less likely to accurately perceive the problem, much less apply an appropriate treatment plan. The checklist approach to social work practice is arguably the reason why the profession has been accused of operating like a wolf in sheep's clothing, especially among diverse groups. While embracing a more holistic approach to secure equitable mental healthcare, it is imperative that the profession decidedly refuse to peddle in the compartmentalization of people's micro and meso needs, which Ehrenreich (2014) dubbed as clinicalism. As the profession pivots toward more inclusive and integrative clinical social work education, it will instantaneously bolster the profession's status and expertise by providing social workers with the tools necessary to competently address mental healthcare-related social justice needs in practice, while earning the trust of the people it aims to serve.

The confluence of pernicious bipartisan politics, the coronavirus pandemic, and the subsequent economic recession lay bare the exploitative, discriminatory, and prejudicial system-wide failures that negatively impact mental health. While many of the initial outcries resulting from the social unrest came from privileged people within systems, such as doctors and nurses during the onset of the pandemic, their voices were instrumental in exposing system-wide breakdowns that were also happening in gross disproportion among African-Americans and Latinos. These systemic inequities serve to elevate the ethical issues related to mental healthcare when social justice issues are present. The most pervasive mental health crisis in this country, according to Ehrenreich (2014), is racism. Wilkerson (2020) reported that while race has become more widely studied, the focus has unwittingly been used to subvert equity by distracting from the institutions that spread and fuel inequality. Understanding how fixed and ubiquitous oppressive structures yoke diverse groups and construct disenfranchisement as well as impose negative stigmas tied to pathologizing normal responses is critical to dismantling structural inequities in our society. As such, the fortification of clinical social justice and advocacy includes an examination of how those institutions intersect with social workers' professional identities.

The United States Bureau of Labor Statistics for Social Work (2021) reported that the amount of people joining the social work profession was expected to grow by 12% in the next decade and The Social Workforce Report according to Salsberg et al. (2017), highlighted that the dominant racial demographic within the profession remains white, which is relevant to the issue of prejudicial and discriminatory practices. Case (2012) reported that because white people are the dominant group, they are not taught to see themselves. To illustrate this point, DiAngelo (2018) discussed white people's limited exposure outside of their geographic location, and Case (2012) pointed out the whiteness that is inscribed in everyday language; this leads white people to essentially cement false and myopic views of themselves in the world in relation to others, which is then reproduced. In a study of white practitioners working in psychotherapy with individuals from diverse ethnic and racial backgrounds, Hall (2001) reported that clients experienced power struggles and defensiveness as a result of clinicians' lack of self-awareness, which led to early termination of mental healthcare services. The notion of a clinician's self-awareness being tied to effective treatment in practice was corroborated by Sorkin et al.'s (2010) study, which found that when clients perceived discrimination from their clinician, there was a lower incidence of treatment adherence and overall satisfaction due to mistrust. Disturbingly, Williams and Williams-Morris (2000) found evidence that suggested clinicians' internalized biases regarding diverse groups led to the prevalence of overdiagnosis and misdiagnosis of people of color, which was validated by Paradies et al. (2015), who reported evidence that stereotypical beliefs among clinicians germinated prejudice, which consistently led to poor mental healthcare outcomes. At the same time, the impact on social workers of diverse backgrounds in a hyper racialized society is of equal importance when examining the issues linked to oppression and privilege. According to Hall (2001), diverse groups are at an increased risk of discrimination because ethnic and racial minorities are often reflexively associated with poverty and dysfunction in the study of mental health. Fries-Britt, George Mwangi, and Peralta (2014) reported that some students of color internalized microaggressions and used it to motivate them. Concealed negative emotions linked to racially motivated acts of discrimination, as stated by Fries-Britt, manifested among other students of color as isolation or withdrawal, which is significant in the quest to raise the voices of people from diverse backgrounds in social work education. Quintana (2007) suggested that it is critical to acknowledge that labels and categories fail to convey the complex phenomenological experiences of diverse groups do not account for psychological differences in processing, and are not useful in predicting psychological variables; yet, the use of them persists. Perhaps, mental healthcare pedagogy should unpack the meaning behind the continued premium on these void labels and categories as a move toward mental healthcare parity.

The need for more social justice and advocacy education and training becomes even more evident when considering that the advent of the Affordable Care Act, which is responsible for delivering mental healthcare access to historically underrepresented groups (Chow, 2011), coincides with the United States Bureau of Labor Statistics for Social Work (2021) report that the largest anticipated growth among mental healthcare occupations is in social work. In order to purge inequities in mental healthcare, the profession must encourage discourse that addresses systemic injustice, especially from within. The impact of a continued dominant perspective in mental healthcare is significant in the education and training of social workers as we seek to invoke a more equitable approach to mental healthcare. With social workers providing the lion's share of mental healthcare treatment to disenfranchised groups, the need for an introspective profession-wide focus on social justice and advocacy is even more apparent.

The social work profession cannot claim amnesty from ingrained practices that prejudice and discriminate, which was brought to light by society's current renewed attention to social justice and subsequent social unrest. Robbins, Coe Regan, Williams, Smyth, and Bogo (2016) described the dismal number of social workers of color in university faculty and administrator positions. The majority of social workers of color, as reported by Robbins et al. (2016), occupied the low paying and poorly supported adjunct positions. In addition to the lack of diversity within the most prestigious university positions, McLaughlin (2009) reported on the diminutive number of advocacy or social justice courses in undergraduate curricula and, worse still, that those courses are housed under optional community development coursework. Despite widespread agreement among clinical supervisors and supervisees, the need for more social justice and advocacy, according to Treichler, Crawford, Higdon, and Backhaus (2020), has not translated into practical strategies to that aim. In a time when social justice and advocacy is so relevant to our society, and specifically to the social work profession, it is no longer merely optional to prioritize these invaluable topics in the university programs.

One of the most current reasons that social justice and advocacy education and training matters now more than ever is that we are in an age of digital activism. People use their smart devices to participate in global discourses; not only that, but they also use social media platforms to self-inform and advocate. Some have used social media to digitally protest by engaging in the *cancel culture*, whereas others have used it to mobilize massive resources, according to Bail (2016). Regardless of how people are involving themselves in this World Wide Web discussion, digital voices are omnipresent. According to Coleman (2010), the long arm of institutional oppression reaches this world as well, and he argued that we must not delude ourselves regarding the encoded white supremacy that permeates the World Wide Web or the proprietary nature of digital platforms on the Internet. The influences that dominate the World Wide Web are especially of note in the current day, according to Torous, Myrick, Rauseo-Ricupero, and Firth (2020), in light of the public's swift and liberal use of deregulated digital mental healthcare, which exploded during the country's stay-at-home orders at the beginning of the pandemic. Torous et al. (2020) reported on concerns regarding clients' technological competency, access to platforms that were culturally and linguistically insensitive, and participation in the data collection process that could be used to exploit. According to Hargittai (2020), there is a danger linked to online harvested and biased data from private companies and the federal government that provide online services, such as therapy, which can worsen social inequities. Even with the unfettered power to bring people together while physically far apart, technology continues to be yet another system that perpetuates categorical separation. If the goal of social justice and advocacy in practice is to make mental healthcare more equitable, then we must seek to uncover the hidden messages that are catalysts to the maintenance of systemic oppression in all its forms.

The future of bolstering social justice and advocacy in social work begins with reflecting on counteractive oppressive practices. In the face of widespread desire to participate in advocacy, social workers are invited to fulfill the National Association of Social Workers' Code of Ethics by upholding social justice values, especially because of our presence in, knowledge of, and access to systems and institutions. The profession must raise its sights toward education that prioritizes social justice values because the fair distribution of power was philosophized by Foucault to be hinged to securing access to knowledge for all (Deacon, 2006). A clinical advocacy framework instructs and encourages social workers to seek out and participate in ongoing advocacy education, training, and networking by engaging with and treating eclectic clients, developing ongoing self-awareness, proactively seeking opportunities to advocate in their communities and in the communities of their clients, collaborating with clients and providers from other disciplines, and knowing that these activities are integral to social work in order to ensure that social justice issues are learned about and addressed (Slater, 2019).

A Solution: Clinical Advocacy Model (CAM)

Excited to begin my private practice after several years of working as a social worker in nonprofit agencies, I set out to find a central location in an urban socioeconomically, ethnically, and racially mixed community. Keenly aware that most socioeconomically disadvantaged people receive mental healthcare services from clinics, I wanted to proffer a type of mental healthcare that was uncommon. My experience as a social worker at an agency highlighted formulaic mental healthcare approaches, which constrained and limited the scope of services and led to ineffective practices and clients' unmet needs. Even more meaningful, in my upbringing, my multiethnic and multiracial family and I have had first-hand experiences with misguided decision-making by the hands of systems. I opened a private practice because I felt I could do a better job and create a path forward for others. Perhaps, naively, I believed that my lived experience as a female Latin American social worker would sufficiently prepare me to treat clients who have experienced ensconced system wide failures, especially in communities of color. After getting started with my private practice, one client after another revealed a mental healthcare need that was inextricably tethered to a social inequity, discrimination, or criminality that endangered or dispossessed them of their human rights. The one-to-one clinical engagement made it possible for me to bear witness to the insidious nature of oppression and its unparalleled havoc on the human psyche. As I became aware of the multiplicity of needs and searched to help my clients, their struggle became my struggle. The profundity of addressing social justice issues related to systemic oppression overwhelmed me in private practice because of my newfound autonomy and, thus, sole ethical responsibility. In the beginning, I panicked when clients would mention social justice-related issues, such as violence or discrimination. I felt like a philosopher with no words or a handyman with no tools. My existing cache of interventions was insufficient at best and inadequate at worst. Although the spirit of the psychotherapeutic alliance is to secure equitable mental healthcare, figuring out how and where to direct those efforts were indistinct. Weaving my clients' parallel humanitarian needs for mental healthcare and political justice through advocacy became an exercise of trial by fire.

Months of hammering away different strategies with my clients revealed progress in the treatment plan. Years of concerted, collaborative, and interdisciplinary effort revealed a set of tools that made it possible to assess and organize clients' interrelated needs in the private practice setting. I honor these psychotherapeutic alliances that served to inform my awareness, instruct my reflective practices, and direct my clinical social work toward a path that embodied social justice and advocacy. My firm belief is that clinical social workers ought to be well prepared and have access to clinical interventions specifically designed to address social justice needs, especially because of the influx of social workers to private practice. CAM can help to bridge the gap between clinicians and address social justice issues in practice effectively. In the portrait of Eylin, a composite case study, the clinical advocacy model will illustrate how CAM shifts the burden of adaptation from the client to the clinician through the development of clinical advocacy acuity, awareness regarding social injustices, assessment through the use of an intervention tool known as HEAL designed to discern the presence of a social injustice, and most importantly, concrete advocacy skills to secure equitable mental healthcare. In no way does CAM suggest that mental healthcare needs evaporate after social justice needs are addressed and or reconciled, only that it makes it possible to have an authentic beginning during mental healthcare treatment, which Eylin's case study will testify.

A central tenet of CAM is the development of clinical advocacy acuity, a skill that promotes a self-reflective practice as a way of becoming acutely aware of how clinical and social work knowledge is interpreted and acted upon by the professional self. Social workers who *Think Big* must develop clinical advocacy acuity by taking active steps to become and remain self-aware in order to engage in self-reflective practice as a way of professional life that contributes to the detection of social injustice. The development of clinical advocacy acuity helps social workers be able to identify and address hardwired beliefs, attitudes, and biases that influence social justice work. The purpose is to expand a social worker's global view of people's life challenges and obstacles, guard against ethnocentrism, and be aware of blind spots that impact professional acuity in order to increase social workers' bandwidths, strengthen critical inquiry, and facilitate productive and sound decision-making in order to produce optimal mental healthcare outcomes for all clients. Moreover, the implementation of CAM's clinical advocacy acuity in the didactic supervisor–supervisee relationship will translate into the development of excellent clinical social work skills.

On turning self-awareness into an analytical skill, the late Supreme Court Justice Ruth Bader Ginsberg famously stated, "the unconscious bias is one of the hardest things to get at" (Hunt, 2018). Recognizing the material world and everything in it as a matrix of interrelated experiences, according to Eglash et al. (2020), has the power to diminish biases' influences. In support of that sentiment, CAM's post humanistic stance recognizes that treating the human condition in a petri dish encourages narrow perspectives and negates the person-in-environment. The preoccupation with essentializing human beings, according to Snaza et al. (2014), sacrifices critical thinking, which is a by-product of real-world engagement. To that aim, Quintana (2007) reported that individuals who possessed a high degree of self-awareness were more likely to detect the presence of bias, discrimination, and intolerance, which is an effective skill in the promotion of social justice that Wakefield (2013) said is the profession's most essential role. According to Slater (2020), personal self-awareness was observed to be influential in social justice work as it served to illuminate the need to redress social injustices in practice. Awareness regarding personal experiences with social injustice was reported by Vera and Speight (2003) to be instrumental in sensitizing social workers. Likewise, Bloom (1995) reported that self-awareness encouraged empathy, a necessary attribute in denouncing social injustices. Furthermore, Hare (2004) reported that self-awareness heightens analytical consciousness, sharpening a practitioner's ability to clearly perceive and effectively respond to social injustice, which Abrams and Moio (2009) correlated with efficacious social justice work. Moreover, practitioners that exemplified self-awareness, according to Lakey, Kernis, Heppner, and Lance (2008), possessed excellent self-regulatory skills that aided in decreased hyperbolic responses and biased decision-making in practice, which Shepperd, Klein, and Rothman (2014) reported liberated them to focus on shared humanity. If Reamer (2013) reported that social workers who really "care" about social justice will do what they can to address social injustice, then the development of clinical advocacy acuity is crucial to social work practice. Hence, sensitizing social workers to social inequities and the mechanisms that drive them is vital to the internal conceptualization and external expression of social justice efforts.

Exploring challenges in the development of clinical advocacy acuity is important to ensuring that social workers are effectively identifying and addressing social justice-related mental healthcare. For the vast majority of people, according to Schlegel, Hicks, King, and Arndt (2011), accurate self-assessment is poor. Nearly 50 years ago, a pioneer in social work named Perlman (1976) reported that in order for social workers to become self-aware, they must work to make their implicit values explicit. She argued that social workers must be able to recognize and transcend their own disquiet regarding their unconscious beliefs in order to be effective in practice. Therefore, helping social workers explore the meanings of oppression and privilege in their own lives without shame and/or guilt is crucial. Wilkerson (2020) reported that the deconstruction of oppressive forces requires more than merely exposing racist beliefs, but rather, it is necessary to explore and challenge the institutions that propagate those distortions. Wilkerson reported that the overemphasis on race as it pertains to systemic oppression places too much attention on the presumed racist individual while obfuscating the systems that reinforce oppression. Systemic oppression is to racism what self-awareness is to advocacy, which is why the application of critical theory as reported by Mattsson (2014) is the ideal portal for social workers to explore their role within institutions of power. Mattson contended that critical theory lowers resistance to tackling systemic oppression by redirecting the focus onto the institutions while providing an opening for what Ortiz and Jani (2010) underscored as social workers developing social justice competency regarding individual and structural variables such as education, class, gender, ethnicity, immigration status, and race as well as their impacts on identity, behavior, opportunity, and access. With that said, CAM places institutional oppression to the forefront as real and problematic to mental healthcare. Social workers developing clinical advocacy acuity is imperative in order for them to constructively question the status quo and become more acutely aware of how institutional fault lines produce social inequities that negatively impact mental healthcare so that they may attain the level of awareness necessary to rightly advocate for others.

How can the profession be the beacon for change in society and instill trust in clients while simultaneously challenging and reinventing itself? Feasibly, the answer lays with introspection. Mental healthcare, according to Shier and Graham (2015), must assume a sociopolitical stance in order to address the conditions that interfere with healthy adaptation. The profession must more wholly embody the equitable practices we seek in other institutions; we cannot impart change without joining in taking accountability for our part. Thus, CAM's clinical advocacy acuity is an invitation for social workers to reflect on the world as it is in order to clearly see opportunities for social justice and advocacy in social work practice.

Pathologizing a healthy response or insisting that an individual adjust to a socially unjust circumstance would be an egregious mistake by any mental healthcare practitioner, but especially by social workers. Socially responsible mental healthcare requires that social workers be armed with social justice and advocacy knowledge, skills, and tools in order to accurately assess clients' needs. CAM guides social workers to *Ask The Right Questions*, which is imperative to the application of HEAL when presumed social justice topics arise. HEAL targets social justice needs related to Health, Economic, Academic, and Legal systems that impact mental healthcare treatment, which is consistent with Bronfenbrenner's ecological systems theory that posited the basis for influencing just environments rests with understanding how individuals interact in their environments (Härkönen, 2007). CAM stresses excellent and robust inquiry, which is extended throughout the HEAL assessment. CAM also urges social workers to look out for subtle and overt abuses of power within systems such as Health needs that are influenced by psychological and medical status, relationships, and spiritual orientation; Economic needs that are influenced by income and employment status; academic needs that are influenced by learning differences, informal and formal education, as well as language; and legal needs that are influenced by interactions with the law. CAM upholds that systems assessment is essential to mental healthcare treatment. As such, it insists that social workers go beyond noticing the difference in access and opportunity in systems for diverse groups of people. In practice, social workers must determine which system guided the client's help-seeking, procure a rich description of the client's need, contextualize the client's need, analyze and organize power in systems as they relate to the client's mental health, resist the proclivity to simplify the client's feelings, express intellectual and affective curiosity with clients, validate the client's reaction to injustice, and prioritize the client's clinical and social justice needs contemporaneously.

To demonstrate the utility for the assessment tool, HEAL, consider a client who arrives for mental healthcare treatment who has reported any of the following: hate crime, sexual assault, mistreatment due to learning disabilities, domestic violence, school bullying, sexual harassment, or forced migration. The primary goal of HEAL is to determine whether and acknowledge if a social injustice is present, understand its impact on the client's mental health, and decide how to advocate for positive change that will secure the client's optimal mental health. A social worker who skips past the assessment of the presumed social injustice risks revictimizing the client by not giving the reported experience attention or even credence, especially by being a member of a system of authority. Such lack of sensitivity to social injustice, according to the NASW Code of Ethics, risks negligence because in the pursuit of equitable mental healthcare, avoidance and inaction are tantamount to complicity. Ergo, the HEAL assessment tool, places a premium on an accurate understanding of the clients' reported experiences and how they intertwine with systems in order to determine most effective clinical advocacy treatment.

Eylin: A Composite Case Study

At the behest of her immigration attorney, Eylin and her father arrived at my clinical private practice office seeking psychotherapeutic services to address her recent traumatic events. The immediacy by which Eylin had recounted the trauma was striking; she indicated that border patrol agents obliged her to recount the details of her traumatic experiences repeatedly. Eylin, a 16-year-old teenage girl, reported that she was forced to migrate from her beloved country of origin after being sexually assaulted by local gang members as payment for her uncle's debt. As Eylin sat across from me detailing the events that brought her to seek my services, any illusions I may have had about my role as a clinical social worker in private practice dissolved into her tearful and despondent gaze. It was clear to me that Eylin's multiplicity of needs made her particularly vulnerable. Her anguish was self-evident, and although I was uncertain how I should proceed, I was bound by the humanity of the moment.

Throughout the consultation, Eylin and her father stood willing to abide by all of my recommendations. Under most circumstances, this strict compliance is a good thing; but, with the combination of my lack of confidence in how to advocate as a private practitioner and their vulnerability, it was not. On top of that, their lack of personal agency made me worried for them in general. Eylin and her father did not make any requests, inquiries, or statements without my direct input, and instead, they waited anxiously for my cues. Had I not disclosed the location of the restroom they would have unlikely asked. As I saw it, Eylin's treatment was hinged to her sense of agency, which she had been robbed of multiple times over. The NASW's Code of Ethics inscribes the notion of a client's right to self-determination presupposes that self-determination exists. Throughout the consultation, I kept circling back to her immigration status, which helped to illuminate the fact that her mental healthcare needs were attached to her immigrant status. I knew that part of our clinical work together must include her political dimension of needs that included asylum.

Despite my keen awareness regarding institutional inequities, my knowledge regarding how to tackle clinical social justice and advocacy issues before meeting Eylin had been limited to providing resource referrals, psychoeducation, and professional membership to organizations. Some of the ways I sought to ensure access to community members after beginning my private practice were by becoming a paneled provider and offering a sliding scale for those without insurance. On occasion, I would advocate in person by accompanying my private practice clients to an appointment. After meeting Eylin, I realized I had essentially only touched the tip of the iceberg with regard to addressing social justice in practice. Despite the fact that her situation was uncharted territory for me as a clinician and as a human being, I felt committed to learning, collaborating, and helping. Before Eylin and her father left my office, I did a number of things that included providing them with psychoeducation, addressing her medical needs after sexual trauma, discussing her healthcare coverage, and asking their permission to speak with their attorney. Immediately after the consultation, I turned to my cell phone and googled "refugee," which sent me on a ricochet search in all sorts of directions. Let the learning commence! I quickly realized that until Eylin entered my private practice in 2016, everything I knew about refugees was through the media. At the time, there was an abundance of anti-immigration rhetoric.

I did not know it then, but my practice would never be the same after Eylin. She continued psychotherapy with me for a year and a half. I was struck by the disproportionate and collective injustices that Eylin had endured and how her circumstances rendered her completely quarantined from participation in society. Eylin thought she was broken and blamed herself for all the injustices that she endured. In her, I could see the importance of reflecting, educating myself, and creating tools and strategies for myself to use in the future with clients whose mental healthcare and social justice needs intersect. Our work together instructed the need to reimagine and strengthen clinical social work in private practice and inspired me to create CAM.

CAM in Practice

To provide a more up-close and personal account of what CAM looks like in practice, let us consider the case of Eylin if we were to apply CAM today. Eylin's forced migration resulting from sexual violence and exploitation caused her to be separated from her family, adapt to a foreign language and culture, and rely on unfamiliar family and acquaintances. First, a clinician with refined clinical advocacy acuity would be easily able to partake in shared humanity and really "care" about Eylin's difficult experiences, even without having had any actual similar life experience or knowledge. The ability to use clinical advocacy acuity to think critically about her circumstances within systems drives effective, empathetic clinical decision-making throughout treatment. Understanding how systems, such as health and legal, have the cards stacked against her is vital to providing genuine affective curiosity in order to honor her lived experience. Although the need for Eylin's psychological care was evident by her presence in my office, less apparent were her other needs tied to varying systems.

The HEAL assessment tool would yield invaluable information regarding how the systems intertwined with Eylin's physiological and psychological healthcare, which would inform the clinical advocacy intervention. To review, Eylin is a notional teenage youth who reported sexual violence and exploitation in her country of origin by local gang members that forced her to migrate. After arriving in the United States, due to fear of retaliation in her home country and fear of deportation, Eylin did not seek medical care. The HEAL assessment tool would reveal the following about Eylin's needs:

Health: Eylin displayed clear physiological and psychological needs related to repeated and protracted sexual violence and exploitation.

Economic: Although Eylin's parents were employed, they had no health-care insurance.

Academic: Eylin possessed a formal education in her country of origin; however, in the United States, she was placed in a bilingual program that did not differentiate language needs from ability needs, which was a concern regarding her appropriate academic opportunity and progress.

Legal: Eylin was seeking asylum, which bears the burden of proof of persecution. Without legal status, her ability to access and navigate any systems would be significantly challenging. Eylin would not be able to reap the benefits of mental healthcare without asylum because she would be under constant fear of deportation; her ability to be a productive citizen would be extinguished.

The HEAL assessment tool made Eylin's interconnecting needs for mental healthcare and social justice clear. Therefore, advocating for Eylin would require a thorough review of interlocking domains within systems in order to secure efficacious mental healthcare outcomes.

The implementation of Eylin's clinical advocacy treatment plan must address her needs identified in the four umbrella systems using HEAL. Addressing her needs regarding *Health* would begin by securing a medical referral. Simply telling her that she needed to obtain medical care for the sexual violence she had endured would not be sufficient considering her legal status, lack of health insurance, and mental state. Therefore, helping secure a gynecological appointment would require that a clinician take initiative and advocate by making the appointment together and ensuring that her father would be able to take her. Eylin's *Economic* needs would have to be ascertained because their financial viability is directly tied to her ability to receive continued mental healthcare treatment. This would need to be unassuming and ongoing; talking about money is difficult for many families and clinicians, especially without feeling like one's rights are not being infringed upon. Clinicians cannot simply ask a client for their W2 form to establish how much a client can afford or decide what to charge. Taking cues from other forms and conversations would inform the clinician of Eylin's family's employment and healthcare coverage, which would provide a starting point for a discussion regarding payment. A clinician, understanding the importance of this discussion as it could make or break a client's second appointment, would then have to speak plainly and matter-of-factly about economic viability with Eylin and her father in order to ensure that they can afford sessions and begin the psychotherapeutic alliance by understanding that no topic is off limits or taboo in session. Following up on her *Academic* needs would call for a clinician to obtain a copy of her academic records in order to get a sense of her ability in her academic placement. This would require a parent's help or written consent to release records to the clinician. Due diligence, in regard to self-educating with the school system and bilingual programs by communicating with school personnel, would be needed to assess Eylin's academic level and advocate to secure the most beneficial and appropriate placement. Advocating for Eylin's *Legal* needs would involve communicating with her immigration attorney to learn about the asylum-seeking process, timeline, what was expected, and how my services fit into the asylum-seeking process. Providing and reviewing with my client a biography of diagnosis, a clinical evaluation that contextualizes her trauma and treatment would be required in order to assist in meeting her legal needs. Legal status would then permit the clinician to focus on attending to her physiological, psychological, educational, and economic needs. Without asylum, Eylin would not have the option to participate in a continued and meaningful psychotherapeutic alliance or transcend the trauma of the forced migration and the asylum-seeking process. While navigating Eylin's needs as identified by HEAL, a clinician must use an interdisciplinary approach which would require that the clinician communicate and collaborate with professionals from other disciplines working on behalf of Eylin so as to ensure clinical advocacy occurs. Allying with other disciplines in an interdisciplinary approach is a powerful tool in the expansion of one's own professional knowledge, network, and influence, which are requisites to advocacy.

A clinician's application of CAM would illuminate the impact that repeated and protracted trauma had on Eylin's mental health and also enable a clinician to recognize that any mental healthcare intervention would be futile without also addressing Eylin's need for asylum status. For Eylin, until the threat of deportation abated, she would be under constant clinically significant stress that would impede her ability to function. The psychotherapeutic alliance fostered through advocacy would reveal a fuller account of the impact of trauma-related forced migration and the asylum-seeking process and their effects on her cognition, communication, and socialization as well as psychological, behavioral, and learning functioning. In order to effectively mobilize services on Eylin's behalf due to her need for asylum, a clinician applying a clinical advocacy framework would need to reflect on their knowledge about the interstices of the various systems as well as their professional jurisdiction. A clinical advocacy framework, such as CAM, helps social workers detect and reflect on a client's needs within systems as well as emphasizes social workers' ethical obligation to exact equitable mental healthcare in practice because the only thing more injurious than a social injustice is mental healthcare that ignores it.

The CAM approach names social justice and advocacy competency as integral and indispensable to productive mental healthcare. Any mental healthcare without a focus on a client's social justice needs would be linked to higher levels of revictimization. CAM provides social workers with the latitude to view their work more holistically and know that equitable mental healthcare is essential to identifying and advocating when there is social injustice. With a clear and comprehensive understanding of a client's needs and the system that exacerbates inequities through the HEAL assessment tool, when and how to advocate on behalf of the client becomes apparent. Social workers can advocate by providing psychoeducation, securing referrals, standing and collaborating with clients, ameliorating among systems, reviewing and providing clients with a biography of diagnosis, engaging in an interdisciplinary approach, effectively communicating, maximizing access to a broad range of clientele through a variety of payment options, engaging in ongoing education and training, and participating in the shared community. The clinical implications are manifold: first, it aligns with the profession's code of ethics, upholds the social work mission's social justice values, adheres to informed and best practices, imparts real-world change, and supports the development of strong psychotherapeutic alliances. Most importantly, CAM provides social workers with the tools to promote optimal mental health outcomes for clients.

Mainstreaming CAM in Clinical Social Work Practice

The time to disabuse social injustice in mental healthcare and society is now. The current unrest has placed social justice on a world stage, which makes this a golden opportunity for the profession to reconnect to its foundation and repledge itself to social justice and advocacy. Social injustices within systems are not aberrations; they are prevalent and account for an alarming rate of mental health concerns, especially among non-majority groups. Social workers' true understanding of how unjust systems intersect with people's mental health ushers an opportunity for a paradigm shift beginning in the mental healthcare system. The profession must promote clinical advocacy in a therapeutic environment that values both nature and nurture as integral to micro, meso, and macro social work. Clinical advocacy ensures that an individual's needs within systems are met as a way of securing equitable mental healthcare. The profession can serve a formidable role in the dismantling of institutional oppression through clinical advocacy competency, awareness that encourages reflective practice, the application of assessment tools that hold institutions accountable for inequities, and concrete skills to advocate. Social workers standing ready to critically reflect, challenging preconceptions, and transforming the status quo to make room for a new approach would bring welcomed equity in mental healthcare.

In order to prepare the profession, we must ensure that social work education and training reflects diverse bodies of knowledge regarding mental health, reckon with our part in mental healthcare that oppresses instead of actively supports clients, lean into our social justice and advocacy role in social work practice, grow the sources of social work knowledge, and encourage mastery of turning awareness into action, especially regarding the systemic inequities that plague society. The goal of successful pedagogy, as Freire (2018) asserted, is to liberate learners to act. The advocates and influencers of tomorrow require education and training today that uphold the profession's core social justice values. According to Reamer (2013), Rawls emphasized that ethical decision-making ought to reflect what a person deems fundamental to one's own basic rights as the guide regarding the rights of others; CAM can help arm social workers with informed and ethical decision-making that upholds a client's rights. Refocused education and training would position the profession to strengthen its role as global leaders in mental healthcare. This must include curating mental healthcare knowledge from diverse groups in order to ensure all people's voices reach the policies that drive institutions.

In the pursuit of equitable mental healthcare and in order to realize the profession's true strength, it must educate and engage its social justice values. If social workers are going to effectively address social injustices, then their education and training should provide them with tools and resources to advocate for their clients, like CAM. Each social worker can then make a difference in the profession's push for social justice and equity.

Close Reading Questions:

1. What skills does Slater illustrate how to address situations in which social workers' personal beliefs are at odds or are unfamiliar with the client's needs?
2. Outline how you might use CAM in your practice to facilitate social justice. Be sure to address any concerns and positive outcomes related to CAM and how they might inform your everyday practice.
3. How do social workers manage and leverage the discomfort that arises from uncertainty during mental healthcare treatment?

Prompts for Writing:

1. What skills are needed in order to help social workers tolerate having their beliefs challenged?
2. The author of this piece identifies as a person of color. How does that impact your understanding of her ideas in this chapter? How do you think a person's own intersectional position affects their stance on social justice? Why is it important to include perspectives from a racially and ethnically diverse array of practitioners?
3. Write a narrative about the connection between the history of immigration in relation to trauma using Slater's case or one from your own experience—or even your own imagination.

References

Abramovitz, M. (2005). The largely untold story of welfare reform and the human services. *Social Work, 50*(2), 175–186.

Abrams, L. S., & Moio, J. A. (2009). Critical race theory and the cultural competence dilemma in social work education. *Journal of Social Work Education, 45*(2), 245–261.

Bail, C. A. (2016). Combining natural language processing and network analysis to examine how advocacy organizations stimulate conversation on social media. *Proceedings of the National Academy of Sciences, 113*(42), 11823–11828.

Beller, S. L. (2014). *Who cares?: Psychotherapy as care work, explored through socialist feminist and relational perspectives.* Northampton, MA: Smith College.

Bernal, D. D. (2002). Critical race theory, Latino critical theory, and critical raced-gendered epistemologies: Recognizing students of color as holders and creators of knowledge. *Qualitative Inquiry, 8*(1), 105–126.

Bloom, S. L. (1995). The germ theory of trauma: The impossibility of ethical neutrality. *Secondary traumatic stress: Self-care issues for clinicians, researchers and educators* (pp. 257–276). Lutherville, Maryland: Sidran Press.

Case, K. A. (2012). Discovering the privilege of whiteness: White women's reflections on antiracist identity and ally behavior. *Journal of Social Issues, 68*(1), 78–96.

Chow, C. C. (2011). *The impact of the Affordable Care Act on behavioral health services: Who, what, how, where, and when?* Philadelphia, PA: Drexel University School of Public Health. Retrieved from https://idea.library.drexel.edu/islandora/object/idea%3A3593/datastream/OBJ/view

Coleman, E. G. (2010). Ethnographic approaches to digital media. *Annual Review of Anthropology, 39*, 487–505.

CSWE Core Competency 5: Engage in Policy Practice. (2019). doi:10.4135/9781529704013. Retrieved from https://www.cswe.org/getattachment/Accreditation/Accreditation-Process/2015-EPAS/2015EPAS_Web_FINAL.pdf.aspx

Deacon, R. (2006). Michel Foucault on education: A preliminary theoretical overview. *South African Journal of Education, 26*(2), 177–187.

DiAngelo, R. (2018). *White fragility: Why it's so hard for white people to talk about racism.* Boston: Beacon Press.

Eglash, R., Bennett, A., Babbitt, W., Lachney, M., Reinhardt, M., & Hammond-Sowah, D. (2020). Decolonizing posthumanism: Indigenous material agency in generative STEM. *British Journal of Educational Technology, 51*(4), 1334–1353.

Ehrenreich, J. H. (2014). *The altruistic imagination: A history of social work and social policy in the United States.* Ithaca: Cornell University Press.

Freire, P. (2018). *Pedagogy of the oppressed.* New York: Bloomsbury Publishing.

Fries-Britt, S., George Mwangi, C. A., & Peralta, A. M. (2014). Learning race in a US context: An emergent framework on the perceptions of race among foreign-born students of color. *Journal of Diversity in Higher Education, 7*(1), 1.

Gough, S. J. (2020). *The role of the Cheltenham Charity Organisation Society, 1905–1929* (Doctoral dissertation). Retrieved from http://oro.open.ac.uk/70728/

Gregory, J. R. (2020). Social work as a product and project of whiteness, 1607–1900. *Journal of Progressive Human Services*, 1–20.

Hall, G. C. N. (2001). Psychotherapy research with ethnic minorities: Empirical, ethical, and conceptual issues. *Journal of Consulting and Clinical Psychology, 69*(3), 502.

Hare, I. (2004). Defining social work for the 21st century: The international federation of social workers' revised definition of social work. *International Social Work, 47*(3), 407–424.

Härkönen, U. (2007). The Bronfenbrenner ecological systems theory of human development, Scientific Articles of V International Conference, pp. 1–17.

Hargittai, E. (2020). Potential biases in big data: Omitted voices on social media. *Social Science Computer Review, 38*(1), 10–24.

Hunt, H. (Ed.). (2018). *Ruth Bader Ginsburg: In her own words.* Chicago: Agate Publishing.

Kumashiro, K. K. (2000). Toward a theory of anti-oppressive education. *Review of Educational Research, 70*(1), 25–53.

Lakey, C. E., Kernis, M. H., Heppner, W. L., & Lance, C. E. (2008). Individual differences in authenticity and mindfulness as predictors of verbal defensiveness. *Journal of Research in Personality, 42*(1), 230–238.

Lord, S. A., & Iudice, J. (2012). Social workers in private practice: A descriptive study of what they do. *Clinical Social Work Journal, 40*(1), 85–94.

Mattsson, T. (2014). Intersectionality as a useful tool: Anti-oppressive social work and critical reflection. *Affilia, 29*(1), 8–17.

McCauley, C. R., & Moskalenko, S. (2011). Friction: How radicalization happens to them and us. New York, NY: Oxford University Press.

McLaughlin, A. M. (2009). Clinical social workers: Advocates for social justice. *Advances in Social Work, 10*(1), 51–68.

Morgaine, K. & Capous-Desyllas, M. (2015). Anti-oppressive social work practice: Putting theory into action. Los Angeles, CA: Sage.

National Association of Social Workers. (2009). Social work speaks: National Association of Social Workers policy statements, 2009–2012. Washington, DC: NASW Press.

Northen, H. (1982). Clinical social work. New York: Columbia University Press.

Ortiz, L., & Jani, J. (2010). Critical race theory: A transformational model for teaching diversity. *Journal of Social Work Education, 46*(2), 175–193.

Paradies, Y., Ben, J., Denson, N., Elias, A., Priest, N., Pieterse, A., . . . Gee, G. (2015). Racism as a determinant of health: A systematic review and meta-analysis. *PloS One, 10*(9), e0138511.

Perlman, H. H. (1976). Believing and doing: Values in social work education. *Social Casework, 57*(6), 381–390.

Quintana, S. M. (2007). Racial and ethnic identity: Developmental perspectives and research. *Journal of Counseling Psychology, 54*(3), 259.

Reamer, F. G. (2013). *Social work values and ethics.* New York: Columbia University Press.

Reisch, M. (2002). Defining social justice in a socially unjust world. *Families in Society, 83*(4), 343–354.

Robbins, S. P., Coe Regan, J. A. R., Williams, J. H., Smyth, N. J., & Bogo, M. (2016). From the editor—the future of social work education. *Journal of Social Work Education, 52*(4).

Salsberg, E., Quigley, L., Mehfoud, N., Acquaviva, K., Wyche, K., & Sliwa, S. (2017). *Profile of the social work workforce.* Retrieved from the Council on Social Work Education website: https://www.cswe.org/Centers-Initiatives/Initiatives/National-Workforce-Initiative/SW-Workforce-Book-FINAL-11-08-2017.aspx

Schlegel, R. J., Hicks, J. A., King, L. A., & Arndt, J. (2011). Feeling like you know who you are: Perceived true self-knowledge and meaning in life. *Personality and Social Psychology Bulletin, 37*(6), 745–756.

Shepherd, C. (2019). Sympathetic knowledge in Jane Addams' democracy and social ethics. *Footnotes, 12*.

Shepperd, J. A., Klein, W. M., & Rothman, A. (2014). Self-compassion, self-regulation, and health: Meredith L. Terry and Mark R. Leary. In *Self-and identity-regulation and health* (pp. 75–85). New York: Psychology Press.

Shier, M. L., & Graham, J. R. (2015). Subjective well-being, social work, and the environment: The impact of the socio-political context of practice on social worker happiness. *Journal of Social Work, 15*(1), 3–23.

Slater, E. L. (2019). Prioritizing the dual needs of asylum-seekers while cultivating psychotherapeutic alliances. *Clinical Social Work Journal*, 1–7.

Slater, E. L. (2020). Private practice social workers' commitment to social justice. *Clinical Social Work Journal*, 1–9.

Snaza, N., Appelbaum, P., Bayne, S., Carlson, D., Morris, M., Rotas, N., . . . Weaver, J. (2014). Toward a posthuman education. *Journal of Curriculum Theorizing, 30*(2), 39.

Sorkin, D. H., Ngo-Metzger, Q., & De Alba, I. (2010). Racial/ethnic discrimination in health care: Impact on perceived quality of care. *Journal of General Internal Medicine, 25*(5), 390–396.

Specht, H., & Courtney, M. E. (1995). Unfaithful angels. New York: The Free Press, a Division of Simon and Schuster.

Tamburro, A. (2013). Including decolonization in social work education and practice. *Journal of Indigenous Social Development, 2*(1).

Torous, J., Myrick, K. J., Rauseo-Ricupero, N., & Firth, J. (2020). Digital mental health and COVID-19: using technology today to accelerate the curve on access and quality tomorrow. *JMIR Mental Health, 7*(3), e18848.

Treichler, E. B., Crawford, J. N., Higdon, A., & Backhaus, A. L. (2020). Diversity and social justice training at the postdoctoral level: A scoping study and pilot of a self-assessment. *Training and Education in Professional Psychology, 14*(2), 126.

U.S. Bureau of Labor Statistics. (2021, September 15). *Home: Occupational outlook handbook*. U.S. Bureau of Labor Statistics. Retrieved January 30, 2022, from http://www.bls.gov/ooh/community-and-social-service/ social-workers.htm

Vera, E. M., & Speight, S. L. (2003). Multicultural competence, social justice, and counseling psychology: Expanding our roles. *The counseling psychologist, 31*(3), 253–272.

Wakefield, J. C. (2013). DSM-5 and clinical social work: Mental disorder and psychological justice as goals of clinical intervention. *Clinical Social Work Journal, 41*(2), 131–138.

Wilkerson, I. (2020). *Caste: The origins of our discontents*. New York: Random House.

Williams, D. R., & Williams-Morris, R. (2000). Racism and mental health: The African American experience. *Ethnicity & Health, 5*(3–4), 243–268.

9 Our Illusion of Separateness

Teaching Social Justice to Social Work Students

Anthony Nicotera

Pre-reading Questions:

1. How would you describe the concept of interconnection from both a scientific or physical, and a spiritual or metaphysical perspective?
2. What does the COVID-19 pandemic, ongoing racial injustice and reckoning, and deepening political polarization have to teach us about connection and disconnection?
3. As Adrienne Maree Brown asserts, "If we want to create a world in which conflict and trauma aren't the center of our collective existence, we have to practice something new," what is that something new that must be practiced? How do we practice it?

Our disconnection, our separation, ultimately, is a myth, at best imaginary, like saying the wave is separate from the ocean. Children seek to make their parents happy because the children intuitively understand that making their parents happy in turn makes them happy. Our suffering and our joy, our harm and our healing, are bound up one with the other. If we see the world as it is, we understand that though separate and distinct, we are composed of the same matter. The law of conservation of mass asserts that matter is neither lost nor gained, created nor destroyed in the universe. This connection invites us to consider that when others suffer, we suffer and when others benefit, we benefit. We are invited to see that, physically and metaphysically, the other is not separate from us, but rather part of us. We are connected in our common human community. As Dr. King asserts, "All life is interrelated. . . . Whatever affects one directly affects all indirectly" (King, 1968, p. 191). No one of us is fully or truly well if one of us is suffering. If we look deeply and are attentive, we see too that our liberation is bound up, one with the other.

Aboriginal Murri activist and educator Lilla Watson captures the heart of this ultimate reality, this truth, when she reflects, "If you've come here to help, you are wasting your time. But if you have come here because your liberation is bound up with mine, then let us work together" (Haga, p. 115). In the midst of a world divided and disconnected, desperately in

DOI: 10.4324/9781003270225-9

need of healing and repair, we are being invited to see that our disconnection, our division, and our devastation exists in the context of a deeper, more profound, more fundamental reality and truth, that of our need for one another, our common humanity, our unity, and interconnection. The truth is that our differences are ancillary and subordinate to our fundamental unity, oneness, and connection. Tragically, however, the us versus them dichotomy commonly presented as fact or truth, though ultimately a lie, can be believed or perceived to be reality. All too often this false dichotomy is used by those who are immature or uninformed or manipulative or cruel to deceive, destroy, and divide. In this way, the falsehoods and deceptions—that we do not need each other, that some have more inherent dignity and value than others—become, in one sense, real. Like the psychosomatic symptoms that affect the body and result in real pain and suffering, so too lies and myths about our disconnection, that we are not interconnected, have devastating, real, even deadly effects and consequences on individuals and society.

The See-Reflect-Act Circle of Insight multidisciplinary framework (Nicotera, 2018, 2019, 2020), which I created over 25 years of teaching, advocacy, activism, and social work practice, combines the concepts from indigenous healing and peacemaking circles, restorative justice processes, Aristotelian philosophical traditions, Catholic social teachings, liberation pedagogy and theology, civil rights era nonviolence trainings, and social science inquiry. In the spirit of educators Paulo Freire (1970/2000) and bell hooks (1994, 2000, 2003), the framework invites both individual and collective connection and movement toward deeper understanding and liberation. Consistent with Bell's (2016) understanding of social justice pedagogy and practice, the Circle of Insight connects analysis to action and is a tool that can be used to transform oppressive patterns and behaviors (Nicotera, 2018, 2019). It challenges us to see, and reflect, and act upon the illusion of our separateness, the myth of our disconnection, and the existential, transformative truth of our ultimate connection. It sheds light on Dr. King's assertion that "violence anywhere is a threat to justice everywhere" (King, 1968). It offers a framework and process that attempts to actualize this insight, that we are inherently connected, and consider its implications for our life together, for society, for the work of justice, for unmasking the myth of disconnection, and deepening our understanding of interconnection.

The Circle of Insight is a dialectical and open process that invites interplay between facts and theory, practice, and principle. Yet, the process is also purposeful, in that it moves toward enlightenment—critical consciousness (Reisch & Garvin, 2016), liberation, and deepened awareness of our illusion of separateness. It invites us to see the other as sister and brother, as oneself. Thus, "one understands that harm to the other results in harm to the self, and harm to the self, results in harm to the other (Nicotera, 2018; hooks, 2003; Nhat Hanh, 1993)" (Nicotera, 2019). It invites and fosters curiosity and calls us to engage all of our senses to absorb the complexity and nuance of our phenomenological, human reality. The Circle of Insight process invites questions that complicate and contextualize the reality of our concomitant connection and disconnection. Applied to the pandemic and structural, systemic racism and injustice, the Circle process reveals how the myth of our disconnection tragically becomes real, as manifested in COVID-19's disparate impact on those most vulnerable and oppressed. The Circle process applied to the pandemic and structural, systemic racism and injustice unveils how a cycle of socialization (Harro, 2018) and social constructs like race perpetuate oppression and false notions, lies, about our connectedness and common humanity. The Circle process applied to the pandemic and structural, systemic, institutional racism and injustice, calls forth action to promote dignity, equity, rights, and justice. In a time of global crisis, the Circle process invites awakening to the fundamental truth of our inherent dignity, our collective humanity, and our interconnection.

In this chapter, I will share some of my experiences, from 2001 to the present, as a teacher of social justice, Lay Chaplain, activist, social worker, and advisor to, and leader with the Fellowship of Reconciliation, the nation's oldest, largest, multifaith peace and justice organization, of which Dr. King, among other Nobel Peace Laureates, was a member. These experiences have shaped the creation of the Circle of Insight framework and affirmed the truth and power of our inherent interconnection. These stories make up a patchwork quilt that invites us to see, to absorb with all of our senses, the truth that we are woven together in a seamless garment of connection. These stories invite us to consider that if we hope to build the beloved community, create a more socially just society, and live the transformative love that can overcome our devastating disconnection, we must learn to see no stranger, to see in the other our sister, brother, and self.

Connection and Disconnection

Terror

On September 11, 2001, I was serving as Chaplain to law students at a large, private university in Chicago. We watched the news as they replayed the footage of planes flying into the twin towers, and then we watched as they reported that a plane had gone down in Shanksville, Pennsylvania, and another had crashed into the Pentagon. Myriad thoughts raced through my mind as my heart pounded at the realization that we were under attack. I wondered if my brother, who often worked in New York City, was there that morning. Having roots in the greater New York City area, I wondered too about the safety and well-being of friends. I looked up at the Chicago skyline and wondered if we were next. I wondered about the well-being of our students and our nation.

Into the afternoon and evening, I joined colleagues in our chaplaincy and university ministry program to attend to the needs of our university community—we gathered together to support one another, to pray, to take care of one another, and to attend to, in particular, the needs of our Muslim students who already were palpably afraid, not only of further terrorist attacks on the United States, but also of being targeted as victims of hatred, ignorance, and prejudice. I realized even in this moment that collectively we were at once experiencing a profound coming together and connection—in our confusion, concern, terror, anxiety, and attempt to console and comfort one another, as well as a tragic division and disconnection—in our labeling, demonizing, attacking, and attempt to disconnect and distinguish ourselves from the other. I had never experienced our nation more concomitantly united and divided at the same time.

In the days, weeks, and years that followed, as we were invited to rally around the flag, I realized that this call to unify, to come together, was in fact a call to dehumanize, to separate us, not only one from another, but also from the truth of our common humanity. The not so subtle insinuation, and often quite explicit proclamation, was that those who did not wave the flag and fully support the Bush administration's response to the September 11th attacks were themselves unpatriotic, on the side of the terrorists. For those who outwardly looked like those who attacked the United States, this simplistic, dehumanizing either/or binary translated into a shattered sense of safety and security. US leadership further fueled the flames of hatred and division, declaring that you are either with us or against us, on the side of good or the side of evil. Tragically, this divisive, us/them, either/or way of seeing the world resulted in more US citizens being attacked and killed, primarily Muslims or those who looked Arab or Muslim. This existentially false us/them dichotomy was used to justify attacks on our students, many of whom were accosted and harassed on public transportation for wearing a hijab or turban. This false dichotomy is precisely that, false, a lie, that justifies the creation of inequities that oppress, demonize, objectify, and dehumanize the other.

I assert that this simplistic, dehumanizing, us/them dichotomy is, like race, a social construct, made real by those who create and perpetuate its myth. It not only divides us, pitting one human being against another but also deceives us into thinking that some human beings are better than others, more worthy of dignity, rights, and justice. This is not to say that there are not real differences among peoples and cultures, and perspectives and beliefs; however, these differences exist in the context of our common humanity. If we examine critically and carefully notions of unity and division, connection and disconnection, and global oneness and global diversity, we see that our division, disconnection, and diversity exist as mere waves on the ocean that is our unity, connection, and oneness. We ignore and remain ignorant of the truth of our common humanity, our unity, our connection, our interdependence, and our interrelatedness, at our own peril.

Virus

In March 2020, the two greater New York City area universities where I was teaching began to shift to remote learning in response to the coronavirus. COVID-19 quickly spread and instilled terror of a different sort, but just as palpable as that felt in September 2001. The enemy was a deadly, difficult to detect virus that spread readily and often imperceptibly. As we learned more and more about the virus, what we knew, and what we did not know, again, myriad concerns surfaced. In addition to worrying about my own well-being, and whether I had been exposed, like most people in the United States and in most countries around the world, I worried about family and friends, especially those most vulnerable and at risk.

Nineteen years later, I felt the same intense, tragic juxtaposition and creative tension between connection and division. Once again, I simultaneously experienced a profound sense of unity and connection, and disparity and division. In response to the pandemic, I helped craft a statement for the Fellowship of Reconciliation (FOR-USA), the nation's oldest, largest, multifaith peace and justice organization, to which Dr. King belonged, stating, "At its core COVID-19 underscores more than ever that we are a world community that is profoundly connected across race, religion, gender, geography and nationality" (https://wagingnonviolence.org/forusa/2020/03/fors-coronavirus-prayer-petition/). This connection seems glaringly self-evident in the face of a virus that in fundamental ways affects us all, regardless of difference. However, the tragic coexistent reality is that the virus underscores a form of disconnection in that it disproportionately affects and devastates the world's most vulnerable, marginalized, and oppressed communities, such as communities of color, the poor, indigenous communities, prisoners, and immigrants. FOR-USA's Gathering Voices campaign featured interviews with people, like the Reverend Starsky Wilson (https://forusa.org/2020/09/03/gathering-voices-rev-starsky-wilson/), discussing their firsthand experience of the profoundly disparate impact of the pandemic. Reverend Wilson recently appointed the President and CEO of The Children's Defense Fund spoke powerfully and poignantly about his community in St. Louis, sharing data that the first 13 victims of COVID-19 were African-American (www.ksdk.com/article/news/health/coronavirus/st-louis-13th-coronavirus-death-black-woman-80s/63-9b048352-d372-4b25–9efb-ef20e74372cc). He spoke of systemic, institutional racism and injustice and the role it played in condemning the poor to death, due to intersectional injustice related to poverty, violence, the lack of fair, adequate housing, healthcare, and nutrition, and heightened exposure to environmental hazards, toxins, and pollutants. Reverend Starsky reminds us that while the pandemic affects us all, it disproportionately devastatingly affects and attacks the poor, persons of color, and communities who are most vulnerable and oppressed. It reminds us of our fundamental human connection and our socially constructed and tragic, divisive disconnection.

In the university classroom, I experienced this connection disconnection tension as it impacted my students. Our students, as well as other faculty, colleagues, and administrators, experienced common fear, anxiety, concern, and the sense that we were in this fight against this deadly virus together. Though we were not able to comfort and support one another in traditional ways due to the need to socially distance and wear personal protective equipment, we grieved together, consoled one another, helped one another in whatever ways we could. We continue to do so. However, the parallel truth, the tragic ancillary reality, no less real because it is ancillary, is that our students have not all experienced the pandemic the same way. Just like our Muslim students after the September 11th attacks in 2001, students of color and lower-income students have been disproportionately impacted by COVID-19. I noticed right away that of the handful of students who were not able to continue with remote learning in my classes, all were students of color. Many students did not have access to the resources or technology necessary to continue. Others were essential workers at higher risk for COVID-19—some contracted the virus, and others had family members who tested positive resulting in the need for these students to become caregivers or breadwinners for their families.

Reverend Starsky's testimony and my experience of the effects of the pandemic on my students are confirmed by the data. The facts are clear and incriminating, "Latino and African-American residents of the United States have been three times as likely to become infected as their white neighbors. . . . And Black and Latino people have been nearly twice as likely to die from the virus as white people" (Oppel, Gebeloff, Rebecca Lai, Wright, & Smith, 2020). Additionally, researchers found that lower-income students were 55% more likely to delay graduation than their higher-income peers. COVID-19 also nearly doubled the gap between higher- and lower-income students' expected GPAs (Aucejo, French, Araya, & Zafar , 2020). This and other data clearly demonstrate that low-income people and persons of color in the United States are disproportionately victimized by the pandemic. In their recent article, "Inequity and the Disproportionate Impact of COVID-19 on Communities of Color in the United States: The Need for a Trauma-Informed Social Justice Response," researchers reported that CDC data confirmed COVID-19's disproportionate impact on communities of color, with Black Americans accounting for 34% of confirmed cases even though Black Americans account for only 13% of the total US population, and Latinos and Hispanics experiencing similar statistics nationwide (Fortuna, Tolou-Shams, Robles-Ramamurthy, & Porche, 2020). What does the reality of the profoundly disproportionate impact of the COVID-19 pandemic on the most vulnerable and oppressed say to us about our disconnection and our connection, our common humanity and our isolating inhumanity? How are we being invited to understand more fully the nature of our connection and disconnection?

Our Illusion of Separateness

Vietnamese Buddhist Zen Master and social worker Thich Nhat Hanh, with whom I have had the privilege of working, who was nominated for the Nobel Peace Prize by the Rev. Dr. Martin Luther King, Jr., asserts that, existentially, "we are here to awaken from our illusion of separateness" (Thich Nhat Hanh Foundation, 2020). Saint Mother Teresa of Calcutta, with whom I also had the privilege of working in Calcutta, India, expressed a similar insight, sharing that if we do not have peace, it is because we have forgotten that we belong to one another (Teresa, 1997). Nhat Hanh refers to this notion of belonging and connectedness as interbeing—we do not exist outside of relationship one with the other and that extends to our connection to the environment and all beings (Nhat Hanh, 2003). Mother Teresa would say that though we are many parts, we are one body, one community. In the African tribal tradition, they have the concept of *ubuntu*—I am because you are (Kaur, 2020; Maathai, 2010; Tutu, 1999). In the Mayan traditions, they speak of, *In La'Kech*, "You are my other me" (Kaur, 2020, p. 11). All of these concepts, from diverse and varied cultures, geographies, religions, and philosophical traditions, invite us to see beyond disconnection, beyond that which separates and divides us, to the fundamental truth of our relatedness, our connection, our belonging to one another. These notions present a common understanding of the fundamental reality that we are one, and our humanity and liberation, our very being is inextricably bound together in relationship one with the other. Arguably, harm to the other results in harm to self. If we do not care for one another, we all suffer.

Legacy of Love

When I was teaching a university social justice and peacemaking course, my students and I palpably experienced the transformative power of our care and interconnection. I gave students a take-home midterm exam that over 70% of the class failed.

We had been studying Arun Gandhi's book, *Legacy of Love: My Education in the Path of Nonviolence*. In the book, Arun, Mahatma Gandhi's grandson, shares the story of how his father, Manilal, Gandhi's son, attempted to parent according to Mahatma Gandhi's teachings.

Arun was 16 and had just learned to drive. He drove into town with his father to run some errands. In the early afternoon, he dropped his father at the bank and then took the car to the garage for repairs. His father told him to meet him back at the bank at 5 pm.

Arun took the car to the garage and the repairs were completed much more quickly than anticipated, so Arun decided to go see a movie. He did not get back to the bank until close to 6 pm.

When Manilal asked Arun why he was so late, Arun told his father that the repairs at the garage had taken longer than expected.

Manilal replied, "Funny, that's not what they said when I called the garage."

Arun had been caught in a lie. Instead of lashing out in anger at Arun, Manilal said simply and calmly, "Clearly I have not conveyed to you the importance of telling the truth."

Accepting responsibility for Arun's failure, Manilal then added, "I will walk home."

Arun drove the car slowly alongside his father. It took them over an hour to get home. Arun's mother was terribly worried. Arun shared that he never lied to his parents again (Gandhi, 2003).

Arun's story was on my mind when I announced to our class that most of them had failed the midterm.

In light of the principles we had been studying, in particular Arun's lesson, I said to the students, "Obviously, I did not convey clearly enough what I expected from you."

I then added,

> We will discuss and decide together how you can redo the exam or do extra credit to help your grade. Also, in the spirit of what we have been studying, I will do a three day liquid fast for your success.

We had read the words of Dr. Martin Luther King, Jr. and Gandhi and others who had engaged in mindful fasting as a way to invite transformation of hearts and minds toward deeper truth and connection.

After I made this announcement, three students raised their hands and asked if they could join me in the fast. I did not expect this. I was deeply moved.

Together we discussed ways in which students could rewrite their exam and do extra credit to help improve their grades. All of the students took advantage of this opportunity, and not only passed, but did quite well. Most raised their grades significantly.

More importantly, the students who joined me in the fast shared their experiences with their classmates. They spoke of the transformative power of fasting. None of them had ever fasted before. They shared that they felt a spiritual power internally and a deeper sense of connectedness to their classmates as a result of fasting. They also said that they felt a bit more connected to those who go without, society's marginalized and oppressed. They expressed a deep, visceral sense that their individual success and well-being was intimately interconnected with the success and well-being of their fellow classmates. They also made a profound connection to Thich Nhat Hanh's notion of interbeing (Nhat Hanh, 2003), which we also had been studying in class.

The students who had fasted felt this connection, our interbeing, deeply, in new ways, beyond mere intellectual understanding, touching a visceral, embodied empathy. Some would even say that they felt a spiritual connection. They shared that they had come to understand more deeply, that our failure or success as a human community depends upon all of us seeing that we are all connected, and that our personal success and well-being is somehow intertwined or woven together with the success of others. Ours is not merely an individual life, but also a life in common. Indeed, these students had become teachers, and the teacher a student.

Together we experienced the truth that if some are deprived of human rights, we all are. If we deprive others of human rights, we are depriving ourselves of the same rights. One of the students who fasted said that she more fully understood the words of Dr. King that we had discussed in class:

> In a real sense all life is interrelated. All . . . are caught in an inescapable network of mutuality, tied in a single garment of destiny. . . . I can never be what I ought to be until you are what you ought to be, and you can never be what you ought to be until I am what I ought to be. . . . This is the interrelated structure of reality
>
> (King, 1994)

The students' stories and insights were a moving testament to the truth and transformative power of our interrelatedness, our interbeing, our profound, and fundamental human connection.

Despite difference, division, and disconnection, this truth—that we are fundamentally connected, that we belong to one another, that we interfere, that our separateness is an illusion, and that we are tied in a single garment of destiny—is universal. It lies at the heart of the world's major religious traditions and is a scientific, phenomenological, and philosophical fact. We need each other. We cannot survive alone. We are comprised of the very same matter, which is neither lost nor gained in the universe. If we look deeply at the world, we understand that all human beings have inherent dignity and rights, and all are equally worthy of respect regardless of race, class, ethnicity, sex, gender, orientation, ability, or any other difference. We understand that across difference, and borders, there exists connection and common humanity. As the COVID-19 pandemic has spread, and religious, racial, and political divides have deepened in the United States and globally, the need to more fully see, reflect, and act on the truth of this insight, that we are existentially, essentially connected, has become even more urgent. I offer the Circle of Insight (Nicotera, 2018, 2019, 2020) as a practical process for exploring and engaging this truth and its consequences in this time of deepened connection and devastating disconnection.

The Circle of Insight, Our Illusion of Separateness, and Pandemic

The Circle of Insight process is presented here as a tool for examining questions of connection and disconnection, and our illusion of separateness, in particular in a time of pandemic, and racial, political, and social unrest and division. Now more than ever, as we experience COVID-19's disproportionate impact on the marginalized, oppressed, and vulnerable, and as we experience renewed and reinvigorated rage at systemic racism and structural injustice as a result of the murder of George Floyd, the Circle of Insight provides a tool and a process to help the social work profession recommit itself to Competency 3 of our Council on Social Work Education's Educational Policy and Accreditation Standards and creatively center our pedagogical commitment to social justice (CSWE, 2015). Social work ethical codes and mandates are clear. A commitment to promoting social justice lies at the heart of the social work profession (Abrams & Moio, 2009; Deepak, Rountree, & Scott, 2015; Finn & Jacobson, 2008; Grant & Austin, 2014; Harrison, VanDeusen, & Way, 2016; IASSW, 2018; IFSW, 2012; NASW, 2017, 2018; Nicotera, 2018, 2019, 2020; Reisch & Garvin, 2016; Sayre & Sar, 2015; Simon, 1994). The Circle process challenges our social work and human community to creatively center our connection and commitment to social justice, holding open the potential for transformative love and justice, healing and hope.

As Adrienne Maree Brown asserts, "the simple act of forming a circle, a wholeness, together, then putting our truths in the center of that circle, is strengthening, clarifying, and can be healing" (Maree Brown, p. 259). The Circle process challenges us to use our hearts and our minds, our intellect and our empathy, to center the truth of our inherent human dignity and connection. From a macro, social justice perspective, the Circle process requires careful and constructive examination of structural, systemic, institutional inequities and inequalities deeply embedded in our society that disrupt, divide, and promote disconnection, keeping us from understanding and experiencing our common humanity and connection. From a micro perspective, the Circle process requires examination of our deepest truths, those found in the core of our being, connecting us to our purpose, to that which animates us and gives us life, to that which gives our life meaning. In centering connection, at all levels of practice and experience, the Circle process beckons personal and collective creative, interdisciplinary, cooperative action and transformation in order to overcome the illusion of our disconnection and move us toward healing and liberation.

Phase 1—To See, Look and Listen Deeply

The first phase of the Circle of Insight process, to see, necessitates that we gather facts and carefully examine the reality in which we exist. It requires that we gather data, quantitative and qualitative, and ask probing questions, listening deeply, and well, without judgment, without assumptions or defenses, like a social worker, an investigative reporter, or a crime scene investigator. "The Indian spiritual teacher J. Krishnamurti once said, 'The highest form of human intelligence is the ability to observe without evaluating'" (Haga, 169) This is the challenge of the Circle of Insight's first phase. We must set aside our own biases, "since any individual's perspectives are limited by their experiences and social locations" (Reed & Lehning, 2014, p. 342). In the spirit of liberation theology and pedagogy, this phase insists that one absorb with all of one's senses the reality of a particular story in order to approximate objectivity, consistent with a social work, clinical, values-based commitment to meet people where they are, not where we might want them to be. Consistent with Freire's liberatory, problem-posing approach to education (Freire, 1970/2000), the Circle's process does not start with answers or preconceived notions, but rather begins with investigation, paying attention, and active listening. It begins with data, observations, stories, and then allows for subsequent critical questions.

The Circle of Insight's first phase also invites us to pay particular attention to stories as told and experienced by those on the margins, the most vulnerable and oppressed. These stories, the stories of persons of color, immigrants, indigenous persons, women, persons identifying as lesbian, gay, bisexual, transgender, queer, or nonbinary, for example, serve as the gauge for our connection, our collective commitment to justice and human dignity. Listening deeply and well to these stories, without judgment, helps us to see and begin to comprehend the reality that reflects and reveals the fault lines in our fundamental human, existential connection. Thus, in the first phase of the Circle of Insight, we gather data and listen to stories of justice and injustice, diversity and disparity, with a focus on the other, in particular those in greatest need. In this extraordinary time of pandemic and racial, political, and social division, revealing with tragic clarity our simultaneous connection and devastating disconnection, our common and disparate vulnerabilities, if we look deeply at the stories of those on the margins, we see that we are presented with a choice, Dr. King's choice, between chaos, disconnection, and community, connection (King, 1968). The story of COVID-19 lays bare the facts and tells a clear and tragic story of the pandemic's disproportionate impact on those most vulnerable and oppressed. The story of COVID-19 exposes more fully and clearly the individual and collective cost of structural, systemic injustice. The story of COVID-19's devastating, disproportionate impact on the poor, persons of color, the marginalized and oppressed reveals our self-inflicted fracture and deadly disconnection. In this way, it incriminates us all.

In the midst of the COVID-19 pandemic, as millions of people flooded the streets to protest of the murder of George Floyd, the Fellowship of Reconciliation (FOR), which counts not only Dr. King but also other prominent civil rights leaders and Nobel Peace laureates, including Jane Addams, as members, initiated FOR's Gathering Voices campaign (https://wagingnonviolence.org/forusa/tag/gathering-voices/). This campaign collected and shared stories of leaders working for peace and justice, in particular in African-American, Latino, immigrant, indigenous, low income, and vulnerable communities. These stories spoke and continue to speak of disproportionate suffering and loss, victimization, and injustice, highlighting our connection and our disconnection. These pandemic stories, the gathered voices, provide phenomenological data, they put names, and faces, on facts and statistics. They invite us to see, and absorb with all of our senses, the reality of our connection, our common humanity, and our disconnection, our inhumanity, the myths that would divide us and assert that some are existentially more worthy than others because of the color of their skin, their status, their gender, orientation, class, or other socially constructed difference.

In addition to pandemic stories from activists, advocates, researchers, social scientists, educators, and community-based leaders, stories from my students spoke of the reality of our profound connection and disconnection. From online learning challenges, to delayed job opportunities and job loss, to increased risk as essential workers, to housing and food instability, to disproportionate cases and impacts on low-income students, immigrant students, and students of color, my students' experiences mirrored national and international data about COVID-19's disparate impact. Indeed, we are all affected, but those most vulnerable are suffering and dying disproportionately. This crisis challenges our commitment to core social work values of social justice, inherent human dignity, diversity, and an understanding of human relationships rooted in belonging. It exposes the disconnection perpetrated by socially constructed myths that would deny our fundamental interbeing and interconnection.

In this time of pandemic and racial, political, and social unrest, engaging the Circle's first phase requires that we pay particular attention to the stories of those who are objectified and reified, dehumanized, and victimized by the social construct of race, resulting in structural racism and injustice. It requires that we look deeply at and acknowledge how the pandemic has exposed the devastating consequences of socially constructed privilege and power, exacerbated oppression, and perpetuated the myth that some are more worthy than others. In a time of pandemic, the first phase of the Circle of Insight invites a particular clarity with respect to the explicit and implicit, conscious and unconscious ways in which we create divides and foment division that contributes to structural, institutional, systemic racism, and social injustice. We must look honestly too at stories of internalized oppression, white nationalism and supremacy, white privilege, classism and other stories of discrimination and marginalization that have been brought more glaringly into the light by COVID-19. These stories too reveal our socially constructed disconnection and its dehumanizing consequences.

bell hooks (1994) challenges us to see that in many cases and places the "biases that uphold and maintain white supremacy, imperialism, sexism, and racism have distorted education so that it is no longer about the practice of freedom" (p. 29). We must look deeply and honestly at this reality in the time of pandemic and invite conversation with students and colleagues in humility and with courage, examining how COVID-19 has unveiled these biases and -isms anew. In and out of the classroom, we must ask probing questions that challenge the privilege and lies that perpetuate disconnection. As social worker educators, as persons in power, we must honestly examine our participation in systems of privilege that deepen divisive, destructive disconnection. We must listen to the voices of students on the margins. For the students of color and the economically poor, the fact that race and class are socially constructed does not change the reality of their horrific consequences—the deadly, disparate impact of the pandemic, and the debilitating, dehumanizing effect of internalized oppression and structural injustice. The classroom must be a place where social workers, teacher–students, and student–teachers alike (Freire, 1970/2000) can critically examine their own story, in order to do the self-care and self-actualization work necessary to realize the radical revolution in values required to confront the injustice of the pandemic's disproportionate impact. In the classroom, we must unabashedly expose stories of socially constructed disconnection and invite creative connection, connection that fosters personal and collective liberation, justice, and the practice of freedom. In the classroom, we must pay attention to students who are vulnerable and living on the margins, and we must invite students to pay attention to the stories of the other, those from whom they may believe themselves to be distanced and disconnected.

A simple practice I have integrated into all of my classes is regular, strengths-based mindfulness meditation practices that seek to foster deep insight and connection. These practices invite students to take mindful moments each class, to connect with body and breath, and to be present to their own deepest truth and desires. These practices of presence are meant not only to help cultivate self-care and self-awareness but also to prepare students to be more present to others, particularly others in great need. These practices invite students to connect more deeply to their own story. They enable students to see and experience their fundamental connection with others. Many students share that these simple mindfulness meditation and mantra practices help them to be more fully present, to pay attention, to their own dignity, strengths, truth, and deep desires, as well as to see more clearly, and be more attentive to, the dignity, strengths, truth, and deep desires of others.

As Adrienne maree brown (2017) asserts, "What you pay attention to grows" (p. 42). The first phase of the Circle of Insight requires that we look deeply at and listen deeply to, our own story, as well as the stories of those who are oppressed, knowing that the stories of those who are most vulnerable, in need, and oppressed hold up a mirror to our own story, and provide the key to our individual and collective conscientization, our critical consciousness and liberation. They shine a light on our connection and our disconnection. The social work profession ethically mandates paying attention, and listening to, stories from the margins, examining questions of power and privilege, and looking deeply at, and unveiling, the reality of dehumanization and oppression. Social work has always challenged structures and systems that disproportionately discriminate against, harm, and dehumanize vulnerable and marginalized populations. Arguably, social workers are well positioned to creatively confront COVID-19 and invite transformation and deeper justice. In a time of pandemic, social workers possess the training and values to lift up stories of injustice and disconnection that must be shared. These stories in turn invite the Circle of Insight's second phase, critical reflection.

Phase 2—To Critically Reflect with Intellect and Empathy

The second phase of the Circle of Insight process builds on the first and invites us to reflect, to ideate creatively. It requires that we critically and constructively apply our learning, using ethical codes, research, core social work values and principles, research-informed best practices, and justice-informed theories as lenses through which to examine the reality observed in the first phase. It also invites and remains open to new learning and is a form of collaborative ideation (Maree Brown, 2017)—an engaged process that calls us together to ask and reflect on challenging and complicating questions. This critical reflection phase, like the practice of social work, engages both empathy and intellect, feeling and thought, intuition and ideas.

In the midst of a pandemic that disproportionately impacts persons of color, the poor, and those most vulnerable, the second phase of the Circle of Insight invites social work educators and practitioners to ask and critically reflect on two overarching questions: in the midst of COVID-19, what does social work's commitment to social justice, the inherent human dignity of all persons, and the importance of human relationships (NASW, 2018; CSWE, 2015) require of social work educators, students, and practitioners? And, in the midst of COVID-19, what does a commitment to engaged, liberatory pedagogy, and practice rooted in an ethic of beloved community and revolutionary, transformative love (Haga, 2020; Kaur, 2020; Freire, 1970/2000; hooks, 1994, 2000, 2003; King, 1968; Nicotera, 2018, 2019, 2020) require of social work educators, students, and practitioners?

The Circle of Insight's invitation to critical thinking and reflection moves us individually and collectively toward deeper, more transformative and liberating dialogue, and praxis—action and reflection upon the world in order to transform it (Freire, 2000; hooks, 1994; Nicotera, 2018, 2019, 2020; Reisch & Garvin, 2016). Perhaps, now more than ever, in the midst of a pandemic,

> this moment requires that we commit to being better educated students, teachers, and practitioners, with respect to social justice theory, skills, and practice such that, consistent with section 6.04(a) of our Code of Ethics, we can better 'advocate for changes in policy and legislation to improve social conditions in order to meet basic human needs and promote social justice' (NASW, 2017)
>
> (Nicotera, 2019)

The second phase of the Circle of Insight invites us to engage in critical thinking and reflection that both applies and deepens our knowledge and theory, recognizing that this requires both intellect and empathy. In this phase, we use social justice and ethical concepts and theories consistent with social work core values as a lens to more fully examine and understand the reality observed in the Circle's first phase.

Social Justice, Inherent Human Dignity, and the Importance of Human Relationships

As COVID-19 spread in the United States in the spring of 2020, I invited students to engage the Circle of Insight's invitation to critically reflect on the pandemic in light of social work's commitment to social justice. We used the seven E's that I proposed in my social work definition of social justice to guide our reflection; social justice in social work invites and insists upon: (1) Equity—equitable distribution of resources; (2) Equality—equal access to basic liberties and opportunities; (3) Empowerment—respect for and cultivation of the power and strengths of all persons, especially the disadvantaged, vulnerable, and oppressed; (4) Environment—a person-in-environment perspective that respects dignity and diversity and challenges discrimination and oppression; (5) Engagement—engagement that centers human relations and is dialectical and restorative; (6) Education—education that is liberatory, relational, and rooted in love; and (7) Enlightenment—insight that recognizes our inherent interconnectedness (Nicotera, 2019). In policy, law, race and bias, and social justice courses, we asked critical questions related to each of the E's. For example, what does social work's commitment to equity, equality, empowerment, and an environment that respects and promotes dignity and diversity have to teach us about the pandemic's impact on our community? What does the pandemic teach and require of us with respect to empowerment, engagement, and education in an environment that disproportionately privileges white, wealthy communities? What does the fact that disturbing, devastating, disproportionate numbers of Black, Latino, Native American, immigrant, and low-income persons have died from COVID-19 teach us about our society's commitment to social justice, to equity, equality, dignity, diversity, and empowerment? How do all of these factors, as a lens via which to critically examine COVID-19, invite deeper insight and help us more fully understand our intrinsic human connection and socially constructed disconnection?

Scholars assert that there is a high likelihood that "preexisting inequities are at the root of the disproportionate impact of the COVID-19 epidemic on racial-ethnic minorities in the United States" (Fortuna et al., 2020, p. 443). These preexisting inequities include, for example, disparities in access to healthcare, housing, jobs that pay a living wage, job training, quality education, technology, affordable childcare, and healthy foods. These current inequities and injustices require social work educators and students to reflect critically on historic, institutional, systemic injustice, and how these injustices are exacerbated, in particular in this moment, by the pandemic. The Circle of Insight framework challenges students to move beyond mere political slogans and scapegoating, such as referring to COVID-19 as the China virus, and to explore with greater insight and deliberate discipline what the pandemic can teach us about social injustice and our collective, societal participation in perpetuating, consciously and subconsciously, dehumanizing, racist, sexist, classist, discriminatory, and oppressive social structures and systems. As a complement to the Circle of Insight, we utilize Bobbi Harro's Cycle of Socialization to explore how we are socialized into prioritizing profit and economic exchanges over people and human relationship (Harro, 2018). Together the Circle of Insight and Cycle of Socialization invite us to see with greater clarity the ways in which socially constructed dehumanizing disconnection creates power, wealth, and privilege for the few, and discounts our connection, our common humanity.

Bobbi Harro created the Cycle of Socialization (Harro, 2018) to explain the perpetuation of systemic, structural, institutional discrimination, and oppression. The Cycle describes the process of socialization that exists, into which we are born in the United States, that teaches us to privilege certain people and oppress others, that asserts that some people, namely white, European, male, cisgendered, Christian, wealthy, land-owning, citizens are more worthy of dignity and respect, are even more fully human, than others. The Cycle persists unless and until we break out of it. Utilizing this Cycle in the classroom, students wrestle with these critical questions and theoretical frames via oral and written reflections, journaling, one-on-one and small group conversations, role playing activities, and creative exercises, including virtual reality simulations where they experience becoming refugees and persons who are homeless. They critically examine the pandemic in the context of social justice theory and they question, complicate, and create theory. They share their stories and concerns, questions and insights, and frustrations and understanding of what the pandemic might be saying to all of us, as social workers and society, about our values and commitment to dignity and justice. They reflect on how the pandemic helps us better understand the Cycle of Socialization and how the Cycle of Socialization helps contextualize and frame the pandemic.

In the context of the Circle of Insight's second phase, student engagement with the Cycle of Socialization helps them refine and focus critically reflective questions. Is it true that all persons have inherent dignity and human relationships are our priority if choices are made that prioritize economics and profit over people and certain communities over others? What disparities exist with respect to access to COVID-19 testing and treatment, and personal protective equipment (PPE), between wealthier, predominantly white communities versus lower-income communities, and communities of color? As a complement to these questions, I share with students stories, including my own, of living and working in and with low-income communities, and communities of color in urban communities in the northeast and midwest as examples of how long-standing wealth disparities, discrimination, and systemic racism contribute to making certain communities far more vulnerable to the pandemic than others.

While working in schools in Camden, NJ, and Newark, NJ, I witnessed the fact that almost every student had an inhaler and suffered from asthma. The prevalence of students suffering with asthma was directly related to the intersection of poverty, pollution, and substandard housing in their communities. In North Camden, housing was so poorly constructed that many students and their families were exposed to rodents, roaches, and excessive dust and dirt, all of which contributed to the development of asthma and other health issues. While living in the Leavenhouse Community in North Camden, an intentional community providing food, housing, referrals to addiction and recovery programs, and social service support to low-income residents, I experienced firsthand toxic unregulated pollution from trash incineration and waste treatment plants in our residential neighborhood. I too lived in the substandard housing in which my students and clients lived. Leavenhouse too had dirt, dust basement floors, rodent infestation, and lack of access to clean water. Social injustice, discriminatory lending and real estate practices, pollution, food deserts, community violence, discrimination, and poverty all ensured that Camden residents, predominantly low-income persons and persons of color, lived in environments that lacked adequate resources, social support, and infrastructure. Furthermore, there was not one grocery store within Camden city limits. It was what is referred to as a food desert. The only place to buy groceries was at the corner store, where food choices were limited, with very few healthy foods. The produce was not as fresh, and the prices were often much higher than at the grocery stores outside the city. However, it was difficult, and expensive for many residents, to get to these larger grocery stores with better prices, produce, and selection.

I also lived in low-income neighborhoods in Detroit and Chicago, and worked in low-income neighborhoods in Boston and Newark, NJ, where residents again were exposed to community violence, air and water pollution, and lacked affordable healthcare, good jobs, and access to quality housing, transportation, and schools. In Detroit, I spent almost two hours waiting at a bus stop to travel to work. Eventually, I called the city to report that I had been waiting over 90 minutes for a bus. They said simply that the driver had called in sick. I asked when the next bus would be arriving. They stated again, the driver called in sick. After a moment, I realized that another bus was not coming. They had one bus driver for our route. There was no bus that day. I invited my university students, some of whom lived in underserved, low-income communities, some of whom had limited access to adequate transportation, housing, healthy foods, and healthcare, some of whom were exposed to pollutants in the air and water, to share their stories and to discuss this reality in the context of a pandemic. I also asked them to reflect critically on connections to disproportionate cases of COVID-19 in their communities. I asked them to reflect on what I suggest is the central question that social workers must ask in assessing social work's pedagogical and ethical imperative to promote social justice: Is this reality fair and just, in particular for the least, the marginalized, the oppressed (Nicotera, 2019)?

Engaged, Liberatory Pedagogy, and Beloved Community

Commitment to engaged, liberatory pedagogy (Freire, 1970/2000; hooks, 1994, 2000, 2003), and beloved community rooted in revolutionary, transformative love (Haga, 2020; hooks, 2000; Kaur, 2020; King, 1968, 1994, 2000) provides another lens via which to critically reflect upon and examine social work's pedagogical commitment to social justice and human dignity in the midst of a pandemic. Later, I will discuss how liberation, love, and beloved community are not only a frame for critical reflection but also the center, the *telos* or goal, of our Circle of Insight process.

As bell hooks (1994) asserts, engaged, liberatory pedagogy requires the we "teach in a manner that respects and cares for the souls of our students" (13); she adds that this "is essential if we are to provide the necessary conditions where learning can most deeply and intimately begin" (13). Freire (1970/2000) and hooks (1994, 2000, 2003) remind us that truly liberatory, engaged pedagogy also must emphasize well-being, and not only student well-being, but teachers too must "be actively committed to a process of self-actualization that promotes their own well-being if they are to teach in a manner that empowers students" (hooks, 1994, p. 14). In particular in a time of pandemic, it is critically important that teachers and students together actively engage in mutual learning, respecting and fostering individual and collective well-being and self-actualization. The classroom, as a microcosm of society, holds the potential for deepened connection or disconnection. The classroom is a place that presents and perpetuates either disconnection—an us/them, divisive pedagogy, insinuating or explicitly teaching and modeling superiority and power over others, or the classroom presents and promotes connection—a both/and, unifying pedagogy, conveying in word and deed the sentiment expressed by Gandhi, that power comes from seeing that everyone holds a piece of the truth.

Social work classrooms, indeed all classrooms, need to be places where we tend not only to the intellectual, academic development of our students, but also to learning and engagement that is holistic (hooks, 1994; Pyles, 2018) that embraces the bio-psycho-social-spiritual bodies and souls of our students. As Dr. King (1968) so prophetically proclaimed, "Enlarged material powers spell peril if there is not proportionate growth of the soul" (182). This growth of the soul, rooted in liberatory pedagogy engages our relational selves, our social interconnection as human persons and human community. This means that engaged, liberatory pedagogy loves and learns in a way that creates beloved community in the classroom. This is challenging for many educators as it requires vulnerability, comfort with ambiguity and uncertainty, and an openness to learning from our students. This vulnerability, uncertainty, and openness in turn hold open the possibility of freedom, connection, mutuality, and learning rooted in co-creation of knowledge and community (Burghardt, 2016; Pyles, 2018; Walter, 2016). As hooks (1994) asserts, "any classroom that employs a holistic model of learning will also be a place where teachers grow, and are empowered by the process" (p. 21). This is pedagogy that fosters openness and freedom. This is pedagogy that encourages students to teach and teachers to learn. This is pedagogy that, in a time of pandemic, risks asking critical questions that invite resistance and a radical revolution in values (King, 2000). This is pedagogy that challenges our culture of disconnection, domination, and reification.

Engaged, liberatory, critical pedagogy "calls for dialogical learning, in which students' perspectives are encouraged and have room (Giroux, 2004, 2011)" (Walter, 2016, p. 166). This room or spaciousness for students' experience and perspective invites social work educators to ask how it is that we, along with our students, as persons-in-environments, are shaped by and are shaping society in the midst of suffering, disease, and pandemic, and its concomitant grief, disruption, death, and devastation. Engaged, liberatory pedagogy offers a lens for critical reflection. What does it mean to care for the souls of our students in a time of pandemic? What does it mean to create a classroom culture of mutual learning and care and of vulnerability and openness? How can we foster beloved community in the classroom? How can we awaken together to critical consciousness, what Freire (1970/2000) refers to as conscientization, an awareness of the reality and dynamics of systemic injustice and power disparities that perpetuate cycles of oppression. This lens utilizes the Circle of Insight's dialectical, open, purposeful, enlightening dynamic (Nicotera, 2019), facilitating pedagogy that does not seek to bank or deposit information (hooks, 1994, 2000, 2003; Freire, 1970/2000), but rather to utilize what Freire calls problem-posing pedagogy (1970/2000) that invites liberation and connection and engages the whole person, body, mind, and soul. Sadly, the experience that hooks (1994) shares here is all too common: "most of my professors were not the slightest bit interested in enlightenment. More than anything, they seemed enthralled by the exercise of power and authority in their mini-kingdom, the classroom" (17). In the midst of the pandemic, it is particularly important to invite critical reflection rooted in mutuality, dialogue, shared uncertainty and vulnerability, and common purpose and connection, which include personal self-actualization and collective well-being, and promote education as the practice of freedom.

This notion of collective well-being and engaged, liberatory pedagogy is ultimately humanizing, acknowledging our connection, our common dignity as human persons, and inviting movement toward beloved community— beloved community that prioritizes people over profit, humanity over humiliation, healing over harm and freedom over fear and oppression.

The work of beloved community as lens for critical reflection in a time of pandemic requires revisioning, refocusing rooted in what Dr. King referred to as a radical revolution in values (King, 2000). It requires a shifting of perspective and priorities, moving from a thing-oriented, material-centered, dehumanizing vision of society to a person-oriented, community-centered, humanizing vision of society. In a time of pandemic, this shifting of perspective and priorities invites compassion, empathy, and requisite healing justice. For, "true compassion is more than flinging a coin to a beggar; it understands that an edifice which produces beggars needs restructuring" (King, 1968, p. 198). So we must ask in the classroom, what restructuring, what radical revolution in values is this pandemic inviting? What does a humanizing response to this pandemic look like? What does building the beloved community in the midst of and beyond a pandemic look like? In the fierce urgency of now (King, 1968, 2000), we ask, as Dr. King did over 50 years ago, what does the lens of beloved community require of us - as individuals, as society, as social workers, as educators, as citizens, as human beings? If the lens of beloved community necessarily includes all persons, leaving no one out, while holding us personally and collectively accountable for harm and responsible for well-being (Haga, 2020), how can we sharpen the focus of this lens and utilize it to create a more just, humanizing response to the disconnection perpetuated by COVID-19's disproportionate, devastating impact on society's most vulnerable communities?

Phase 3—To Act Individually and Collectively

What does engaged, liberatory pedagogy look like in practice, in the classroom and community? How do we teach and work and live in a way that moves us toward deeper insight, love, and liberation? What practices surface as a result of a disciplined, deliberate application of the Circle of Insight process in the midst of a pandemic? It is my conviction that the Circle of Insight can help educators and social workers and human beings actualize engaged, liberatory pedagogy in this time of pandemic, and help us all move toward a more just, beloved community in the classroom and community. Modeling this engaged, liberatory Circle of Insight pedagogy in the classroom in turn can reverberate out into the field and help transform society, exposing socially constructed myths of difference and disconnection. In the midst of COVID-19, pedagogy that emanates from engaging the Circle process will help us move toward deeper connection, liberation, justice, and beloved community.

The third phase of the Circle of Insight, to act, builds on the first two. After looking deeply at the reality of pandemic, and reflecting critically in light of a commitment to social justice, human dignity, liberation and beloved community, the Circle invites thoughtful, constructive, and creative action. In a time of crises, the temptation can be to act impulsively, to react without first looking carefully at the data and research, and reflecting critically using the lens of core social work values and principles. This third phase, applied in the classroom, challenges teacher/students, and student/teachers (Freire, 1970/2000; hooks, 1994, 2003) to refrain from acting until the first two phases of the Circle have been fully engaged. Students must research and collect data, understand theory and concepts, and investigate and share stories that relate to the pandemic, before considering appropriate action.

Students often want to begin with action. They ask, understandably, What can or should I do? How can we make a difference? What actions are most just? What does our commitment to social justice require of us? These are good, important questions, but they can be premature if asked before engaging the first and second phases of the Circle of Insight. A common mistake is to react, to act first, without gathering information, looking carefully and critically at, in this case, the data and stories related to the pandemic's disproportionate impact on the oppressed and vulnerable. Another common student desire, in addition to wanting to (re)act immediately, is the desire for certainty, to want to know generally what constitutes just, right, and appropriate action. What is the answer? What will help us create a more just, liberated society? What specifically do we need to do to confront the implicit bias and structural racism that have contributed to the pandemic's disproportionate, devastating impact? The challenge is that there is no cookie-cutter response, no single action appropriate for every situation (Nicotera, 2019). However, engaging the Circle of Insight process will help ensure that action steps and recommendations respond most directly to sources of oppression and move us most thoughtfully and purposefully toward deeper connection, liberation, justice, and beloved community. This step invites action that holds open the possibility of transformation of hearts and minds and affirms our innate connection.

When teaching social justice, peacemaking, spirituality, and social work courses at an urban university in the midwest, I had the privilege of working with civil rights leader and activist Diane Nash. As a student at Fisk University, along with the late Representative John Lewis, she helped lead sit-ins in Nashville, Tennessee. Ultimately, they were effective in desegregating the city's lunch counters and advancing the work of civil rights and social justice nationally. This movement was led by and composed primarily of college students and young people. Ms. Nash came to my social justice classes and led our students in a nonviolence training similar to the one in which she had engaged as a student. At the time, those trainings were facilitated by civil rights leader, and Southern Field Secretary of the Fellowship of Reconciliation, Reverend James Lawson. She described a process taught to her by Rev. Lawson that mirrored the Circle of Insight. She emphasized the strict discipline of their preparation. She shared that they tried never to react to any situation, but always first to gather facts and data, then reflect critically in light of their commitment to *agape*, the Greek word for selfless, other-centered love, a reflection of God's love, at the heart of Dr. King's teaching and preaching (King, 1968), and then and only then did they discuss creative action.

The full-day training included stories about the challenges that Ms. Nash and fellow civil rights advocates and activists faced in desegregating lunch counters. Ms. Nash also shared how she and fellow students educated themselves in the strategic tactics of nonviolent direct action and its economic, social, and political impact. She discussed how the students and activists genuinely hoped for the transformation of the hearts and minds of their oppressors—that their oppressors would ultimately come to see the common humanity and inherent connection they shared. She taught us the principles they practiced, in particular their collective commitment to active nonviolence, which Ms. Nash preferred to call agapic energy—soul force or the energy of selfless love. She led conversations and reflections on these principles and talked about some of the tensions and challenges they faced in embracing agapic energy. She also led my students in role plays similar to those that she and others went through in preparation for the sit-ins, practicing being spit upon and yelled at, and even attacked.

We were amazed at the discipline, critical thinking, strategizing, and careful preparation she detailed. Ms. Nash told us that they trained in such a way so that in the midst of their sit-in, they would be prepared to remain focused and true to their convictions, so that they would not react, but rather act deliberately, with discipline and purpose. She shared that their preparation always included information gathering, critical reflection, and role playing various potential scenarios. Ms. Nash also confirmed that in all of their preparations for action throughout the civil rights movement they would always assess a situation and gather information before acting. King scholar Kazu Haga (2020) affirms this process as part of Dr. King's strategic thinking: "In his 'Letter from a Birmingham Jail,' Dr. King said that the first step in any nonviolent campaign is the 'collection of facts to determine whether injustice exists'" (p. 168). This embraces both the first and second phases of the Circle of Insight, seeing, gathering information, and critically reflecting, determining, in light of values and convictions, whether an injustice exists. Ms. Nash also told us that they would prepare so that they would never act rashly, so that in the face of racism and even violence, they would respond with thoughtful, compassionate action rooted in love with their eyes on the prize, the goal of creating a more just beloved community. She added that even when Dr. King's house was bombed, though some wanted to respond impulsively and violently, their commitment was to maintain what I would refer to as their Circle of Insight discipline—pausing, looking and listening deeply, collecting facts, reflecting critically, and then, and only then, carefully, creatively acting. This process was rooted in a conviction that despite hatred, division, and discrimination, their liberation was bound up with, connected to, that of their oppressor.

I continue to share Ms. Nash's story in the classroom with my current students as an example of the Circle of Insight in action. I invite students to reflect on and discuss what Ms. Nash's story has to teach us about connection and disconnection, and about the pandemic and possibility for justice and liberation. Students are surprised and often impressed by the discipline, practice, preparation, and commitment of Ms. Nash and her fellow civil rights activists. They also are challenged, even baffled by how Ms. Nash describes the interconnection of her liberation and that of her oppressor. She acknowledges our disconnection, and the harm wrought by divisive social constructs like race and class, and yet, she insists on our fundamental connection and common humanity. She also asserts, with Dr. King, that her convictions call her to love, with agapic energy, even those who oppress and discriminate and perpetrate violence. I invite students to consider courageous, creative love in action, consistent with Ms. Nash's witness and wisdom. What would this action look like as a way to confront the pandemic and contemporary racial injustice? I ask students to suggest creative, disciplined action, maybe using social media, the arts, virtual reality, technology, political action, or education to tell the story of how the pandemic's disparate devastation on the poor, persons of color, and vulnerable populations, is exposing the destructive fallacy of privilege and social constructs that divide and disconnect. What action would be most effective in achieving the goals set forth by Ms. Nash—affirming our interconnection; building the beloved community; transforming hearts and minds; transcending our disconnection, that which would divide us; and affirming our connection, our common humanity, worth, and dignity?

My effort to co-create with students the beloved community in the classroom, consistent with our commitment to engaged, liberatory pedagogy is one way I seek to model the third phase of the Circle of Insight. Over the years in light of my work with Thich Nhat Hanh, Mother Teresa, Married Maguire, Arun Gandhi, and Diane Nash, I have observed the power of education to transform and liberate hearts and minds. Reflecting critically on lessons learned from these inspirational leaders and my own experience teaching for over 20 years, I have come to understand that it is important to act, as an educator, in a way that builds connection. Thus, I work to create a classroom and educational environment that centers justice and invites the reimagining of the world we want to see outside the classroom. I work to make the classroom not only a place for learning but also for modeling the beloved community and thus for building something new. As Maree Brown (2017) asserts, "if we want to create a world in which conflict and trauma aren't the center of our collective existence, we have to practice something new" (pp. 149–150). We have to practice transformative, healing justice that recognizes and builds trust, resilience, and interdependence (Birkenmaier et al., 2011; Haga, 2020; Kaur, 2020; Maree Brown, 2017; Pyles, 2018; Reisch & Garvin, 2016). Thus, we practice creating something new in the classroom, what I refer to as transformative justice in action. Transformative justice, or what Pyles (2018) refers to as healing justice, in the classroom in a time of pandemic invites action that acknowledges: the synergistic relationship between the personal and political; the need to change the structures and operations of historic oppression; the need to decolonize spaces in which we work and live; the need to attend to means and process as vital to our collective liberation; the negative impact oppression has on our bodies; and the fact that personal and collective care practices and healing are necessary for sustainability and transformation. All of these aspects and dynamics of transformative justice, toward which the Circle of Insight moves, show up in the classroom and university setting. Thus, to create a classroom culture consistent with transformative justice, social work educators and students together must acknowledge and grapple with oppression, colonization, systemic injustice, as well as with liberation, love, and healing. The Circle of Insight offers a process for doing so, for naming, reflecting on, and actively working to understand and transform oppression, divisiveness, and colonization, and lift up and foster connection, liberation, and healing.

In a time of pandemic, classroom oppression can take the form of pedagogical omission, failure to acknowledge or discuss COVID-19's disproportionate impact on communities of color, low-income communities, indigenous, immigrant, and vulnerable communities. It can take the form of pedagogical commission, akin to Freire's banking form of education (1970/2000), whereby educators deposit knowledge into students without creating a safe, compassionate, loving culture for true praxis. Action consistent with the Circle of Insight and transformative justice in the classroom, on the other hand, is participatory and responsive to the dynamics and reality of the students. It centers healing, liberation, and creativity. It engages and invites healing, transformative justice and whole self-care. Practically, this includes introducing and inviting personal practices, such as regular mindfulness meditation, or other holistic practices that cultivate not only intellect or mind but also body, heart, and soul, bio-pyscho-social-spiritual well-being. This process also includes promoting and protecting a classroom culture that fosters conversation across difference, acknowledging social, systemic injustices associated with the pandemic, and creating safe spaces for students to discuss personal experiences and perspectives. It requires Circle of Insight engagement with action-focused, challenging questions, such as "What does it take to reclaim wonder now after so much trauma and devastation?" (Kaur, 2020, p. 23) What concrete steps need to be taken to build the beloved community and practice transformative justice in the classroom, on campus, and in the community, in a time of a pandemic? What is required for us in order to confront disparities faced by the students and the university and larger community as a result of the pandemic? What classroom, campus, even community policies and practices need to be instituted, amended, or abolished?

In the midst of the pandemic, the action required, the new world we are being challenged to create in and beyond the classroom, "at once looks back to the roots of our profession . . . while simultaneously moving relentlessly and boldly forward" (Nicotera, 2019). Nobel Peace Laureate and social work cofounder, Jane Addams, was on the front lines of battling the 1918–1919 influenza pandemic (Gore, 2019). As the Jane Addams Hull-House Museum reports, "Addams was a leader in providing aid to those struck by the flu in the crowded tenement district where Hull-House was located in Chicago" (Jane Addams' Leadership, 2020). Today, the NASW and CSWE provide updates, reports, and educational resources for social workers laboring to confront COVID-19 in the classroom and the community. Social workers have been working on multiple fronts, clinically, with other public health and medical personnel, and politically as advocates for just policies regarding everything from access to adequate treatment and healthcare, to social justice for vulnerable and disproportionately impacted populations. As we consider appropriate action in light of looking deeply at the disproportionate impact of the pandemic on communities of color, I invite the Circle of Insight process to help foster appropriate and transformative action that integrates learning from the past and invites bold action moving forward to foster deeper connection and creatively confront injustices and disconnection.

Political theorist Gene Sharp (1973) categorizes 198 methods of nonviolent action that have been used by individuals and peoples globally to foster connection, transform societies, and promote peace and social justice. As a way to engage the third phase of the Circle of Insight, I invite students to consider how Sharp's methods might be applied to the pandemic. One creative example of protest that can be applied to our current COVID-19 reality took place in Madrid in 2015. The government banned all protests in front of the Parliament, so activists created history's first known holographic protest, projecting protestor holograms onto the street in front of Parliament. Hundreds of protestors were marching, but nowhere near the Parliament. They did not break the law but were able to use technology to creatively act for justice to confront unjust laws (Jegroo, 2015). In the classroom, I share stories of this type of creative action, consistent with the Circle of Insight's engaged liberatory pedagogy, as well as invite students to consider their own creative action consistent with the Circle of Insight process. I introduce various concepts, resources, and practices, such as peacemaking circle processes, tools for contemplative practice, cooperative learning exercises, critical, engaged pedagogy principles and practices, role plays, and self-care strategies that help engage and actualize healing and transformative justice in the classroom (Adams et al., 2018; Barbezat & Bush, 2014; Bell, Goodman, & Varghese, 2016; Birkenmaier et al., 2011; Freire, 1970/2000; hooks, 1994, 2000; Kaur, 2020; Marree Brown, 2017; Nicotera, 2018, 2019, 2020; Pranis, 2005; Pyles, 2018; Pyles & Adam, 2016; Reisch & Garvin, 2016; Van Soest & Garcia, 2008). All of these actions can help shine a light on fissures and divides, disconnection that is the result of social constructs and systems of injustice that exacerbate harm and oppression. These actions can also help foster connection. They can help us see more clearly the illusion of our separateness.

In this spirit, Valarie Kaur (2020) offers one simple but profound example of a practice of revolutionary love that can transform how we see the other and remind us of our ultimate connection. This is the Circle process in action, continually inviting us to see again, after we have acted, and then to reflect again, and act, all in continual movement toward deeper connection, love, justice, and liberation. She shares,

> As I move through my day and come across faces on the street or subway or on a screen, I say in my mind, *Sister. Brother. Sibling. Aunt. Uncle . . .* I say in my mind: *You are a part of me I do not yet know*
> (Kaur, 2020, p. 27)

In the fierce urgency of now, our world desperately needs social workers, indeed all of us, to renew our commitment to social justice, to embrace Valarie Kaur's revolutionary love, and to commit to actualizing anew Dr. King's beloved community. In this way, we not only see and critically reflect on the truth of our innate connection, but also act on it and invite others to do the same.

The Circle's Center—Insight, Liberation, Beloved Community, and Revolutionary Love

The center of the Circle of Insight is that toward which the circle purposefully moves, its *telos*, goal, or objective. For Freire (1970/2000) and hooks (1994, 2000, 2003), it is critical consciousness and liberation. For Dr. King (1968), it is *agape* and beloved community. For Kaur (2020), it is revolutionary love. For Thich Nhat Hanh (1993, 2003), it is insight, interbeing, and love in action. For Frankl (1984), it is meaning. In the African tribal tradition, it is *ubuntu*—I am because you are (Kaur, 2020; Maathai, 2010; Tutu, 1999). "It is the ancient Sanskrit truth that we can look upon anyone or anything and say: *Tat tvam asi*, 'I am that'" (Kaur, 2020, p. 11). For many social scientists, activists, and social workers, it is social, restorative, or transformative justice (Adams, Bell, Goodman, & Joshi, 2016; Adams et al., 2018; Austin, 2014; Bell, 2016; Bent-Goodley & Hopps, 2017; Birkenmaier et al., 2011; Colby, Dulmas, & Sowers, 2013; CSWE Learning Academy, 2016; Gill, 1998; Hodge, 2010; Hutchison, 2011; Marree Brown, 2017; Marsh, 2005; Nicotera, 2018, 2019, 2020; Pyles, 2018; Pyles & Adam, 2016; Reisch & Garvin, 2016; Van Soest, 1996; Van Soest & Garcia, 2008). All of these notions lift up and celebrate the fundamental truth of our inherent connection. They are the ocean of which the waves of our disconnection and difference are merely a part. These concepts convey in various languages, from varying cultures, geographies, and times, our innate connection; they exist at the center of the Circle of Insight, its telos, that toward which it beckons us to move, its end and its beginning.

The Circle's center thus is both means and end; it is both purpose and process. It invites movement toward justice, and it engages the work of justice in the present. It is both now/already and not yet/that toward which we strive (Nicotera, 2019). As Dr. King proclaimed, "Peace is not merely a distant goal that we seek but a means by which we arrive at that goal" (King, 1968, p. 194). In this time of pandemic, the Circle of Insight invites us to awaken from our illusion of separateness. As we rage and grieve together in the midst of a pandemic that has caused so much suffering, we see that our collective anger and grieving is itself an act of connection and transformation. This rage and grief "creates new relationships, and energizes the demand for justice. . . . It is how we build real solidarity, the kind that shows us the world we want to live in—and our role in fighting for it" (Kaur, 2020, p. 44). Echoing Thich Nhat Hanh, and Dr. King, and core social work principles, Valarie Kaur (2020) affirms that "separateness is an illusion. . . . We are part of one another" (p. 54). In the midst of the pandemic, we are being invited to see our fundamental connection, the fact that the well-being, the liberation of the other, the stranger, is bound up in our own. We are being called to Valarie Kaur's (2020) revolutionary love:

> If you "see no stranger" and choose to love all people, then you must fight for anyone who is suffering from the harm of injustice. This was the path of the warrior-sage: The warrior fights, the sage loves. *Revolutionary love*"
>
> (p. 92)

This is who we are, our calling, as social workers and social work educators in the midst of this pandemic and beyond, to be, and to cultivate in our students, warrior-sages. Warrior-sages see, and help others see, beyond socially constructed difference and disconnection to the fundamental reality of our connate connection. Warrior-sages invite awakening from our illusion of separateness.

Prompts for Writing:

1. How has the pandemic, political polarization, and racial reckoning in the United States, and globally, unveiled injustice and the need for healing? What does justice and healing require of us personally and collectively? Reflect on ways in which you might apply the Circle of Insight framework to explore notions of interbeing, interconnection, disconnection, and polarization.

2. What lessons did you take away from the author's recounting of Diane Nash's story and nonviolence training? What personal stories would you consider sharing with others as a means to promote nonviolence?

3. In the context of a devastating and ravaging pandemic, ongoing racial injustice and reckoning, and paralyzing political polarization reflect on

Valarie Kaur's question, "What does it take to reclaim wonder now after so much trauma and devastation?" How is wonder connected to understanding our disconnection and connection and to moving toward healing and hope? What does Kaur's invitation to see no stranger and practice revolutionary love, and social work's ethical mandate to center and practice social justice, require of us in this moment?

Close Reading Questions:

1.   How does the Circle of Insight's See, Reflect, Act process invite deeper understanding of our inherent interconnection and disconnection? What is the deep listening that is being invited by the author as central to the first, See phase of the Circle of Insight? How does the Fellowship of Reconciliation's Gathering Voices campaign help elucidate and demonstrate this phase?
2.   How does the author's presentation of the seven E's of social justice help deepen your understanding of the Circle of Insight's second, Reflect phase? How does the author present notions of liberation, love, and beloved community as not only a frame for critical reflection, but also the center, the telos or goal, of the Circle of Insight process?
3.   How does Harro's Cycle of Socialization complement the Circle of Insight process? How does Kaur's refrain "You are a part of me I do not yet know" serve as a practical application of the Circle of Insight process?

References

Abrams, L., & Moio, J. (2009). Critical race theory and the cultural competence dilemma in social work education. *Journal of Social Work Education, 45*, 245–261.

Adams, M., Bell, L. A., Goodman, D. J., & Joshi, K. Y. (2016). *Teaching for diversity and social justice*. New York: Routledge.

Adams, M., Blumenfeld, W. J., Chase, D., Catalano, J., DeJong, K. S., Hackman, H. W., . . . Zúñiga, X. (Eds.). (2018). *Readings for diversity and social justice* (4th ed.). New York: Routledge.

Aucejo, E.M., French, J., Araya, M.P.U., Zafar, B. (2020). The impact of COVID-19 on student experiences and expectations: Evidence from a survey. *Journal of Public Economics, 191*, 1–15, Retrieved from: https://doi.org/10.1016/j.jpubeco.2020.104271

Austin, M. J. (Ed). (2014). *Social justice and social work: Rediscovering a core value of the profession*. Washington, DC: Sage.

Barbezat, D. P., & Bush, M. (2014). *Contemplative practices in higher education: Powerful methods to transform teaching and learning*. San Francisco, CA: Jossey-Bass.

Bell, L. A. (2016). Theoretical foundations for social justice education. In M. Adams, L. A. Bell, D. J. Goodman, & K. Y. Joshi (Eds.), *Teaching for diversity and social justice* (pp. 3–26). New York: Routledge.

Bell, L. A., Goodman, D. J., & Varghese, R. (2016). Critical self-knowledge for social justice educators. In M. Adams, L. A. Bell, D. J. Goodman, & K. Y. Joshi (Eds.), *Teaching for diversity and social justice* (pp. 397–418). New York: Routledge.

Bent-Goodley, T. B., & Hopps, J. G. (2017). Social justice and civil rights: A call to action for social work. *Social Work, 62*, 5–8.

Birkenmaier, J., Cruce, A., Burkemper, E., Curley, J., Wilson, R. J., & Stretch, J. J. (Eds.). (2011). *Educating for social justice: Transformative experiential learning.* Chicago, IL: Lyceum Books.

Burghardt, S. (2016). "By the end of the term, you will have gained power in the classroom and I will have lost none": The pedagogical value of discomfort and vulnerability in the teaching of community practice. In L. Pyles & G. J. Adam (Eds.), *Holistic engagement: Transformative social work education in the 21st century* (pp. 83–100). New York: Oxford University Press.

Colby, I. C., Dulmas, C. N., & Sowers, K. M. (Eds.). (2013). *Social work and social policy: Advancing the principles of economic and social justice.* Hoboken, NJ: Wiley.

Council on Social Work Education. (2015). *Educational policy and accreditation standards.* Retrieved from www.cswe.org/Accreditation/Standards-and-Policies/2015-EPAS.aspx

Council on Social Work Education Learning Academy. (2016). *Teaching for social justice.* Retrieved from https://learningacademy.cswe.org/products/teaching-for-social-justice#tab-product_tab_overview

Deepak, A. C., Rountree, M. A., & Scott, J. (2015). Delivering diversity and social justice in social work education: The power of context. *Journal of Progressive Human Services, 26*, 107–125.

Finn, J., & Jacobson, M. (2008). Social justice. In T. Mizrahi & L. Davis (Eds.), *Encyclopedia of social work* (Vol. 4, 20th ed., pp. 44–52). New York: NASW Press and Oxford University Press.

Fortuna, L. R., Tolou-Shams, M., Robles-Ramamurthy, B., & Porche, M. V. (2020). Inequity and the disproportionate impact of COVID-19 on communities of color in the United States: The need for a trauma-informed social justice response. *Psychological Trauma: Theory, Research, Practice, and Policy, 12*(5), 443–445.

Frankl, V. E. (1984). *Man's search for meaning: An introduction to logotherapy.* New York: Simon & Schuster.

Freire, P. (2000). *Pedagogy of the oppressed* (M. B. Ramos, Trans.). New York: Herder and Herder (Original work published 1970).

Gandhi, A. (2003). *Legacy of love: My education in the path of nonviolence.* El Sobrante, CA: North Bay Books.

Gil, D. G. (1998). *Confronting injustice and oppression: Concepts and strategies for social workers.* New York: Columbia University Press.

Giroux, H. (2004). Critical pedagogy and the postmodern/modern divide. *Teacher Education Quarterly, 31*(1), 31–47.

Giroux, H. (2011). *On critical pedagogy.* New York, NY: Continuum.

Gore, K. (2019). *The remarkable life of the first woman on the Harvard faculty.* Retrieved from www.nytimes.com/2019/08/29/opinion/alice-hamilton-harvard.html

Grant, J., & Austin, M. J. (2014). Incorporating social justice principles into social work practice. In M. J. Austin (Ed.), *Social justice and social work: Rediscovering a core value of the profession* (pp. 357–369). Thousand Oaks, CA: Sage.

Haga, K. (2020). *Healing resistance: A radically different response to harm.* Berkeley, CA: Parallax Press.

Harrison, J., VanDeusen, K., & Way, I. (2016). Embedding social justice within micro social work curricula. *Smith College Studies in Social Work, 86*, 258–273.

Harro, B. (2018). Cycle of socialization. In M. Adams, W. J. Blumenfeld, D. Chase, J. Catalano, K. S. DeJong, H. W. Hackman, . . . X. Zúñiga (Eds.), *Readings for diversity and social justice* (4th ed., pp. 27–34). New York: Routledge.

Hodge, D. R. (2010). Social justice as a unifying theme in social work education: Principles to realize the promise of a new pedagogical model. *Journal of Comparative Social Welfare, 26*, 201–213.

hooks, b. (1994). *Teaching to transgress: Education as the practice of freedom.* New York: Routledge.

hooks, b. (2000). *All about love.* New York: HarperCollins.

hooks, b. (2003). *Teaching community: A pedagogy of hope.* New York: Routledge.

Hutchison, E. (2011). *Social justice and social work: Oxford bibliographies online research guide.* New York: Oxford University Press.

International Association of Schools of Social Work. (2018). *Global standards for social work education and training.* Retrieved from www.iassw-aiets.org/global-standards-for-social-work-education-and-training/

International Federation of Social Workers. (2012). *Statement of ethical principles.* Retrieved from http://ifsw.org/policies/statement-of-ethical-principles/

Jane Addams' leadership and the crises of our time: Racial unrest, pandemic, and war. (2020). Retrieved from www.hullhousemuseum.org/programs-and-events-at-hullhouse/2020/7/17/jane-addams-leadership-and-the-crises-of-our-time-racial-unrest-pandemic-and-war

Jegroo, A. (2015). *Spaniards continue protesting as new "gag law" takes effect.* Retrieved from https://wagingnonviolence.org/2015/07/spaniards-continue-protesting-as-new-gag-law-takes-effect/

Kaur, V. (2020). *See no stranger: A memoir and manifesto of revolutionary love.* New York: Random House.

King, M. L. (1968). *Where do we go from here: Chaos or community?* Boston, MA: Beacon Press.

King, M. L. (1994). *Letter from the Birmingham jail.* San Francisco: Harper.

King, M. L. (2000). *Beyond Vietnam: Address delivered to the clergy and laymen concerned about Vietnam,* at Riverside Church. Retrieved from http://kingencyclopedia.stanford.edu/kingweb/publications/speeches/Beyond_Vietnam.pdf

Maathai, W. (2010). *Replenishing the earth: Spiritual values for healing ourselves and the world.* New York: Doubleday.

Maree Brown, A. (2017). *Emergent strategy: Shaping change, changing worlds.* Chico, CA: AK Press.

Marsh, J. C. (2005). Social justice: Social work's organizing value. *Social Work, 50,* 293–294.

National Association of Social Workers. (2017). *Code of ethics.* Washington, DC: NASW Press.

National Association of Social Workers. (2018). *Social justice priorities.* Retrieved from www.socialworkers.org/Advocacy/Social-Justice/Social-Justice-Priorities

Nhat Hanh, T. (1993). *Love in action.* Berkeley, CA: Parallax Press.

Nhat Hanh, T. (2003). *Interbeing: Fourteen guidelines for engaged Buddhism.* New Delhi: Full Circle.

Nicotera, A. (2018). Teaching note—circle of insight: A paradigm and pedagogy for liberation social justice social work education. *Journal of Social Work Education, 54*(2), 384–391.

Nicotera, A. (2019). Social justice and social work, a fierce urgency: Recommendations for social work social justice pedagogy. *Journal of Social Work Education, 55*(3), 460–475.

Nicotera, A. (2020). A history of spirituality, religion, and social work: Using the "circle of insight" to challenge, question, and create a framework for spiritually sensitive practice. In M. Jaffe, W. Nicola, J. Floersch, & J. Longhofer (Eds.), *Spirituality in mental health practice: A narrative casebook*. New York: Routledge, Taylor & Francis Group.

Oppel, R. A., Gebeloff, R., Rebecca Lai, K. K., Wright, W., & Smith, M. (2020, July 5). The fullest look yet at the racial inequity of coronavirus. *The New York Times*. Retrieved from www.nytimes.com/interactive/2020/07/05/us/coronavirus-latinos-african-americans-cdc-data.html

Pranis, K. (2005). *The little book of circle process: A new/old approach to peacemaking*. New York: Good Books.

Pyles, L. (2018). *Healing justice: Holistic self-care of change makers*. New York: Oxford University Press.

Pyles, L., & Adam, G. (Eds.). (2016). *Holistic engagement: Transformative social work education in the 21st century*. New York: Oxford University Press.

Reed, B., & Lehning, A. (2014). Educating social work students about social justice practice. In M. J. Austin (Ed.), *Social justice and social work: Rediscovering a core value of the profession* (pp. 339–356). Thousand Oaks, CA: Sage.

Reisch, M., & Garvin, C. D. (2016). *Social work and social justice: Concepts, challenges, and strategies*. New York: Oxford University Press.

Sayre, M. M., & Sar, B. K. (2015). Social justice in the social work classroom: Applying a professional value to social work education. *Social Work Education, 34*, 623–635.

Sharp, G. (1973). *The politics of nonviolent action (Parts 1–3)*. Boston, MA: Porter Sargent Publishers.

Simon, B. L. (1994). *The empowerment tradition in American social work*. New York: Columbia University Press.

Teresa, M. (1997). *No greater love*. Novato, CA: New World Library.

Thich Nhat Hanh Foundation. (2020). Retrieved from https://thichnhathanhfoundation.org/what-we-fund

Tutu, D. (1999). *No future without forgiveness*. New York: Doubleday.

Van Soest, D. (1996). Impact of social work education on student attitudes and behavior concerning oppression. *Journal of Social Work Education, 32*, 191–202.

Van Soest, D., & Garcia, B. (2008). *Diversity education for social justice: Mastering teaching skills* (2nd ed.). Alexandria, VA: Council on Social Work Education.

Walter, U. M. (2016). Improvisation: A practice for praxis. In L. Pyles & G. J. Adam (Eds.), *Holistic engagement: Transformative social work education in the 21st century* (pp. 157–174). New York: Oxford University Press.

Index

For Product Safety Concerns and Information please contact our EU
representative GPSR@taylorandfrancis.com
Taylor & Francis Verlag GmbH, Kaufingerstraße 24, 80331 München, Germany

www.ingramcontent.com/pod-product-compliance
Lightning Source LLC
Chambersburg PA
CBHW050353270326
41926CB00016B/3721